PANFISHING

F. PHILIP RICE

Illustrations by Charles Berger

Drawings of lures by Sylvia Schwartz
and John Dahl

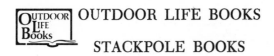

OUTDOOR LIFE BOOKS

STACKPOLE BOOKS

CONTENTS

INTRODUCTION

Panfishing. The word stirs memories of a lazy creek laced with branches and logs, the mirror-like surface of a quiet pond surrounded by rustling bullrushes, the gentle lap of waves on the side of an anchored boat, a bobber dancing on the shimmering water, and the throb and pulse of the line. These are some of the reasons so many people go panfishing. It is a sport which digs deeply into man's inner being, carving its own place in his time and thoughts.

But for those who have yet to know these sights and sounds, and who are strangers to the sport, perhaps a few introductory remarks are in order.

The word "panfish" is sometimes applied to any fish small enough to fit into a frying pan. With this definition, however, one would have to include dozens of different species of fish of many different families. Rather than make this book so all-inclusive, my final selection includes some twenty species of smaller fish which are most known, sought after and most usually called panfish. These include four basic families of fish:

1. The sunfish family: Green, orangespotted, redear, pumpkinseed, longear, yellowbreast, spotted, Sacramento perch, rock bass, warmouth bass, bluegill, white crappie and black crappie.

2. The perch family: Yellow perch.

3. The sea bass family: White bass, yellow bass and white perch.

4. The catfish family: Black, brown and yellow bullheads.

This book attempts to be both a scholarly work, incorporating the latest scientific information, and a practical book, which will help you with the every-day problems of fish catching. In gathering scientific information, I have delved into hundreds of books, periodicals, biological abstracts, reprints of scientific articles and published reports of studies and surveys. I am especially thankful to the fish and game departments of all fifty of our states, each of which has responded to my questionnaire concerning panfish in their state. Many departments have sent me copies of scientific reports which have proven extremely helpful.

My goal has been to write the most complete and comprehensive book ever published on panfishing. Into it has gone the results of fifty years of personal experience on streams, rivers and lakes in many parts of the United States. I am grateful also to dozens of other writers whose published articles have added to my own knowledge of methods and techniques. In addition, dozens of tackle companies have sent full information regarding tackle, equipment and lures. All this—and other valuable data—has been incorporated in this book.

F. Philip Rice

1

BLUEGILL

The bluegill (*Lepomis macrochirus*) is undoubtedly the most popular panfish in the United States. In fact, it has been said that more anglers fish for bluegills than for any other freshwater fish. There are a number of good reasons for this distinction, the most important being its wide distribution and its abundance.

As it is found in all the states except Alaska and Maine, the bluegill is widely enough distributed to provide sport for millions of fishermen from coast to coast. Its abundance in so many areas is due to the fact that it is a prolific breeder, several females laying up to 67,000 eggs in one nest and one male guarding the nest and young fry from predators so as to enable them to achieve a high rate of survival in suitable waters. So abundant is the bluegill in some states that fishermen are urged to keep every fish they catch regardless of size, to prevent stunting the population.

The bluegill is one of the largest and gamest of the true sunfishes. The world's record was a 4-pound 12-ounce fish caught in Ketona Lake, Alabama, in 1950. In a few waters of the country where the growing season is long and food is plentiful, the fish will consistently run half a pound or more. A spunky fighter, the bluegill will hit a fly or lure with gusto and then fight to the bitter end, turning its broad side toward the fisherman, darting to and fro, never giving

Distribution of the bluegill.

up until it is landed. On ultra-light tackle, it provides a real thrill and wonderful sport.

Live-bait fishermen like the bluegill because it will take a varied assortment of insects, larvae, worms, grubs or nymphs. Fly fishermen like it because it will hit popping bugs, dry flies, wet flies, nymphs or small streamers. Spinning enthusiasts like it because they can use a fly and bubble, weighted spinners or small spoons.

And, finally, the bluegill makes a tasty dish when fried until golden brown in creamery butter in a hot skillet. Sometimes I even fillet a bluegill, especially the larger ones, enjoying the succulent, bone-free meat to the utmost.

The bluegill is a member of the sunfish family Centrarchidae, which includes the crappie, Sacramento perch, rock bass and warmouth bass, largemouth and smallmouth black bass, and eight species of "true sunfish"—the green, orangespotted, redear, pumpkinseed, longear, yellowbreast and spotted. Although similar in appearance to other true sunfish, the bluegill has several distinguishing features. Its color varies, but generally it is dark olive-green on the back with a purple or blue iridescent cast to the sides. The breast of the female is white or pale yellow, that of the male is yellow or a bright, rusty red. In muddy water, the colors will be more pale. There are usually six to eight vertical dark-colored bars on each side of the fish, and the sides completely lack the bright-colored spots which other sunfishes have. The ear flap is short and has only a very narrow membrane; the black spot on the flap is wide and comes to the edge of the flap, covering the membrane. There isn't any trace of a red spot on the border of the opercle flap. The rear margin of the gill cover is flexible.

The pectoral fins are long and pointed; there is a dark blotch on the posterior part of the soft dorsal fin next to the body of the fish. The dorsal fin is continuous and unbroken with ten spines and ten to twelve soft rays in that fin. The fish has three anal spines and ten to twelve soft rays in the anal fin. The tail is weakly forked and has rounded tips. Ctenoid scales cover the fish with thirty-eight to forty-eight scales in the lateral line.

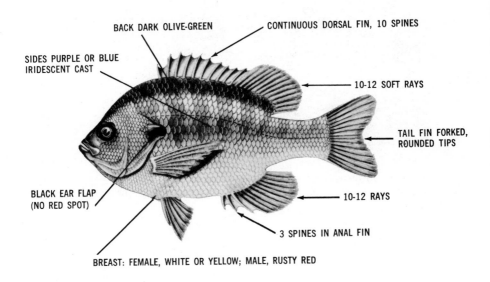

Bluegill

STEVE PRICE PHOTO

Bluegills prefer warm, weedy lakes with underwater vegetation. The fish travel in small schools from deep-water resting places to shallow-water feeding areas.

HABITS AND HABITAT

The bluegill is predominantly a lake fish, preferring warm water and clear-water lakes with an abundance of aquatic vegetation. It is seldom found in small streams, although it will live in large and quiet rivers and streams. It is less likely to occur in cold, swift-flowing streams and large, cold, barren lakes. It prefers the weedy areas of a lake, moving among the weeds, eating insects and some vegetation. The kind of warm, weedy waters that largemouth bass prefer are also ideal for the bluegill. Given a choice, the bluegill prefers underwater vegetation rather than stumps or brushpiles.

Bluegills inhabit water from about 1 to 20 feet deep, the depth depending primarily upon the season of the year, time of day and temperature of the water. Bluegills prefer water temperatures of from 65° to 75°, with 70° to 72° being ideal. Take temperature into consideration when fishing for bluegills, therefore, in order to be able to locate the largest fish.

These fish travel in small, loose schools, with usually ten to twenty fish swimming together. They do not roam all over a lake as do crappie, white bass or white perch, but have a home range over which they move back and forth from their deeper-water resting places to the shallow, weedy waters where they feed. If removed from their normal haunts, they attempt to return. Usually, in hot weather, the fish will move into the shallows to feed sometime during every twenty-four-hour period. When you catch one fish, try to remain in that spot and to keep quiet, so that you can catch others from the same school. Excessive noise will scare the fish away or make the larger ones so wary they will not bite.

Bluegills will not tolerate a low oxygen content in the water as will northern pike, yellow perch or bullheads. If the dissolved oxygen in the water gets below 0.6 ppm (parts per million), mortalities can be expected. This is why bluegills are among the first fish to die from winter kill in shallow lakes which are frozen over for too long during the winter. Interestingly enough, however, some lakes that are subject to winter kill provide excellent fishing for bluegills since the excessive numbers of these fish are killed off.

The food of the bluegill varies. Very young fish eat plankton (the small animal and plant organisms that float in the water), vegetation and small crustaceans. As the fish grow larger, they eat larvae or nymphs of insects, snails, worms and adult insects. Occasionally, they will eat small fish or fish eggs when these items are easily found, even though bluegills are not considered fish eaters.

During the early summer, bluegills thrive especially on mayfly nymphs. Also, they can be seen feasting on the emerging insects as they hatch out and come to the surface of the water. Some of your finest dry-fly fishing can be enjoyed during these periods when insects are hatching.

During the winter months, when insects become scarce, bluegills feed on vegetation. They eat lightly during the cold months, but will indulge in a variety of foods. They seem to prefer various larvae when caught through the ice, probably because they like the change in diet which the larvae afford. One study in Michigan indicates that from May to October these fish consume 336 percent of their body weight, while during the remainder of the year, only 13 percent is consumed. This is because food consumption is determined by the metabolism of the fish, which in turn depends upon water temperature. When water temperatures are below 55°, food consumption is drastically reduced. This is one reason why very small baits, particularly larvae, are best in the winter.

SPAWNING AND REPRODUCTION

Bluegills begin their spawning activity when the water temperature attains approximately 67°. This may be as early as late March in Florida or other warm states, or as late as early June in the northernmost states. The following are some representative spawning periods in various states.

Oklahoma—Middle of April until middle of July.
Ohio—Late May to late July with peak in June.
Wisconsin—Late May to early August with peak in late June.
Michigan (Upper Peninsula)—Early June to early September.

The reason the spawning activity is spread out over a period of time is that not all female bluegills become ripe at the same time, and also the eggs from a single fish may mature gradually. A single female may deposit eggs in batches over a period of a week or two. The long spawning season assures some successful reproduction and provides the fisherman with shallow-water fishing over a period of time.

The bluegill differs from other members of the sunfish family in that it makes its nest in colonies without much separation between nests. Each nest is prepared by the male fish on a sandy or gravelly bottom in shallow water from about one-half to 4 feet deep. The male hollows out a shallow depression, 2 to 6 inches deep and about 1 to 2 feet in diameter, by violently swishing his tail and body. He then courts the female and induces her to lay her eggs after which he emits milt on them. The eggs are deposited among the clean pebbles and sand at the bottom of the nest. On the average, about 18,000 eggs are laid in one nest, not necessarily all from the same female. As many as 67,000 eggs have been taken from a single nest. After the eggs are laid, the male keeps a constant vigil over them and keeps them aerated and clean by gentle fanning with his fins. The nesting territory is vigorously protected by the male, and although there may be many nests almost touching, each male drives others from his nest.

Hatching usually takes two to five days under normal weather conditions. Once hatched, the school of fry is protected by the male for a few additional days before he drives them toward cover and then deserts them.

SIZE AND BAG LIMITS

Newly hatched fry are usually from 2 to 3 millimeters in length. Growth rates vary from one body of water to another. In waters of low fertility, there may be stunted fish no longer than 6 inches regardless of age. In warm climates such as in the southern United States, and in waters of high fertility, these fish may consistently grow to be over 10 inches long and over a pound in weight. Needless to say, lakes containing these mammoth-size bluegills provide excellent sport.

Usually, however, the average size is much smaller. The following table shows the average growth of bluegills in three states, and the average from eighteen sample states, which represents a national average.

STATE	NO. OF FISH	LENGTH IN INCHES AT END OF YEAR					
		1	2	3	4	5	6
Okla.	5,454	3.2	4.9	6.0	6.8	7.2	—
Minn.	2,248	1.9	3.4	4.9	6.1	7.1	7.8
Ohio	1,000	1.6	3.6	5.1	6.0	6.8	7.5
U.S.	4,492	1.9	3.7	5.3	6.0	6.8	7.7

Most bluegills do not live more than about five years. Out of a total of 5,464 fish used in a study in Oklahoma, only eight fish were older than five years of age. Ninety-one percent were less than four years old. Thus, it is extremely important that the fish have ample food available from the beginning of their life in order for them to grow the maximum amount during the few years they live.

The natural mortality of bluegills, as with most fish, is high. In a study at Murphy Flowage in Wisconsin, out of 100 fish which started the fishing season, 24 were caught, 32 lived and 44 died sometime during the year. Thus, only about one-third survive from one year to the next. Of those which do survive, only 1 out of 5 is caught by anglers. Actually, angling has little effect upon fishing populations of bluegills. It has been shown time and again that there is no need for size limits or creel limits on bluegills; the season ought to be open all year round; all fish caught should be kept and anglers ought to be encouraged to catch as many as possible. A very fertile pond will produce around 200 pounds of fish per acre and some fisheries biologists estimate that at least 50 or more pounds of fish per acre should be removed yearly from these ponds to keep bluegill populations down. This means that most ponds will stand more fishing pressure for bluegills than they are receiving.

FINDING THE FISH

If you go about your fish-finding systematically, you should not have trouble determining where to fish for bluegills, even in waters that are comparatively new to you. There are several factors that ought to be considered in finding them.

First, consider the season of the year. Is it spawning time, the hot period of midsummer, the cool weather of fall, the cold of winter, the period during which the bluegill water is frozen over, or is it thawing time?

During spawning time, look for the spawning beds in shallow, sandy, gravelly water, sometimes in or near weed beds. The spawning nests appear as light-colored basins, usually 1 to 2 feet in diameter, sometimes close together. Once located, you can fish these areas easily.

After spawning is over and during the heat of midsummer, the fish retire to the deeper water during the day, coming into the shallows only during certain periods of early morning, late evening or night. The hotter the weather and water, the later the bluegills seem to feed at night. Thus, during the daytime fish only the deep weed beds, the deep drop-offs along steep banks and shady, cool spots affording cover. Very early morning, late evening and at night you can fish the weedy shallows where the bluegills come in to feed.

In early fall, after the water temperature has cooled to about 70°, the fish will be found all over the lake—sometimes shallow, at other times deep. When the water is below 70°, usually the shallow water is good when it is being warmed by a hot sun; if the weather is cold and the water is getting below ideal temperatures, the blue-gills will move into deeper and deeper water. After the cold weather of fall really begins in earnest, most large bluegills are about 10 to 15 feet deep. I find these depths satisfactory for most ice fishing as well.

Right after ice out in the spring, the fish are scattered. On warm, sunny days, they go into quiet, shallow bays to warm up. On cold days, before the water is warmed, they remain in the depths. One good spot in the early spring is by inlet streams where the incoming

STEVE PRICE PHOTO

These anglers, drifting quietly along a slow-moving river, are fishing weedbeds and drop-offs for bluegills on a hot summer day.

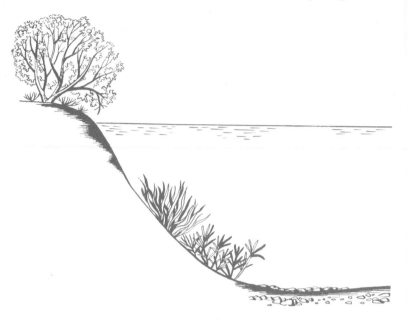

During spring spawning, which begins as the water temperature approaches 67°, look for bluegills in the shallow weed beds and sandy bottoms along the shoreline. Spawning beds appear as closely grouped, shallow basins 1 to 2 feet in diameter.

water is warmer than the lake or river. Bluegills swim up these warmer channels and inlets to find food and to begin spawning.

Second, be certain to look for the best possible cover available. As mentioned, bluegills prefer weed beds to areas of brush, stumps and logs. I have always liked areas of huge boulders where the fish can hide. Also, boat houses, rafts and docks in deep water are favorite spots. Sometimes large bluegills hide out in the shade under old piers, especially if the water is deep. Weed beds and overhanging banks provide excellent cover in creeks and rivers.

Third, be willing to try different depths until you find spots where there are schools of fish. Approach each likely spot as quietly as possible, or you'll spook the fish. If you're catching only small fish and you know there are larger ones in the water you're fishing, then probably you need to get down deeper with your bait or lures. Depth is of primary importance in all types of bluegill fishing. Once you

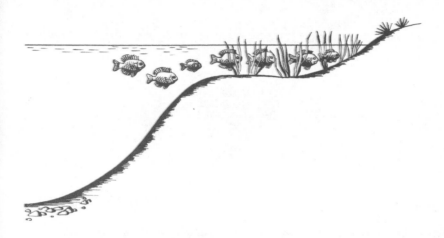

locate the depth where the larger fish are located, stay at that level.

Fourth, just because you had good luck in one spot during one season of the year does not mean the fish will still be there at different seasons. Water in which the fish spawned may be completely barren in late summer. The cold depths where you found the fish in late fall may be vacated as the waters warm up in the spring. Usually, however, areas that produce during certain seasons produce year after year during similiar seasons and with similiar water temperatures, unless something has radically changed in that area which has affected the fish.

LIVE-BAIT FISHING

Insects in their larva, pupa, nymph, or adult stages are the best baits for bluegills. The single exception to this rule is the earth-

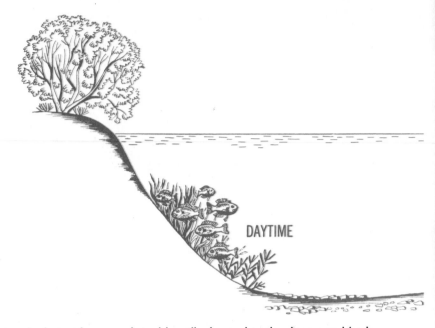

During the hot midsummer days, bluegills descend to the deep weed beds and drop-offs along steep banks in water up to 20 feet deep. Late in the evening and at night they return to the weedy shallows to feed.

worm, which is always a good bait. Actually, the favorite bait will depend upon which part of the country you are in and what time of the year you are fishing. The favorite live baits include: earthworms, crane-fly larvae or pupae (mousees), grasshoppers, crickets, cockroaches, catalpa worms, meal worms, grubs, gall worms or maggots. The larger baits—earthworms, grasshoppers, crickets, catalpa worms and cockroaches—are better during the warm summer months when the fish like a big mouthful. The small baits—mousees, meal worms, grubs, gall worms and maggots—are the standard diet for ice fishing.

SPINNING TACKLE

Ordinarily, the fly rod is better all-round equipment for bluegills than is spinning or spincasting gear. However, you can use your

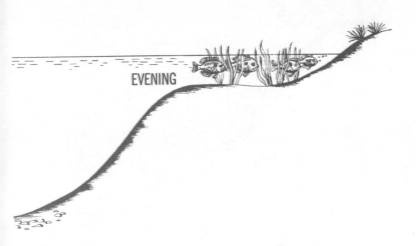

spinning tackle for these fish in several ways.

1. Use spinning tackle for live-bait fishing.

2. Use a plastic bubble and either dry or wet flies or poppers with it. The bubble gives you enough weight to cast the flies.

3. Use a small plug, usually a surface plug, with a fly attached to it by means of a short piece of monofilament. The bluegill will investigate the splash of the larger plug and then bite on the fly or panfish popper.

4. Use ultra-light spinning lures—primarily weighted spinners, wobbling spoons or jigs. None of these lures is as effective for blue-gills as are flies, however. Your best bet is to learn to fly fish or stick to the first three methods mentioned.

FLY FISHING

A complete discussion of fly fishing is found in Chapter 10, but I want to summarize some information here which applies partic-ularly to bluegills.

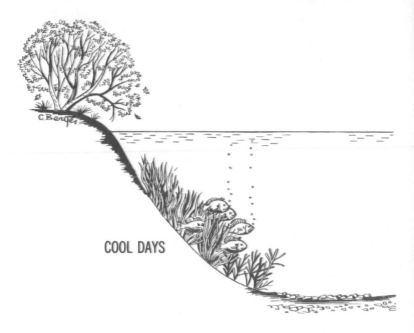

COOL DAYS

In early fall, when the water temperature drops to 70° and below, bluegills roam all over the lake, seeking shallow water when the sun is warm and deeper water as the water cools.

When the fish are rising to the surface, use dry flies or panfish poppers with rubber legs. Some of the dry-fly patterns recommended in Chapter 10 are suitable for bluegills. The best patterns include:

Dry Flies

Bivisibles: grizzly, brown, black or gray
Black Gnat
Light Cahill
Adams March Brown
Iron Blue Dun
White Miller
Mosquito
Pink Lady
Royal Coachman
Gauze Wing Drake (blue dun, yellow, ginger)
Brown Hackle Yellow
Gray Hackle Red
Irresistible
Goofus Bug
Wulff flies in black, white, blonde, or grizzly

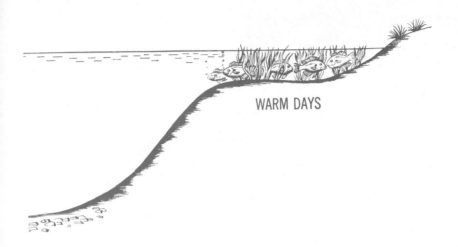

WARM DAYS

Actually, bluegills are not too particular when it comes to dry-fly patterns. If possible, I try to "match the hatch." Somber patterns usually work best for me.

In panfish poppers, a variety of finishes is satisfactory: black and white, red and white, all white, all yellow, all black or all tan are all good. Sometimes, the bluegills will prefer one color more than another. The following poppers are recommended:

Poppers

    Dylite Deluze Creepy Popper (Weber)
    Screwball (Glen Evans)
    Water-Waif (Glen Evans)
    Firelure Nitwit (Weber)
    Firelure Halfwit (Weber)
    Sizzler (Falls)
    Marathon Grasshopper Fly
    Mountain Hopper (Phillips)
    Ruf-Rubber: Waterbug, Varmint, Skit-It (Glen Evans)

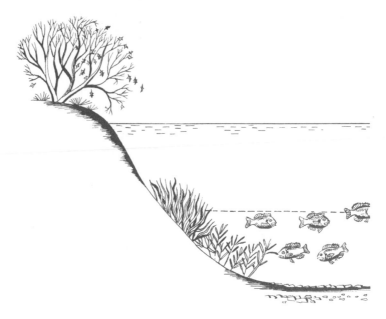

With the coming of colder weather in late fall, the bluegills, particularly the larger species, seek depths of between 10 and 15 feet.

More often than not, bluegills will bite better on wet flies than on dry. If the fish are not hitting on the surface, sink your flies down as deeply as needed to catch the large fish. You can use more than one fly by adding dropper loops to your leader. Some of the recommended patterns are:

Wet Flies

Black Gnat
Cowdung
Royal Coachman Gold
   Ribbed Hare's Ear
Parmachene Belle
Professor
Wooly Worm (green,
   brown)
Picket Pin
Fall's Spider

Bream Wiggler, Black
Weber Brim-Fli

Weighted Nymphs

Tan Shrimp
Mayfly Nymph
Stonefly Nymph
Gray Nymph
Black and Yellow

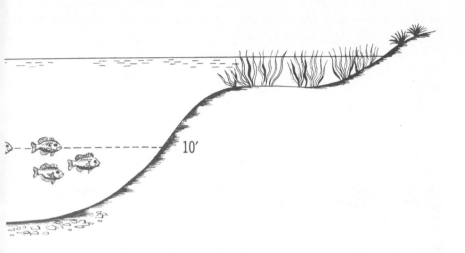

Ordinarily, fly-rod lures, spoons, spinners or jigs are not as effective for bluegills as are the lures or flies mentioned. Bluegills will hit plugs, spoons and spinners, but you will miss too many strikes. Use the various flies or poppers which I have suggested, in size 10 or 12, and you can't go wrong.

Occasionally, a small spinner added to your fly will produce better than the fly alone. This is especially true when the fish are deep or in cloudy water. A tiny piece of pork rind or live bait put on the hook of the fly also works wonders when the fish are hesitant about taking the lure into their mouth.

One of the most important considerations in fly fishing for bluegills is to fish the fly or lure slowly. This applies to both dry and wet flies. Cast the dry fly or popper and let it rest for thirty seconds or more before even twitching it. Never drag it across the water; fish it very slowly, just barely making it flutter and waiting quite awhile between twitches.

In fishing wet flies, let them sink for some seconds or even two or three minutes at a time, depending on the depth desired. If the flies do not sink deeply enough, add a spinner or a small split shot. Bluegills will often examine the fly for some time before moving up and striking. If you jerk or pull the fly along rapidly, the fish may not even touch the fly, or the fly may never get down deep enough to catch the larger fish.

You should always try to set the hook the instant a strike is felt or seen. Watch your line carefully and if you see or feel even the slightest touch, strike quickly to set the hook.

Another consideration is to cast and pick up the line carefully so that other fish of the school are not frightened. Don't slap the water with your line, or pick up the fly or lure so as to splash the surface of the water. Raise the rod tip slowly until the slack is out of the line and the fly or popper is coming out of the water already before sharply raising the rod for the back cast. Each time you move the bait, row or anchor quietly. You'll get more big ones if you do.

DAVE RICHEY PHOTO

Bluegills take flies readily and provide good sport on light tackle. Key to fly fishing is to retrieve lure slowly.

ICE FISHING

There are three principal methods of catching bluegills through the ice: live-bait fishing, primarily with the larvae, small worms and grubs; fishing with nature lures; or using ice flies. Nature lures are plastic imitations of live baits. Ice flies are weighted flies that are used by slowly jigging at various depths under the ice. At certain times, bluegills will hit nature lures or ice flies fiercely; at other times, you will do better on live bait. See the chapters on fly fishing, spinning and ice fishing for suggestions about patterns and types of nature lures and ice flies and how to use them.

2

CRAPPIE

There are two distinct species of crappie: the black crappie (*Pomoxis nigro-maculatus*), commonly called the calico bass, and the white crappie (*Pomoxis annularis*). Of the two species, the white is more common in the South and the black more common in the northern part of the United States.

It is not difficult to tell the two species apart. Both have a sunfish-like shape with a deep, flat body which is rather thin for its size. The dorsal and anal fins are large and of equal size; the dorsal fin is single and without notching; the caudal or tail fin is large with rounded corners and very little notching in the middle. Both species of crappie have a snout that turns up from the eye forward. The mouth is large and extends beyond a line extending down from the middle of the eye. Although large, the mouth is quite delicate, with thin membranes surrounding it. You have to be careful in playing your fish, therefore, or you'll tear the hook out of its mouth.

The black crappie, as the name implies, is darker in coloring, with black, irregular speckles over a silvery background. It has a mottled appearance and black or blackish-green coloring on the dorsal and anal fins. The white crappie is more silvery in color with several dark bands extending downward from the back. The dorsal fin of the black crappie is as long at the base as is the distance of the front

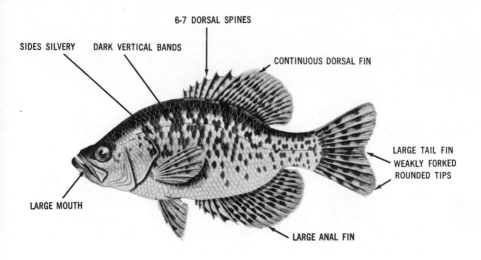

6-7 DORSAL SPINES

SIDES SILVERY   DARK VERTICAL BANDS

CONTINUOUS DORSAL FIN

LARGE TAIL FIN
WEAKLY FORKED
ROUNDED TIPS

LARGE MOUTH

LARGE ANAL FIN

White Crappie

of that fin to the eye. The dorsal fin of the white crappie is shorter at the base than is the distance from the front of that fin to the eye. Furthermore, there are usually seven or more dorsal spines on the black crappie and usually seven or less dorsal spines on the white crappie. The majority of black crappie have seven spines; the majority of the white crappie have six. Both species have five or more anal spines. The eye of the black crappie is deep blue with a golden circle about the iris; the eye of the white crappie is lighter in color.

Crappie are among the largest of our panfishes. I used to catch black crappie in a Minnesota lake that were all between 1½ and 2 pounds. The largest white crappie on record weighed 5 pounds 3 ounces. Louisiana claims a record black crappie of 6 pounds.

Black crappie are found in forty-eight states and white crappie in thirty-nine. Although black crappie are found in more states in the United States, the white crappie are often more numerous in those states having both fish. Where the two species are found together in the same water, the white will eventually dominate the population. The reason for this is that white crappie are more prolific and will stand more adverse water conditions than will the black. In the years ahead, therefore, we should expect a gradual shift in the population from black to white crappie. This has already taken place in some lakes. Years ago, for example, in Chautauqua Lake, New York, black crappie was the predominant species, but in recent years the white crappie appears to be in greater abundance.

HABITAT

The black crappie prefers clear, cool waters having hard bottoms and an abundance of aquatic vegetation. The white crappie thrives over a soft mud bottom, is not adverse to roily water and does not require aquatic vegetation as an essential. Because of these preferences, the white crappie is by far the best to stock in the average artificial impoundment or reservoir, especially if the water is inclined to get muddy during certain seasons of the year. The white crappie is completely dominant over the black in nearly all large Missouri watershed reservoirs. For example, the first few years after impoundment a few black crappie were taken in Clearwater Lake, Missouri, but from then on the white rapidly gained in number. This is a typical situation in similar impoundments. Apparently, the white

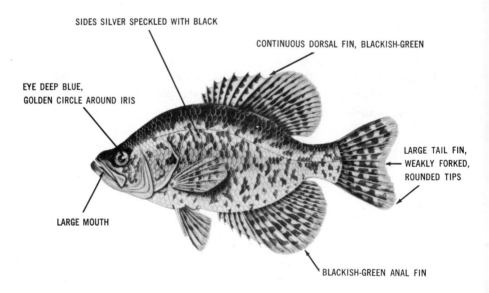

Black Crappie

STEVE PRICE PHOTO

TV fisherman Bill Dance shows off a nice crappie taken on a jig. He likes to fish for crappie with a fly rod and spinning reel.

Distribution of the white crappie.

crappie can do well in large, turbid, open waters where there is sparse aquatic vegetation.

Both species of crappie prefer the larger waters, however. They are seldom found in small ponds, lakes or streams. If found in streams, they inhabit only the more sluggish areas, the bayous or overflow parts. They can also be found in the sheltered bays and mouths of large rivers. Both species compete with black bass for food, and often become more abundant than the latter where both are present in the same lake.

It is well to remember that the white crappie, particularly, is very much a fish of the tangled brush, the deep-water willows, the rotting stump beds or the fallen trees. Look for deadfalls and piles of driftwood, edges of log jams and deep-water piers and pilings. When the fish are in deep water, an old river channel or stream bed forming a submarine canyon is a natural hiding place. Crappie also will be found over underwater islands and bars, or off rocky ledges or points of land. The black crappie loves these deep-water edges,

Jerry Gibbs, *Outdoor Life* fishing editor, casts a small streamer fly for crappie among old pilings along a lakeshore.

particularly if there are lots of underwater weedbeds growing near the bars or ledges.

Many fishermen construct their own hot-spots by sinking huge brush piles or old auto bodies. Such a spot in water about 20 to 30 feet deep makes a wonderful warm-weather spot. This method is used successfully also by the operators of fish docks on the large impoundments of the South.

Another clever scheme is to select an appropriate spot and bait it over a period of days with cottonseed cake or some other bait. The cake dissolves slowly and attracts schools of minnows which, in turn, lure the schools of crappie.

One important principle to remember in fishing for crappie is that these fish do not stay in one place. Most of their spawning is done in water from 4 to 8 feet deep. After spawning is over, the schools begin roaming all over a lake. They may be in sheltered bays and along shallow shorelines in the evening or at night, or rest-

Distribution of the black crappie.

ing or cruising during the day in 20 to 25 feet of water. They may be in one part of the lake one week and in another part the next. One reason, undoubtedly, is because they are carnivores, eating bait fish which they follow around from place to place. In the artificial impoundments of the South and Southwest, they chase the gizzard shad from one end of the lake to another. This is why an area that was marvelous at one time, may be terrible the next. This is what drives the crappie fisherman mad, but it's part of the sport.

When the warm weather begins in earnest, the very large schools break up and crappie cruise around individually or in small schools of ten or fifteen fish. This habit makes them much harder to locate in mid and late summer, and this is when some fishermen hang up their rods for the year. However, for the fisherman who is willing to hunt, much as is required in fishing for the black bass, fine sport is available. The crappie are there; all you have to do is find them.

SPAWNING

The spawning activities of the crappie are similar to those of other

Fishing along the fringes of weedbeds and shoreline trees, this angler landed a hefty crappie on a minnow.

sunfishes. The principle differences between crappie and bluegills are in the depth and type of water in which each spawn. Crappie may seek water as deep as 8 feet, although 2 to 6 feet is more usual; bluegills may sometimes spawn in water not more than 6 inches deep. Furthermore, while crappie do spawn in weedy, sandy, gravelly areas (like bluegills), they may also lay their eggs on hollow sunken logs, in beds of debris or near brush piles. Sometimes the nest is made right in the end of a hollow log, or in the center of an upright, hollow stump. I've taken lots of crappie off their spawning beds right next to large brush piles. Stump-filled, sheltered bays are excellent spawning areas for crappie. Weedy bays with open pockets are especially good for black crappie.

Like other sunfishes, it is the male crappie which hollows out a nest, drives a female or two into it to lay her eggs and, after fertilization, guards the nest until the fry can shift for themselves. These males will attack anything that comes near the nest, so love-making time for crappie is fishing time.

The exact time of spawning will depend on the latitude and the resulting temperature of the water. I'm a water-thermometer enthusiast myself and can tell more about the activities of all fish by measuring water temperature than by any other method. Crappie spawn when the water temperature ranges from 64 to 68 degrees. That's the time when you should be on the water. This may be as early as March in the South, or as late as the first of July in the northern United States. The following months are the usual spawning months for crappie in some representative states.

New York—Late May to July.
Ohio—May and June are usually the best months.
Oklahoma—April is usually the best.
Tennessee or Kentucky—Late March, April.
Mississippi or Florida—March.

If you are planning a trip to go crappie fishing, try to check with the local residents to see when the spawning activity is beginning. Early or late seasons may throw you off. Nothing is more disconcerting than to go south for the spring crappie run and to have a spell of freezing weather to delay spawning.

If you have never witnessed the spring crappie runs, and the mad scramble of fishermen who seek them, then you have a real treat in store for you. When the dogwood, the honeysuckle and redbud begin to bloom, it is crappie time in hundreds of places. Literally several million fishermen hurry to the lakes, some driving hundred of miles. The warming weather brings the crappie to the shallow water to begin their spawning activities, and the sunny days bring out the fishermen to catch the crappie. The shorelines of some lakes are literally lined with fishermen. Hundreds of others paddle about in every conceivable type of boat.

It is very easy to catch crappie during this time of year. If you catch the fish right on the spawning beds (water temperature 64° to 68°), you can fish for them any time during the day. Look for the fish in the best spawning areas: near the mouths of streams and inlets to lakes, in the shallow reaches of tributaries, coves and bays, particularly around brush, beds of stumps, willows, weeds, lily pads, logs and other cover. The best areas are 2 to 6 feet deep and with plenty of cover. Cast your lures, flies or baits as close to the actual beds as possible; give the crappie plenty of time to inhale the lure or bait, then strike gently and play the fish until it's ready to be brought in.

If the fish are already off the spawning beds, but the water is still fairly cool (72° or less), the fish will be cruising around the lake after food. They will usually move into selected bays and shorelines to feed in the late afternoon and at dusk. This is the best time for the fly rod or shallow-running spinning lures.

SEASONAL TACTICS

It has been mentioned that after the hot weather of summer begins crappie move out to deep water; the large schools begin to break up and so the fish are much harder to find. There are ways and means

STEVE PRICE PHOTO

Fishing at night for crappie can be very productive. These anglers hung a lantern over the gunwale of their boat to attract minnows, the crappie's favorite food.

to catch crappie during hot weather, however, so don't put away your fishing tackle.

One way is to fish for them only late evening or at night. On a calm, "buggy" summer evening, row around your favorite crappie lake quietly, watching and listening for signs of crappie feeding. Usually you can locate some and, if you can get near the school without scaring them, you'll catch crappie about as fast as you can cast.

If you can use a dock or swimming raft, particularly one in deep water, place a lighted gasoline lantern on it at dusk and let the lantern stay there for a couple of hours until there are thousands of insects swarming around it. The light attracts the bugs, and the bugs will attract the crappie—by the hundreds!

I learned of this method from a crappie fisherman on Lake Chautauqua, New York. This man had added the refinement of an electric light on his dock, however. Every night he would take a pail of minnows to the end of his dock and catch crappie by the dozens. He let me help one night; I think I caught over twenty in about forty-five minutes.

If you object to such methods, then you will simply have to troll slowly and deeply, either drifting or with a motor, or fish the deepest bars, underwater brush piles and weed beds you can find. During one summer when our family spent several weeks on Lake Mille Lacs, Minnesota, one of the favorite crappie spots was a boat which had sunk in about 25 feet of water. The crappie always swarmed around the place.

If the water you fish is a newly created impoundment, look for the tops of trees just sticking out of deep water, drowned willows, large bushes and other deep-water cover. One of my favorite spots in Lake Spavinaw in Oklahoma used to be a sunken tree near a deep drop-off. We could always count on catching crappie there, even in the middle of hot summer days. For this type of fishing, live minnows or jigs are usually best. Sinking spinners and spoons will also produce, if fished near the bottom. Hot-weather crappie are fairly well scattered though, and sometimes move around a lot, so you'll have to really work to find them.

With the cooling of the lake waters and the complete turnover of the water that accompanies the fall weather, the crappie become much more active again and can now be found all over the lake. Sometimes they are in shallow water; at other times they are in the depths. The shallows are now cool enough for them to be comfortable there; the depths now contain enough oxygen to support life.

You will seldom find the crappie surface feeding on insects in the fall, but you may find schools of fish chasing minnows or shad; if so, you'll have good fishing. Spinners, spoons or streamer flies are best.

After the first frosts begin, and the lake cools below 60°, the crappie will retreat to their deep-water hangouts. Live bait or artificials fished very slowly just off the bottom are now the best baits.

After crappie waters freeze up and the ice is thick enough to bear your weight, you can have wonderful sport ice fishing for crappie. Minnows or the various larvae are good baits. Occasionally, the crappie will hit jigging spoons or ice flies, but live bait is usually better. Look for the schools of fish in water from 20 to 30 feet deep, usually in areas of brush, stumps and other cover.

BAITS FOR CRAPPIE

In considering the best baits for any fish, it is wisest to consider first what the fish most often feed on. Young crappie feed primarily on crustaceans and aquatic insects; their nymphs or larvae. As the crappie grow older, they begin feeding on minnows and other small fish. Young perch were found to comprise a main item in the diet of black crappie from Silver Lake, New York. Others had eaten dragonfly nymphs and largemouth-bass fry. In some lakes, gizzard shad comprise a mainstay of the diet of adult crappie. Crappie are also especially fond of mayflies and other adult insects in early summer. At times, they will take a variety of food: earthworms, crawfish, grasshoppers, crickets, nymphs and larvae.

By far the best all-around bait for crappie is minnows from 1 to 2 inches long. It is important that you fish minnows of about this size; if your bait is too large or too small, it is not as effective. Choose a size that makes a good mouthful, yet is small enough for a crappie to get into its mouth. Also, be certain your minnow is lively and wiggling. More crappie are caught on minnows than on any other bait, probably because crappie are primarily fish eaters and have a decided preference for these small fry.

My next choice of baits would be nymphs: dragonfly nymphs, mayfly nymphs and stone-fly nymphs. If the larger nymphs can be obtained, they make wonderful crappie bait, although they are rather delicate and ought to be wired or tied on the hook.

My next choice for crappie would be various land insects: grass-hoppers, crickets and cockroaches. These insects are particularly effective when the crappie are feeding on or near the surface.

My last choice would be earthworms, crawfish and various larvae: catalpa worms, meal worms, caddis worms, crane-fly larvae, grubs, gall worms and maggots. The worms and larvae are not nearly as good bait for crappie in either spring or summer as are minnows or the various nymphs and insects; but they are excellent baits to use for ice fishing. Like other panfish, crappie like a delicate mouthful, especially in cold water, and the worms and larvae seem to be appealing.

How you fish your bait is perhaps just as important as the bait you use. Choose light monofilament line or leaders, small hooks (size 8 is about right) and bobbers with little resistance. Your bobber should pull under with the slightest touch, which means that either the bobber should be small, or, if a larger bobber is used, your sinker should be heavy enough to pull it nearly under. If you are fishing fairly deep water, a sliding bobber is easy to use since you can reel your line in and then cast only a short line with bobber, sinker and hook attached. Of course, you'll have to put a rubber band, knot or other stop on your line so your bobber will let only that much line slide through and then stop at the right depth. The sinker should be heavy enough to pull the line through the sliding bobber.

There is also a knack to hooking crappie. They usually bite gently, just sucking in the bait gradually and then turning and heading for the depths. If you strike too soon, you'll pull the bait right out of the fish's mouth, so let your bobber go way under and stay there before striking. When you do set the hook, do so gently, and play the fish without pulling too much on your rod, or else you'll tear the hook out of the fish's mouth. If your tackle is ultra-light, you will thoroughly enjoy catching the larger fish because of the good fight they will give you on the limber rod.

If you troll for crappie with live bait, you must do so very slowly, letting the bait drift down to the proper depth. If you are going to use worms or larvae, attach an Indiana or Colorado spinner in front of the baited hook, weight your line so you can get down deep, and then troll just as slowly as you possibly can and still keep the spinner spinning. You can also troll minnows by using either a minnow rig or by sewing the minnows on. (See Chapter 11.)

You can increase your catch by using a spreader or several drop hooks on your line and fishing two or three baits on one line. Since crappie are school fish, you'll often hook two at the same time.

When you catch a fish, mark that spot with a buoy, or by taking cross-bearings on landmarks. Anchor there and begin casting in that spot. Stay in one place until the fish quit hitting, then begin casting around in a circle to find out in which direction the school is moving. Try to follow the school as they move along and you'll soon have your limit.

LURES

Although usually not quite as productive as the minnows, you can have the most fun in crappie fishing by going after them with artificials either on your fly or spinning outfit. Of these two types of equipment, I think the spinning or spincasting outfit is by far the most appropriate for crappie, primarily because minnow-like imitations are the best lures. Various types of flies will catch lots of fish, especially streamer flies or flies and spinners, but the use of spinning-size plugs, weighted spinners, spoons and jigs is usually more effective, especially when the crappie are in deeper water. Deep, open-water fishing with the fly rod is almost impossible, yet it is managed easily with sinking-spinning lures.

What types of spinning lures should you buy for crappie? Of the many lures suggested in Chapter 9, I would use the following for crappie:

Surface Plugs

Whopper Stopper and Pop 'n' Jig (Whopper Stopper)
Rebel Popper (Plastic Research and Development Corp.)

Floating-Diving Plugs

Creek Chub Darter (Creek Chub)
Flatfish, 1¾″ and 2½″ (Helin)
Rainbow Runner (Phillips)
Rapala (Normark)
ThinFin Super Shiner Minnow (Storm)

Rebel, Deep Runner Minnow (Plastic Research and Development Corp.)

Tiny River Runt Spook (Daisy-Heddon)

Sinking Lures

Deep Inch (Falls Bait Co.)

Harrison's Rocky Lure, Jr. (Harrison-Hoge)

Inch Minnow (Falls Bait Co.)

L and S Spin-Master (L & S Bait Co.)

L and S Trail-O-Lure (L & S Bait Co.)

Rapala (Normark)

Tiny Ike (Daisy-Heddon)

Wobbling Spoons

Al's Goldfish (Al's Goldfish Lure Co.)

Dardevle, Skeeter Plus or Lil' Devle (Lou Eppinger)

Feathered Shad King (Hildebrandt)

Johnson's Bucktail Spoon (Louis Johnson)

Little Bantam (Southern Tool and Die Co.)

Marathon Dictator (Marathon)

Midge (Glen Evans)

Phantom Wobbler (H & J)

Slim Spoon (Webber)

Williams Nymphs (Williams)

Weighted Spinners

Abu-Reflex (Garcia)

Colorado Spinner, 3|0 Blade (Glen Evans)

Flicker-Spinner (Hildebrandt)

Hep (Daisy-Heddon)

Marathon Spin-O-Hawk (Marathon)

Mepps Aglia (Sheldons)

Worden's Rooster Tail (Yakima)

Worth Pearlie (Worth)

Jigs

Baby Lead Head Jig (Glen Evans)

BJ Bucktail Jig (Horrocks-Ibbotson)
Crappie Killer (Weber)
Full Tail Jig (Assassinator)
Hot-Line (Arndt & Son)
Little Crappie Killer (Cordell)
Little Doggie Marabou Jig Fly (Glen Evans)
Marathon Canadian Minnow (Marathon)
Plain Jig Head (Assassinator)

Nature Lures

Weber 2″ Spinner Minnow, Shiner

Pork Rind

Uncle Josh, Fly Strip, White

There are, of course, many other fine lures which will take crappie. I have tried to give you a varied assortment to meet different situations. When the crappie are surface feeding, you can use a wide variety of lures: the surface plug, floating-diving plugs and weighted spinners or spoons are all wonderful fish catchers when cast right into the schools of fish.

When the crappie seem to be down deep, then your best bait is a jig. Jigs can be fished in or around the brush piles so that the hook is kept upright and you won't get snagged. Fish the jig as slowly as possible. Of course, sinking plugs, weighted spinners and spoons are also good, but you'll have more trouble getting snagged with these. However, if you let them sink to just above the cover or fish them alongside the cover, you'll have good luck. Unlike most game fish, crappie like a slow, steady retrieve; do this and you'll catch more fish.

When you can't seem to find the fish, then I would troll as slowly as possible, using the floating-diving or sinking plugs, the spoons or the plastic minnow. If a slight breeze is blowing, try drift trolling with the wind. If you are rowing or using your outboard motor, then go as slowly as you can and still give action to your lure. Usually, enough weight added to your line to bring your lure down near the lake bottom brings the best results, unless you're trolling right through schools of crappie that are chasing minnows or shad on the surface.

Two of the most effective lures for crappie (other than jigs) need special mention. A spinner and pork strip or a spinner and fly make good lures to use on your ultra-light spinning outfit. You can simply add a fairly large spinner and sinker to a bare treble hook to which a pork strip has been attached, or you can put a small piece of rind on a weighted spinner like the Heddon Hep. The Paul Bunyan No. 66S or No. 66F is essentially just a spinner, weight and fly attached. The fly is removable so that you can add others as the need may arise.

FLIES

As has been mentioned, the fly rod is not as good as the spinning outfit for all-round crappie fishing, but this does not mean that you can't have good sport with the fly rod. The fly rod is wonderful for crappie when the fish are shallow or when you're live-bait fishing. It's simply too hard to fish deep enough with the fly rod to make it convenient to use at times.

I would suggest the following flies for crappie:

Dry Flies

Bivisible: Black, Gray
Black Gnat
Light Cahill
Iron Blue Dun
March Brown
White Miller
Yellow May
Royal Coachman
Blue Dun
Ginger
Brown Hackle Yellow
Gray Hackle Red
Goofus Bug
Wulff Blonde or Grizzly

Wet Flies

Black Gnat
Coachman

McGinty Montreal
Parmachene Belle
Western Bee
Professor
Wooly Worm (green, brown)
Marathon Red Tail Crappie Fly

Streamer Flies

Blacknosed Dace
Black Ghost
Gray Ghost
Mickey Finn
Muddler Minnow
Nine-Three
Red and White Bucktail
Supervisor
Yellow Marabou

Terrestrials

Worth Special Hornberg Fly (Worth)

The above assortment gives you enough variety of type and pattern to meet most any condition. Note that crappie like a lot of color in wet flies—unlike the bluegill which takes somber patterns better. Buy most of your flies in size 8 or 10, only occasionally a size 6 (such as in a streamer) for large crappie.

In fly-rod lures I would recommend the following:

Popping Bugs

All black, all white, red and white, or yellow are good. Weber Dylite Deluxe Creepy Popper and the Weber Nitwit or Half-Wite are recommended. The Creepy Popper has rubber legs; The Nitwit is a slim, well-designed popper. Both are of light plastic.

Spoons

Feathered Shad King (Hildebrandt)
Dardevle, Skeeter Plus (Lou Eppinger)

Plug

Flatfish, Baby, 1¾"

Spinner

Standard Colorado Spinner, for use with wet flies.

Use the dry flies or the popping bugs late in the evening when the crappie move in at dusk to feed along the shoreline. Ordinarily, standard wet flies work better with a small spinner, sometimes with a piece of pork rind attached. Streamer flies are excellent either casting or trolling; in fact, I would rate streamer flies as the best of the flies for crappie, probably because they imitate minnows. Although hard to cast with the fly rod, the spoons and plugs which I have suggested are wonderful lures. The spoons can be allowed to sink and so are used fairly deep; the flatfish is one of the best all-around fly lures for crappie when the fish are shallow.

In fishing your dry flies or surface bugs, work them ever so slowly; just barely twitch them. Crappie do not bang them like bluegill; they just take them in gently, so give the fish plenty of time to see, take and partly swallow them, or else you'll pull the fly or lure away from the fish.

In fishing spinners and wet flies, fly-rod plugs, spoons or streamers, let them sink as far as needed before retrieving very slowly, usually with a steady motion. Crappie do not seem to like erratic retrieves.

3

ROCK AND
WARMOUTH
BASS

This chapter is about two fish that are both called bass, but which aren't really bass but species of sunfish. In Chapter 7, I discuss the white perch, which is not really a perch but a member of the sea-bass family. The only true perch discussed in this book is the yellow perch and the only true bass are the white and yellow bass. All of this goes to prove that panfish can't be classified by their common names, but only by the scientific family to which they belong.

The rock bass and warmouth bass belong to the sunfish family Centrarchidae. That is about as closely as they are related, however, since each belongs to a different genus within that family. The rock bass is a member of the genus *Amblopites* and is given the species name *rupestris*; thus its scientific name *Amblopites rupestris*. The warmouth bass is of the genus *Chaenobryttus*, and its species name is *gulosus*; thus it has the scientific name *Chaenobryttus gulosus*. The two fish are somewhat similar in appearance, but they each have definite physical characteristics and habits which distinguish them from one another.

The rock bass has a definite sunfish shape, a chunky body, a single dorsal fin with ten to twelve spines, an anal fin with five to seven

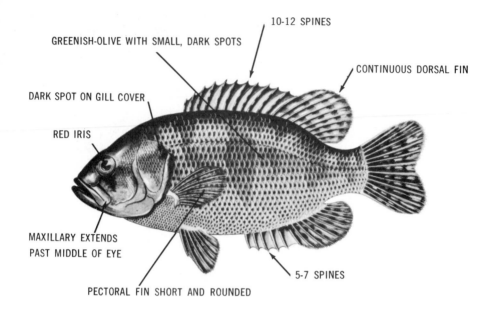

10-12 SPINES

GREENISH-OLIVE WITH SMALL, DARK SPOTS

CONTINUOUS DORSAL FIN

DARK SPOT ON GILL COVER

RED IRIS

MAXILLARY EXTENDS
PAST MIDDLE OF EYE

5-7 SPINES

PECTORAL FIN SHORT AND ROUNDED

Rock Bass

spines, a large mouth with the maxillary or upper jaw extending past the middle of a large red eye, dark spots on the scales which form lengthwise stripes below the lateral line, a dark spot on the gill cover and short and rounded pectoral fins. The general coloring is greenish-olive with brassy reflections or bronze coloring and with small dark spots in lines along the body. The fish is sometimes called "redeye" or "goggle-eye" due to the red color of the iris of the eye.

The warmouth bass is similar in general shape to the rock bass. It has a short, heavy body, a single dorsal fin, a short and rounded pectoral fin and a large mouth, but the warmouth bass has only two or three spines in the anal fin and lacks the longitudinal streaks of dark spots of the rock bass. Instead it has four dark lines or color bars on the cheek and gill cover; the bony part of the opercle flap (ear flap) is very dark with a lighter border around it. The warmouth can also be distinguished from all other panfish by the presence of teeth on the tongue. In coloring, the warmouth has the appearance of being brassy in hue, mottled with dark brown. Like the rock bass, the iris of the eye is red.

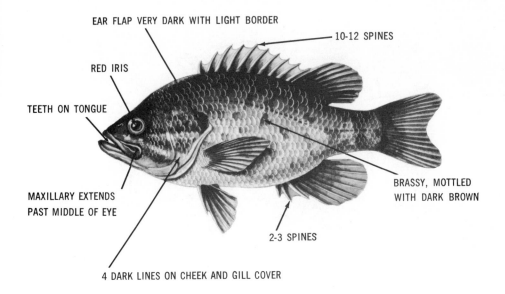

EAR FLAP VERY DARK WITH LIGHT BORDER

10-12 SPINES

RED IRIS

TEETH ON TONGUE

MAXILLARY EXTENDS
PAST MIDDLE OF EYE

BRASSY, MOTTLED
WITH DARK BROWN

2-3 SPINES

4 DARK LINES ON CHEEK AND GILL COVER

Warmouth Bass

RANGE AND HABITAT

Rock bass are found in thirty-six states and warmouth bass in twenty-eight states. Their general distribution can be seen on the maps. Note that the warmouth bass is found primarily in the south-central and southeastern part of the United States with the fish also distributed along the west coast. The rock bass is more widely distributed and is found in most states except the western United States and some states in the South, Southeast and in New England.

Rock bass are found primarily in clear-water lakes or streams. They do well in the kind of water inhabited by smallmouth bass—water with gravel or rocky bottoms, streams with running water, or lakes with sandy, hard, rock-strewn bottoms. One illustration of this can be seen from a study in Missouri. Before impoundment, rock bass made up 19 percent of the creel from the upper Black River in Missouri. The river was then dammed to form Clearwater Lake. A year after impoundment, rock bass made up only 3 percent of the creel from the lake, and each year after that the percent declined

Distribution of the rock bass.

until the catch of rock bass was negligible. It was evident that rock bass failed to spawn successfully in the lake. They just do not do well in the average artificial lake with mud bottom and cloudy water.

Warmouth bass thrive in either clear or cloudy water, although the rate of growth is slower in continuously turbid waters. They prefer quiet waters over mud bottoms where there is adequate vegetation, sometimes even dense beds of weeds. They are found in both lakes and streams but are far more numerous in lakes, preferring the large bodies of water. They do not grow as fast in small streams or ponds.

The kind of habitat preferred by each of these species of fish is an important key in determining where to fish. In fishing for rock bass in streams, look for them in and around any kind of underwater obstructions. These fish like to lurk in the middle or under piles of brush in streams. Look for them right under an overhanging bank, beside rocks and boulders or in or around aquatic vegetation. They like shady spots in hot weather, deep pools if there is plenty of cover, the well-oxygenated water below riffles and dams and the eddies off of the foaming swirls in streams.

Distribution of the warmouth bass.

Warmouth bass are lovers of bayous and shallow, weedy places. They are not as partial to rocks or logs as the rock bass, preferring dense weed beds instead. At times, these fish have a distinct muddy taste because of the kind of water areas they inhabit, and so they are not nearly so sought after as a food fish as are some of the other sunfishes.

In lakes, rock bass definitely prefer the rocky shoals and bars; sometimes they are found over very shallow bars when the water temperatures are ideal (65° to 75°). In hot weather, they like the rocky drop-offs in deeper water, the shade of huge boulders and steeply cut banks, or the protection of underwater brush, stumps or logs. In lakes lacking rocks and boulders, but offering areas of stumps, brush and sunken logs, you should fish for them by brush piles, fallen trees and stumps sticking out of the water.

Always try to find the weed beds, lily pads and other vegetation in lakes when searching for warmouth bass. When water temperatures are moderate, you'll find the fish in shallow-water weed beds; when the hot weather sets in, try the deeper underwater weeds.

Rock bass in streams lurk under piles of brush or overhanging banks, beside rocks and boulders, or near aquatic vegetation.

REPRODUCTION AND GROWTH

The spawning habits of both the rock and warmouth bass are similar to those of other sunfish. Both of these fish spawn from early April until July, the exact time depending upon the water temperature conditions. Rock bass spawn in usually 1 to 4 feet of water over gravelly bottoms. A bar over which a slight current is flowing is a favorite place in streams. Shallow, sandy, or gravelly shoals or sheltered bays are favorite places in lakes. The warmouth bass prefers to spawn in isolated clearings in shallow water among dense growths of aquatic vegetation. In the case of both fish, it is the male which digs out the nest and guards it after the eggs are laid and for a few days after the fry are hatched.

44

Under favorable conditions, in fertile water which is not over-populated, these fish may average half a pound, although this is above average for most waters. Michigan boasts a record rock bass weighing 3 pounds 5 ounces. A study of growth rates of warmouth bass was made in sixty-eight representative bodies of water in Oklahoma. The largest of 1,131 fish checked was 10.8 inches in length and weighed 1 pound 5 ounces. Many of the fastest-growing fish came from newly created lakes which are extremely fertile for the first several years after impoundment. The growth rate of warmouth bass in large lakes and reservoirs was also significantly above that in small lakes, ponds and streams. The average warmouth bass of half a pound is about 8½ inches long. To weigh a pound, the fish must reach approximately 10½ inches. The record warmouth was a 2-pound, 2-ounce fish caught in South Carolina in 1973.

In lakes rock bass prefer rocky shoals and bars, the shade of large boulders and steeply cut banks, the cover of fallen trees and underwater stumps.

Warmouth bass, in both lakes and streams, inhabit shallow weed beds, water thick with lily pads and other vegetation.

FEEDING HABITS

One of the important characteristics of these fish from the point of view of the angler is their eating habits. Knowing what they eat helps you in knowing what baits and artificials to use in catching them. The young of both of these species feed upon miscroscopic crustaceans, the nymphs, larvae and adult forms of aquatic insects, and worms and snails. The adults feed upon insects and worms but also upon small fishes much more than do others of the true sunfishes. In addition, the rock bass will eat many kinds of food found in the rocky habitat where it lives. Hellgrammites and crawfish are excellent baits for rock bass. Small minnows are excellent for both the rock and warmouth.

It is important to remember that both of these fish like plenty of cover. When fishing for rock bass, you'll have to drop your bait or lure right in the middle of the hollow stump, or right next to it, or let the bait drift completely under the brush pile or undercut bank. Many bait fisherman put their live bait right through a small hole in the brush. Look for the warmouth in the small holes or pockets in the densest weeds and then fish right in these small openings. Neither fish likes to leave its protective cover, except in the late evening and at night, so you'll have to find the cover where they are holed up.

Both of these fish feed both day and night. In warm weather, perhaps the best time of all to fish for them is late evening during the hour before dark. You can also have success with small black poppers after dark. Both fish strike with a hard bang, fight viciously for a short time with fast, quick rushes and then turn quickly to be brought in. Some will fight all of the way in, but most give up after a short, hard fight.

One of the most delightful characteristics of these fish is their willingness to strike. They will hit almost any kind of bait or artificial, and are usually in a striking mood. The total abandon with which they hit lures and flies brings joy to an angler's heart.

These are school fish, so when you hook one be extremely careful not to disturb the rest while you're playing the first fish in. This is particularly necessary in clear, shallow water.

LURES AND BAIT

The rock and warmouth bass are among the few sunfishes that can be caught readily on both fly and spinning tackle and with both live bait and artificials.

The best live baits for rock bass are earthworms (one of the best), small minnows, hellgrammites, small crawfish or crawfish tails, stonefly nymphs, grasshoppers, crickets, cockroaches, catalpa worms and meal worms. The best live bait for warmouth bass are earthworms, small minnows, dragonfly nymphs, mayfly nymphs, grasshoppers, crickets, cockroaches, catalpa worms and meal worms. Certainly, the fact that these fish will take such a wide variety of baits gives the angler a lot of leeway to use what is most readily available.

There are also a large number of spinning lures that will take both species of these fish.

Surface Plugs

Baby Crippled Killer (Phillips)

DAVE RICHEY PHOTO

Rock bass like plenty of cover, but when they see a lure or bait they strike readily. This angler used light tackle and a weighted spinner to get down deep.

Creek Chub Plunker (Creek Chub)
Jitterbug (Fred Arbogast)

Floating-Diving Plugs

Creek Chub Pikie Minnow (Creek Chub)
Finn-Oreno (Gladding-South Bend)
Flatfish, 2½″ (Helin)
Rebel Shiner Minnow (Plastic Research and Development Corp.)
Tiny River Runt Spook (Daisy-Heddon)

Sinking Plugs

Deep Inch (Falls)
Harrison's Rocky Lure Junior (Harrison-Hoge)
Inch Minnow (Falls)
L & S Mirrolure, Joined (L & S Bait Co.)
Rapala (Normark)
Tiny Ike (Daisy-Heddon)

Spoons

Al's Goldfish (Al's Goldfish Lure Co.)
Dardevle Midget (Lou Eppinger)
Geminini Spoon (Al's Goldfish)
K-B Spoon (Prescott)
Little Cleo (Seneca)
Midge (Glen Evans)

Weighted Spinners

Droppen (Garcia)
Little Fooler (Hildebrandt)
Marathon Bream Buster (Marathon)
Mepps Black Fury (Sheldon's)
Worth Scamp (Worth)

Nature Lures

2″ Spinner Minnow (Weber)
Panfish Worm Lure (Sportsman's Products)

Of all of the above which are suggested, those lures which will work sub-surface are generally superior to the surface lures. The nature lures—particularly the plastic worm—are real killers; the weighted spinners and spoons will also work well. Generally, the plugs are not quite as good as these others, not because the fish won't hit them, but because the plugs are so big it's hard for the fish to get hooked.

For fly fishing, we have an infinite variety to choose from. Actually, rock bass and warmouth bass will take all types of dry flies, wet flies and fly-rod lures. I prefer dry flies that are a little larger and bushier than those used for bluegills and other small-mounthed sunfish. Also, streamers work well on these fish, since the fish eat more minnows and small fry than the other true sunfish. Fly-rod lures are also quite productive.

Nature Lures

Crawfish (Burke Flexo-Products Co.) (Creme Lure Co.)
Flyrod Frog (Burke)
Brown or Green Frog (Creme)
Cricket, Tru-Life (Weber)
Grasshopper, Green or Yellow (Creme)
Grasshopper, Brown (Burke)
Baby Hellgrammite (Burke)

Fly-Rod Lures

Colorado Spinner (to use with wet flies, pork rind, as needed)
Dylite Deluxe Creepy Popper (Weber)
Firelure Nitwit (Weber)
Marathon Grasshopper Fly (Marathon)
Mountain (deer hair) Hopper (Phillips)
Ruf-Rubber: Waterbug,
Ruf-Rubber: Waterbug, Varmint, Skit-It (Glen Evans)
Screwball (Glen Evans)
Wisp (Falls Bait Co.)
Flatfish, Baby, 1¾" (Helin)
Uncle Josh Pork Rind, Fly Strip, White

Dry Flies

Bivisible: Black, Brown, Grizzly

Royal Coachman
Gauze Wing Drake
Gray Hackle Red
Goofus Bug
Irresistible
Wulff Black, Blonde, Royal

Wet Flies

Black Gnat
Coachman
Gold Ribbed
Hair's Ear
Parmacheene Belle
Western Bee
Professor

Wooly Worm

Fall's Spider (black, yellow, green)

Weber Brim-Fli: Black/White or Red Tail

Nymphs (Weighted)

Mayfly Nymph
Ted's Stonefly Nymph
Tellico

Streamer Flies

Black Ghost
Edson Tiger Dark
Gray Ghost
Mickey Finn
Muddler
Nine-Three
Professor
Red and White Bucktail
Yellow Marabou

Ordinarily, size 8 is about right for rock and warmouth bass since they have large mouths. If the fish are running large, size 6 in some types of flies may be all right; if the fish are running small, size 10 is probably better. If you are missing too many strikes, use smaller flies or lures.

When spinning for rock bass in flowing streams, if you are using a surface or floating-diving plug, cast the plug so it will drift past the suspected hiding place of the fish. Just twitch the lure slightly, giving it enough motion to make it appear alive. The floating-diving lure can be retrieved very slowly past the hideout, just fast enough to make it swim lazily along. For a fuller explanation of fishing surface, floating-diving, and sinking plugs, see Chapter 9.

When using sinking plugs, weighted spinners, spoons and nature lures, let the lures sink into the deep holes, under banks and by underwater cover before retrieving. You may have to get your lures nearly to the bottom of the stream or lake in which you are fishing before the fish will strike.

When fly fishing, use your dry flies and poppers on calm evenings or nights, especially in warm weather when the fish are surface feeding. A black popper makes a good fly-rod lure at night. In the middle of the day in warm weather, and whenever the fish are deeper, let your wet flies, streamers and nymphs sink before retrieving. If you need to get down deeper, add split shot on a spinner. You can cast your wet flies and nymphs up and across stream and let them float down naturally with the current past the hiding places of the fish. Streamers can be fished downstream, across or up; it doesn't matter as long as you are able to make them swim and dart past the best cover.

When fishing for warmouth in lakes, let the streamers sink near the bottom and retrieve in slow jerks, making them dart like minnows. The wet flies or nymphs can be twitched just as in fishing for other sunfish.

When live-bait fishing in flowing streams, use your fly rod with only split shot added to the leader, letting the bait wash down naturally with the current past the fish lairs.

In quiet waters, either lake or stream, I prefer to use a bobber if not fishing too deep. If the bobber is set for deep water, you can't take in line nor pull all of the line out of the water without doing it by hand, as the bobber interferes with retrieving. If you are fishing water 10 feet deep or more, you can either still-fish without a bobber or use a sliding bobber. For this type of fishing, your spinning tackle works best.

4

SUNFISH

One of the most helpful guides to identifying the different species of sunfish is the structure and coloring of the ear flap, the elongated rear edge of the gill cover. The ear flap consists of a long part plus a membrane of varying width. On all of the true sunfishes there is a black spot on this ear flap; sometimes the spot is just on the bony structure of the flap; sometimes it is just on the membrane; sometimes it is on both. On some sunfish, there are other colors in addition to black on the ear flap. Thus, the dimensions, structure and coloring of the flap help to identify the various species.

GREEN SUNFISH (*Lepomis cyanellus*)

In a survey of the United States, thirty-nine states reported green sunfish within their boundaries. There may be other states where green sunfish are found, but these others did not think it important enough to report this fact in the survey.

The green sunfish has several distinguishing marks. The black spot on the ear flap is on the bony portion only and does not extend to the membrane. There is a single dark area on both the dorsal and anal fins, located on the posterior part of those fins next to the body of the fish. The dorsal, anal and caudal (tail) fins have a yellow edge on the tips. The body is usually green in color and often shows longitudinal lines.

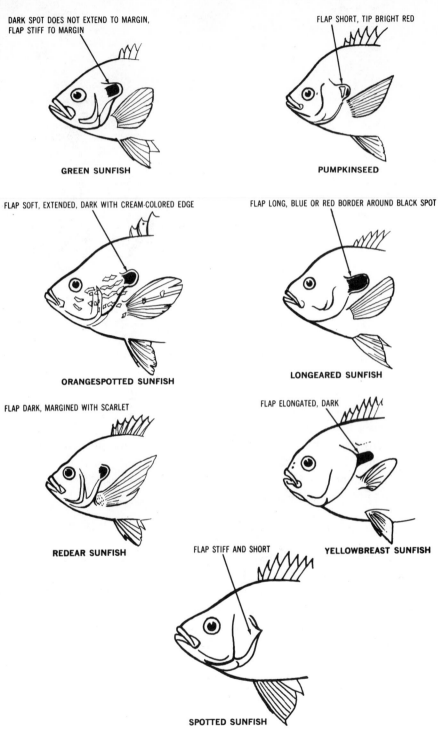

DARK SPOT DOES NOT EXTEND TO MARGIN, FLAP STIFF TO MARGIN

GREEN SUNFISH

FLAP SHORT, TIP BRIGHT RED

PUMPKINSEED

FLAP SOFT, EXTENDED, DARK WITH CREAM-COLORED EDGE

ORANGESPOTTED SUNFISH

FLAP LONG, BLUE OR RED BORDER AROUND BLACK SPOT

LONGEARED SUNFISH

FLAP DARK, MARGINED WITH SCARLET

REDEAR SUNFISH

FLAP ELONGATED, DARK

YELLOWBREAST SUNFISH

FLAP STIFF AND SHORT

SPOTTED SUNFISH

Comparison of ear flaps of different species of sunfish.

54

Distribution of the green sunfish.

This is one of the sunfish of average size, usually reaching from 4 to 8 inches. However, in the Southern states the fish tends to grow more rapidly and to reach a larger average size. The following table shows the rate of growth of green sunfish.

This table would indicate that this rate of growth is considerably faster than in more northern states. Thus, the rate of growth (in inches) in Ohio and Minnesota, as compared with Oklahoma, is as follows.

LENGTH AT END OF YEAR

	1	*2*	*3*	*4*	*5*	*6*	*7*
Ohio	2.3	4.3	5.6	6.3	6.8	—	—
Minnesota	1.7	2.9	3.9	5.0	5.9	6.6	7.2
Oklahoma	3.8	6.0	7.3	7.9	8.9	9.0	—

In the studies made in Oklahoma, most of the fish (96.3 percent) studied (1,656 specimens from 110 bodies of water) were less than four years old. Apparently only a few fish live longer than that. Fish living in streams show the slowest growth rate whereas those in ponds show the fastest growth. Those fish which are spawned in small or large lakes show a slightly slower growth rate than those in the ponds. The world's record green sunfish was caught in Minnesota and weighed 2 pounds, 2 ounces.

The green sunfish is found predominantly in streams, creeks or small ponds. If placed in larger bodies of water with other sunfishes, it does not do well and is sometimes entirely eliminated. It also does poorly in clear, cold waters. It prefers streams or creeks with muddy bottoms, and slow, sluggish creeks rather than those that are clear and swift. Turbid water does not seem to affect this fish too much except slightly to impede growth rate. This is a good fish to stock in small farm ponds where other sunfishes are not present.

These fish spawn from early spring into the summer months, the time depending entirely upon the climate and temperature. Thus, in Ohio the fish spawn from early April to late July with most of the spawning taking place in May and June. They can be caught easily during this period.

The adult fish eat plants, insects, worms and larvae, crawfish and various small fish and can be caught with most all of the very small minnows, land and water insects and their larvae or nymphs.

I have also had outstanding success in fly fishing for these fish. They take panfish poppers, dry flies, wet flies, nymphs and small streamers readily. Their large mouth (compared to the bluegill's) makes it possible even to use panfish lures on these fish: sponge-rubber spiders, plastic worms and larvae, very small wobbling spoons, fly-rod plugs, and fly and spinner combinations. In general, though, the lures (except sponge-rubber spiders) are not as good as flies. I sometimes add a little strip of pork rind to the fly and find it works well.

The spinning or spincasting outfit is not ideally suited to these fish. You can, of course, use a plastic bubble and fly, or cast tiny lures, or fish live bait with your spinning equipment, but the ultra-light fly rod is more ideally suited for green sunfish.

ORANGESPOTTED SUNFISH (*Lepomis humilis*)

Since this is one of the smallest sunfishes it was not included in the survey, but this omission is justified since this fish has no sport or commercial value at all, and its only importance is as a forage species.

This fish has a shorter life span and a smaller maximum size than any of the other sunfishes discussed in this book. In a survey conducted in Oklahoma, no orangespotted sunfish were found older than three years of age; most were less than two years of age. The largest fish found was only 4.8 inches in length; most were less than 3 inches. No fish weighed as much as .1 of a pound.

This fish can be identified in several ways. The black spot on the ear flap is almost entirely on the membrane rather than on the bony structure; there is a white margin around the dark spot. The fish has three spines and seven to nine rays in the anal fin and twenty to thirty squarish orange spots on the body of the fish behind the gills.

REDEAR SUNFISH, OR SHELLCRACKER
(*Lepomis microlophus*)

Twenty-eight states reported that this fish was found within their borders, although a few others may have neglected to mention it. This sunfish can be identified in several ways. There is a broad scarlet border on the ear flap which surrounds the black spot; the fish has a small mouth; the body is without spots or bars, the pectoral fin is long and pointed and reaches to or beyond the middle of the anal fin.

This fish gets the name shellcracker from its habit of eating snails and other shelled animals. The lower pharyngeals of the fish are provided with thick, heavy teeth which enable it to crush shells. The fish seems to prefer a steady diet of plankton, various organisms from the bottom and only an occasional small fish.

The redear is one of the fastest growing and one of the largest of the true sunfishes and so it is very popular among the fisherman of the South. In a survey conducted in Oklahoma, involving 2,046 fish, the average redear reached a catchable size during the second summer, the slowest growing not until the fourth year of life, while those displaying the fastest growth grew to a length of 7.3 inches during the first year of life. The largest fish was 12 inches long and weighed 1 pound 6 ounces. The record redear weighed 4 pounds, 8 ounces and was caught in Virginia.

Distribution of the redear sunfish.

This fish prefers small lakes, reservoirs and slow-moving rivers, particularly those with clear waters, where it exhibits a far-above-average growth rate. It sometimes enters brackish water but does not spawn there. It seems to prefer the deeper areas of lakes and can be caught readily by fishing deep with earthworms—a bait which is universally the favorite for these fish.

Since the redear sunfish seems to prefer deep water, it is not well suited to the fly fisherman. As far as I know, it will not take flies or lure readily, being caught almost exclusively on live bait.

The spawning habits of the fish are the same as other sunfish with the male scooping out the nest and then guarding it after the eggs are laid.

PUMPKINSEED SUNFISH (*Lepomis gibbosus*)

Thirty-five states reported the presence of the pumpkinseed sunfish, although others may have it but do not consider it important. As can be seen by the map, the fish is unevenly scattered across the northern part of the United States.

Deep-bodied in proportion to its length, the pumpkinseed is one of the most brightly colored of the sunfishes. It generally is greenish-

Distribution of the pumpkinseed.

olive on the back with a series of darker vertical bands running from the dorsal fin to slightly below the lateral line. The sides are dotted with scattered orange and crimson spots and the cheeks have a series of wavy blue stripes over a deeper orange color; these stripes radiate from the mouth to the edges of the gill cover. There is a single red or crimson spot on the hind portion of the short ear flap. The opercle (gill) flap is stiff and cannot be bent forward easily. The belly of the fish is a bright yellow or orange; the pectoral fin is long and pointed and the dorsal fin is quite high. The mouth is small so only small-size baits or flies should be used.

This fish does not usually grow to a large size. The following table shows the average total lengths of these sunfish from several states. The lengths are given in inches.

STATE	NO. OF SPECIMENS MEASURED	YEAR						
		1	2	3	4	5	6	7
Rhode Island	258	1.6	3.1	4.4	5.5	6.2	6.7	7.1
Minnesota	1,582	1.7	3.1	4.4	5.5	6.4	7.2	7.7
Michigan	4,184	3.3	4.9	5.9	6.8	7.5	8.0	8.1

As can be seen, this fish is large for its species when it grows to a length of 8 inches. It also is not very prolific in comparison with the bluegill. The number of eggs in the pumpkinseed ranges from 600 to 3000 whereas the egg count in the bluegill may be four to twenty times that figure. Furthermore, the pumpkinseed spawns only once a year, whereas the bluegill is almost a continual spawner; the same female bluegill may spawn more than once a year if the water is warm enough. Thus, in waters where the bluegill and pumpkinseed are in competition, the pumpkinseed usually declines in numbers.

This fish seems to prefer two types of cover: weedy areas and rocky areas. I have had my best luck, particularly early in the season, when some fish were still on the spawning beds, fishing over rocky shoals and along rocky shorelines of a lake. In sluggish, warm-water streams with a profuse growth of water plants, pumpkinseed sunfish do not do so well, as is evident from the fact that these fish are less common in the southern half of the United States.

During the spawning season, do most of your fishing for them over the spawning beds in water from 1 to 4 feet deep. The spawning season in Maine usually lasts from the beginning of June until the first of August with the peak near the end of June and the beginning of July. In warm states, spawning will begin earlier, usually in May. During the heat of the summer, you will have to fish for them in deeper water, usually up to about 15 feet deep, depending upon the temperature.

About half the diet of these fish is small mollusks such as snails and clams; the other half is mostly insects, nymphs and larvae of various kinds. The best live baits are earthworms, nymphs and lar-vae. Live crickets, grasshoppers and other insects are not nearly as good.

In fly fishing for pumpkinseeds, I have had the best luck on small artificial nymphs. These fish will also take small wet or dry flies but not with the same abandon as will the bluegill. Pumpkinseeds like to nibble at the bait more. They will hit panfish poppers with or without rubber legs, but I have trouble hooking the fish with these larger lures so I prefer dry flies. Use them on calm evenings in the early summer; you'll have a lot of fun.

You can catch pumpkinseed sunfish as readily in the winter through the ice as during the summer. Use small larvae as the best baits:

Panfish will consume surprisingly large baits for their size. Here a pumpkinseed sunfish devours a large earthworm.

Caddis worms (uncased), crane-fly larvae (mousees), catalpa worms
(cut in pieces), meal worms, gall worms and maggots are all good.

LONGEAR SUNFISH (*Lepomis megalotis*)

Twenty states indicated that the longer sunfish is found in their
waters. As can be seen on the map, this fish is found primarily in the
southern and south-central parts of the United States. It is relatively
unimportant as a sport fish, however, because of its small size. The
majority never reach 5 inches in length. In a survey of 656 fish from 52
bodies of water in Oklahoma, the largest fish was only 6.3 inches in
length and weighed only .2 of a pound. Most of the fish in this survey
were less than 3 years of age; most never grow to be 4 years old.

This fish is most often found in clear streams of medium size. It
does, however, show about equal growth when placed in reservoirs,
large and small lakes, ponds and streams. It does better in clear than
in turbid water, however.

The longear can be identified by its long ear flap, which is all
black except for a blue or red border. The fish has a steep back and
forehead, a low dorsal fin, rounded pectoral fin and small mouth. It
is very beautiful, with brilliant colors of blue, orange, crimson, yellow and red, and many wavy lines and spots. The iris of the eye is
reddish in color.

Distribution of the longear sunfish.

Because of its small size, this fish is seldom stocked intentionally; it feeds mostly on insects, their nymphs and larvae, and can be caught with small live baits, particularly worms or larvae, and with small artificial flies and nymphs.

The longear spawns in May and June in Ohio, somewhat earlier in the South, with most of the nests to be found in sandy gravel, in water from 1 to 3 feet deep.

YELLOWBREAST OR REDBREAST SUNFISH
(*Lepomis auritus*)

Twenty-one states indicated that the yellowbreast or redbreast sunfish could be found in their waters. There may be a few other states which consider this fish insignificant and so did not report it. The fish is primarily distributed along the Atlantic seaboard and in the Gulf states.

The yellowbreast can be identified by its elongated ear flap which, unlike the longear sunfish, has no border, being all black. The body

Distribution of the yellowbreast sunfish.

is uniformly colored, but its belly is bright orange. The anal fin has three spines; the mouth is fairly large for a sunfish.

This fish runs to a pound in weight, although most species, particularly in the northeastern states, are much smaller. The record fish was 1 pound, 8 ounces and was caught in Florida. This is primarily a stream fish, preferring clear, running water. The fish also does well in warm-water lakes with thick vegetation. The fish feeds on crustaceans, insects and their nymphs or larvae and on small fish.

The yellowbreast takes artificial bait readily and affords real sport on fly tackle or ultra-light spinning gear. The best artificials to use are the standard wet and dry flies, nymphs, very small streamers and plastic nature lures. The rubber spiders, popping bugs and small fly-rod lures, particularly the flatfish, are also good. The fish will hit small spinning lures such as ultra-light spoons, but, as is true for all sunfishes, flies are better.

The males begin to make their spawning nests in early June in Maine, the exact date depending upon the water temperature, which should be 65° to 70° F. The nests are about 12 inches in diameter in

Distribution of the spotted sunfish.

shallow water with a gravel bottom. The male attends the eggs and the young for a short period.

SPOTTED SUNFISH, SPOTTED BREAM
OR STUMPKNOCKER (*Lepomis punctatus*)

This fish has a limited distribution in eleven states, mostly in the southern and southeastern states. It is found in ponds, streams and brackish water. It has a fairly uniform coloring with small dark specks over a lighter background. It develops a brick-red color during the breeding season. It usually grows to be 6 to 8 inches in length. The mouth is small.

It can be caught on live bait or artificial flies using most any of the common methods already described. It is not very important as a sport fish; this is due mostly to its limited range. Southerners most often use live bait in fishing for it.

Distribution of the Sacramento perch.

SACRAMENTO PERCH *(Archoplites interruptus)*

This fish also has a limited distribution; it was native originally to California and is now found in the waters of only six states. It used to be very numerous in the sloughs and slow-flowing channels of the Sacramento-San Joaquin system and in the Pajaro and Salinas Rivers, but it is not now seen very often except in a few places such as Clear Lake, California.

The fish spawn in warm, shallow water. The only published record of their spawning describes about fifty of them spawning in 1 or 2 feet of water. There was no nest-building or guarding of eggs of the young. All of the fish were concentrated in one area, 4 by 12 feet, in a space covered by boulders and algae. There was some exchange of mates and each pair spawned in a different area about 1½ feet in diameter. The spawning activity lasted about six hours; the fish then wandered away leaving the eggs adhering to the algae or the rocks. On the following day, few eggs remained, however, suggesting that other fish had probably eaten most of them.

The fact that this fish does not guard its nest, as do the other sunfishes, suggests why its numbers may be on the decline. It cannot compete with other fishes which are introduced into its waters.

The Sacramento perch can be identified in several ways: the mouth is large with the corner of it extending back to a line through the middle of the eye. There are pronounced dark, vertical bars on each side; the fish has twelve or thirteen spines in the dorsal fin with very little dip between the spines and rays of that fin. There is also a typical sunfish dark spot at the rear angle of the gill cover. The Sacramento perch grows to about 1 foot in length. It can be caught readily on live bait or with various fly-rod artificials.

LAKE FISHING FOR SUNFISH

If I had to choose one best time to fish for sunfish, I would pick the spawning season, since the largest specimens are in shallow water during this period and are easily caught. And don't worry about catching these fish off of their nests. As has been mentioned, the greatest problem with sunfish is keeping the number under control so the fish may grow to a reasonable length. You will ordinarily be helping to improve the fishing in a lake by catching as many sunfish as possible.

The exact time the spawning season begins in your state will depend upon the water temperature. These fish begin to spawn as the temperature approaches 60° to 65°, with most of the spawning taking place when the water temperature is between 65° and 70°. In the northern part of the United States, May and June are the times when spawning begins, with the peak of the activity coming usually in June. Spawning may continue until the middle of July or later. In the southern states, spawning may take place in March or April, depending upon the temperature. By keeping a close watch on the weather and thermometer, you can usually tell when the activity is starting.

One good indication of when to fish is when the trees are well leafed out and the lilacs are in bloom. When this happens, the fast action with the sunfish will begin, particularly if there is a series of warm days with the air temperature over 70°. The sunfish then stay in fairly shallow water until the water temperature gets between 70°

and 75° and until the spawning is over.

After the spawning season and the hot summer weather begins, the sunfish retire to deeper water, usually 6 to 15 feet deep, depending upon the temperature. It is important during the time that the water is warming up in the early summer to fish at the right depth, since there is a temperature gradient between the surface and bottom of a lake or pond. Even fairly shallow ponds and lakes have a temperature gradient in early summer before the water is thoroughly warmed from top to bottom. For example, ponds 6 to 8 feet deep in Missouri had the following temperature gradient during June of one year.

Surface 72°
1 ft.   71°
2 ft.   69°
3 ft.   68°
4 ft.   68°
5 ft.   64°
6 ft.   62°
7 ft.   61°
8 ft.   60°
9 ft.   60°

Obviously, the early-season sunfisherman ought to fish in water not over about 3 to 4 feet deep for best results.

After the water gets much over 70°, the sunfish will usually stay in deeper water until late afternoon, night or early morning. During the hot weather of summer, the late evening hours, just before dark, are usually wonderful times for fly fishing in bays and along shorelines (particularly in calm water) as the sunfish come into shore late in the evening to feed. You will also have success after dark, especially with surface bugs and flies. Early morning is also good, but this time is usually not as good as the late evening.

If you fish during hot summer days, you'll have to fish fairly deep. Large, deep lakes form definite temperature layers: the epilimnion (warm surface layer), thermocline (temperature gradient) and hypolimnion (bottom cold layer), but only during the really hot, still days of late summer. Sunfish are usually found near the top of the thermocline or near the bottom of the hypolimnion, except when they come into the shallows to feed. In order to get down deep enough, use a split shot when fishing wet flies or nymphs or add a spinner to your wet fly and then allow the fly to sink before retrieving. Live bait is also always good fished close to bottom in hot weather. You can use small nature lures on your fly or spinning outfit, weighted so they can be fished down deep. Occasionally, a small spoon or weighted spinner will take sunfish, particularly if a bit of pork rind or live bait has been attached to the hook. Small plugs will work but are not as good.

As the lake cools off in the fall, and the water turns over, the fish will range in both the shallow and the deep areas. When the cool weather begins again in earnest, the sunfish will again retire to the deeper water and can be caught most easily using live bait at approximately 10- to 12-foot depths. For some reason or another, I have never done well with the fly rod and flies on sunfish in the late fall. After the water has cooled to about 65° and below, the fish just aren't very active and have to be caught with very deliberate techniques and with small baits.

The principal job in lake fishing is to locate the schools of sunfish. Look for them in rocky areas, particularly around large boulders or over rocky or sandy bars or shoals. By boat houses, docks, floating rafts, anchored boats, trees, stumps, brush, lily pads and weed beds are good places. Look for sharp drop-offs and fish right along the steep banks leading into deeper water. This is particularly effective during warm weather. During the spawning season look in the bays and sheltered areas over sandy, gravel bottoms in water 1 to 4 feet deep. During hot weather, you may have to seek the deeper weed beds or rocky areas.

Since most lake fishing is done from a boat, use one that can be moved gently from spot to spot without scaring the fish. This means one you can row or paddle easily.

If you are fly fishing, try to pick a calm area near good cover so you can cast and work your fly or lure properly. If you are still-fishing, move around occasionally until you find the fish but always try to pick spots where there is likely-looking cover.

When fishing for sunfish through the ice, the fish will usually be in water 8 to 15 feet deep, although they may swim around just under the ice occasionally. However, fishing about a foot off of the bottom is usually best.

STREAM FISHING

One of the most enjoyable experiences is to wade and fly fish streams and creeks for sunfish. It's far better sport than fishing from the bank and much more productive. During hot days when the water is just warming up in the spring, look for the fish in very shallow, calm water, usually in small inlets and bays out of the mainstream. The fish are either there spawning or up in the shallows warming up.

During hot weather and with the water warm, the fish seek shady spots under overhanging banks and deep pools. Usually the deepest water is found on the outside of the curve at the bend in the stream and where the water undercuts the bank. Also, deadfalls, brush, trees and weedbeds are likely spots in the stream or creek. During the colder weather of fall, the fish may be anywhere, depending on the time of day and temperature of the water, but usually they seek the deep, calm-water holes.

One must be extremely careful to avoid splashing, thumping the stream bottom or bank and other unnecessary commotion while stream fishing, or else the best specimens of sunfish will be scared off or become too wary to bite. Usually in clear, shallow streams and creeks the finest terminal tackle and utmost caution are necessary to catch the largest fish. I prefer small bugs and nymphs, or flies without a spinner. Only in the larger, deeper, cloudier water do I use small spinners with flies in fishing for sunfish. Ultra-light spoons or spinners with a bit of pork rind or live bait are also very effective in deep, turbid water. Usually, though, the flies are best. If the fish are spitting out your lures without getting hooked, add a tiny worm or larva to the hook; this technique really helps.

In fishing flowing streams with live bait, attach a split shot and let the bait drift along naturally into the deep holes, under banks, past logs and brush, past boulders and rocks and weedbeds. Play out your line as the bait floats downstream, keeping enough slack in it so it doesn't pull taut and jerk the bait up short—a sure give-away to the fish that it is not what it pretends to be.

If your creek is too deep in spots to wade, use an innertube float with canvas cover and seat. It is the most efficient method I have ever found to fish a deep, slow-moving stream.

5

YELLOW PERCH

The yellow perch is the only fish discussed in this book which belongs to the true perch family Percidae. Fish of this family can be distinguished from the sunfishes and those of the sea bass family in several ways. The perches have a completely divided dorsal fin on the back with the spiny portion separate from the soft. Also, the anal fin of the perch has only one or two spines.

The perch family is divided into three genera: 1) the *Stizostedion* genus, including the walleye (*Stizostedion vitreum vitreum*), and the sauger (*Stizostedion canadense*); 2) the *Perca* genus, including the Eurasian and American yellow perches; and 3) the *Percina* genus, including about ninety species of darters in North America, the largest of which is the logperch (*Percina caprodes*). All of the darters except the logperch are small, 1 to 3 inches in length. The yellow perch belongs to the second group, the *Perca* genus.

The yellow perch (*Perca flavescens*) is sometimes called the ringed perch, raccoon perch or common perch. Its color varies, but it is usually yellow or yellowish-green, blending to a lighter yellow or greenish color on the side with the belly almost white. In dark water, the back may be blackish or dark olive-green, with a lighter green on the sides and a yellowish cast to the belly. There are conspicuous dark vertical bars on the sides, six to eight in number, with seven most common. The fish has a humpbacked appearance due to an upturned head and snout forward of the eyes. The body of the fish feels rough to the touch because of the ctenoid-type scales. The first dorsal fin contains twelve to fourteen spiny rays: the second dorsal fin has two or three spiny rays and twelve or thirteen soft rays. The anal fin has two spiny rays and seven or eight soft rays; there are fifty-seven to sixty-two scales along the lateral line.

The yellow perch has a prominent curved lateral line; the tail is weakly forked and rounded on the tips. The fish has a large mouth with bands of small teeth, but there are no large canine teeth such as occur in the walleye and sauger. Before and during the breeding season the lower fins may be a brilliant orange color.

Under better than average conditions, a yellow perch may reach 12 inches and a weight of a pound in about nine years. A very fast-growing female may attain a length of 12 inches in five years. The all-time record is a 4¼-pound specimen taken in the Delaware River, New Jersey, in 1865, by Dr. C. C. Abbott.

Forty-two states report the presence of the yellow perch within their boundaries. Of these, New Mexico has only a few; Oklahoma has practically none. Others that did not mention it also probably have limited numbers, especially some of the southern states which reported them.

As can be seen by the map, these fish are found primarily in the northern latitudes of the United States with none found in many of the south-central states. This distribution is due to the fact that yellow perch are really a cool-water fish, somewhere in between the cold-water fish (the trouts and salmon) and the warmwater fish (sunfish and others) in their preference for cool temperatures. It has been found that yellow perch prefer water temperatures of 69.8°, and concentrations can often be found at that temperature stratum in the summer.

HABITAT AND HABITS

Yellow perch are an adaptable type of fish, adjusting to a wide variety of water conditions. They are most numerous, however, in large, deep, clear lakes with modest amounts of vegetation. The yellow perch is primarily not a stream fish, unless the stream is deep

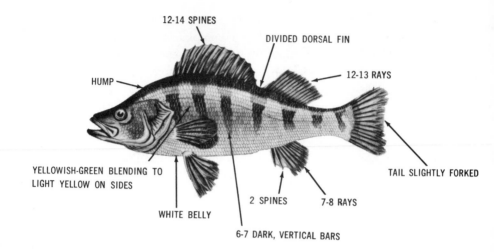

Yellow Perch

and sluggish and has a fair amount of aquatic vegetation.

The fish move about a lake in schools of from 50 to 200 fish. The schools are stratified by size and age of fish, so if you can locate a school of large specimens, you can catch a whole string.

Extensive studies and observation have revealed that the largest perch are those which inhabit fairly deep water. The young adults and young of the year congregate about aquatic plants in shallow water; but if you want to catch the largest fish, you have to move out deeper. Along the shores of Lake Michigan, Lake Erie and other Great Lakes, for example, anglers fishing from the piers on shore consistently take smaller fish than do the commercial fishermen farther out in the lake.

The exact depth at which to fish will depend upon the time of year and day and the water temperature and oxygen conditions. After the ice is out in the spring, and before spawning, the perch will be located all over a lake and at all depths from about 10 to 50 feet. They seem fairly well distributed. As the water gradually warms up, however, and approaches 45°, which is the approximate temperature at which the fish begin spawning, they start their shoreward migration. Some will migrate up rivers to spawn, others just move to the weedy shallows to deposit their eggs. Usually the males

Distribution of the yellow perch.

will be the first to the spawning beds and the last to depart. The females move in, spawn and then depart. Many times you will catch more males than females in shallow water just before and after the spawning period. During this season of the year, you can have some very fast action casting in the bays and along weedy shorelines. This is really the only time of year when you can catch many large perch while fishing in shallow water.

Spawning may occur anywhere between March and early May, the exact time depending upon latitude and temperature. In lakes containing northern pike and walleyes, the northerns are the first to spawn right after ice out, then come the walleyes, followed closely by the yellow perch.

Spawning is usually over by the time the water temperatures have reached 52°. After this, the fish move gradually to deeper water, but they usually can be found for some time in medium-depth water, from about 10 to 25 feet.

When the warm weather of summer begins, the fish are usually found in the cooler water in the thermocline, if the lake is deep enough to have temperature stratification. Studies in Lake Mendota,

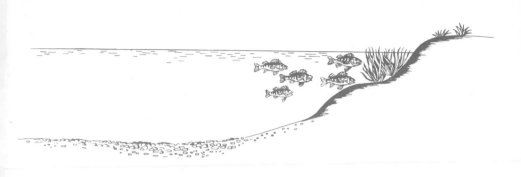

In the spring, as the water approaches 45°, the fish begin spawning. Look for them in the weedy shallows along the shoreline or at the mouths of inlets.

Wisconsin, have shown that during the early summer and in the daytime, the fish usually swim below the surface at depths ranging from 25 to 35 feet. By July, the adult perch are most numerous at the 35–55 foot levels. By August, however, as the oxygen begins to be depleted at the lower levels, the fish begin to rise toward the 22-foot level. The fish are caught at various levels, however. The general conclusion is that most of the adult perch remain in the deepest water which contains enough oxygen to sustain life.

Most of the time the fish can be caught close to the bottom at the appropriate depth. Nets placed 6 feet off the bottom at Green Bay, Wisconsin, seldom catch perch. Perch will occasionally linger well off the bottom at a level where they find sufficient oxygen, but usually you will do better to find a depth that is right and then fish only a foot or two off the bottom.

What about fishing in the autumn? After the water has cooled enough for the lake to turn over, the fish scatter all over the lake. You can catch some in fairly shallow water during this period, but most larger fish still are found in deeper water where they remain during the winter. Most of your largest fish will remain under the ice in depths of from 15 to 50 feet, unless forced out of the depths by oxygen depletion. Apparently there is some variation from lake to lake, but don't make the mistake of fishing too shallow for yellow perch. You'll catch bigger ones in deeper water.

There is one other perch habit that you ought to know about. Perch are strictly daylight feeders. This means that toward sundown they move in to shore until they touch bottom. There, the schools break up and scatter and the individual perch sink to the bottom

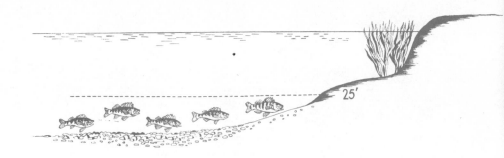

By early summer, after the water has reached 52°, yellow perch are through spawning and gradually migrate to deeper water. Fish for them just off the bottom at 25-35 foot depths.

where they rest for the night. At daybreak, the fish rise, congregate into schools, and, shortly after sunrise, they swim back into deeper water. The fish are completely inactive during this resting period in shallow water so, unfortunately, you can't have much luck catching them there very early or late in the day. You'll do better to wait until the schools have congregated and begun their daytime feeding, even though they are in deeper water.

The food habits of perch vary, but the small backward-slanting teeth which line the jaws, and the inner edges of the gills which are lined with comb-like gill rakers, equip the fish for a diet of small, live animal foods. The gill rakers strain out small organisms from the water. Commonly, the stomachs of small fish are filled with nothing but microscopic crustaceans or midge larvae which the fish strain from the water and mud. Midge larvae form a principal diet of the fish in winter.

Other common foods of the adult fish are insect larvae of all kinds, small crawfish and small fish. An analysis of the stomach content of fish taken from rivers revealed that about one-half of the food was crawfish. Fish found in lakes often are filled with minnows and crawfish. Thus, both of these make extremely good live baits. Earthworms are also good, but crawfish tails or minnows will usually take the larger fish. I've also caught large perch on small live frogs. Cut minnows will sometimes work very well.

Yellow perch seldom feed on the surface. They will gobble up mayflies but usually those which are water soaked and half drowned. Thus, you can fish for them with wet flies. Dry flies or bugs are very

75

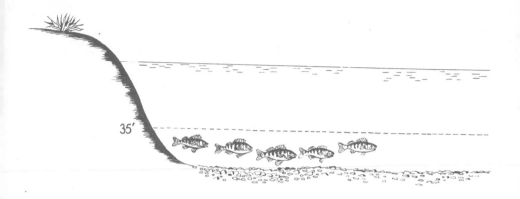

Later in the summer—around July in the North—the adult fish are driven by the heat into really deep water. Get your bait down below 35 feet.

poor lures for yellow perch. Better lures are small streamer flies or fly and spinner combinations which represent minnows. Of course, various nature lures and small spinning lures work very well.

METHODS OF FISHING

The principal problem in fishing for yellow perch is getting your bait down deep enough to catch the largest fish. This is not too difficult early in the spring, just before, during and after the spawning season, but it is a real problem during the best part of the summer when the fish are deep.

If you like to fly fish, the best time is early spring. You can use streamer flies, wet flies and spinners (sometimes with a little pork rind attached), plastic nature lures or small fly-rod plugs or spoons.

The best all-round tackle for yellow perch is spinning or spin-casting equipment. When the fish are deep, 20 or 30 feet or so, small, heavy, sinking spoons or weighted spinners work very well when you're casting. If you are going to troll, you can have good luck with small sinking plugs to which weight has been added to sink the lures down to the fish. Or, plastic worms on gang hooks with a spinner attached make a wonderful bait.

When the fish are in water from 30 to 50 feet deep, your best bet is to still fish with small live minnows or crawfish tails. Cut bait,

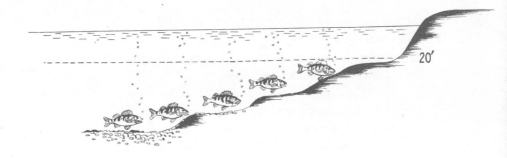

By August the oxygen in the depths of some lakes has been depleted and the fish rise toward the 22-foot level where breathing is easier. Fish for them at various depths, from 20 to 50 feet, however, since the oxygen content of lakes varies.

worms, fish eyes or various types of meat: beefsteak, shrimp and other types will also produce, but these are usually not as good as the minnows or crawfish, except in the winter. The reason I prefer live-bait fishing in this very deep water is simply that it is the easiest method to use to get the bait down deep enough to take the large fish. It's really much more fun catching the fish by casting, but I'm just not patient enough to let my lure sink down 40 to 50 feet each time I cast.

Yellow perch can be caught readily through the ice in the winter time, since they will bite all year around. My favorite bait is yellow perch eyes. Use any sort of bait to catch several perch, then take one of these fish, press below the eye with your thumb until the eyeball pops out; pull the eye loose, and impale it on a size 8 hook. Sometimes two eyes can be used at once.

There are certain times that are better than others for fishing for yellow perch. As has been mentioned, your best shallow-water fishing will be in early spring. After the hot weather of summer, you'll have to get down deep to find the big fish, since adult perch prefer water of 69.8 degrees. You can catch just as many perch in the summer as in the spring, but in the summer you'll have to search the depths to find them. In the fall, you may find them all over the lake, but usually in water from 10 to 50 feet. In winter, look for them at depths of from 15 to 50 feet.

What about the time of day? Unlike most fish, yellow perch seem to bite best during the day. From 10 a.m. to 2 p.m. and again from 4 p.m. to 6 p.m. are usually the best times to fish. Don't try to catch them at night; it doesn't work. Also, there is usually no use getting up early in the morning, since the middle of the day is usually better.

When ice fishing, I prefer the period from 10 a.m. to about 4 p.m., depending on the weather. I have the best luck on warm, sunny days in winter. If the day is dark, the perch don't seem to bite as late in the afternoon as on sunny days.

In the middle of the summer, you may be able to catch them earlier or later in the day than at other seasons, probably because the days are longer, with the fish beginning to feed soon after daylight and not stopping until near sunset.

I've never noticed that wind conditions or direction, barometric pressure or moon phase made any difference in fishing for perch. You'll do better to watch water temperature and to select your fishing depths accordingly, remembering that the fish begin to come up out of the depth (30 to 50 feet) in both late summer and late winter when the oxygen supply is beginning to be depleted in the deep places.

LIVE BAIT

I feel that two live baits are best for yellow perch: small live minnows about 1 to 2 inches long or crawfish tails. During the summer months, however, you will also have good luck on very small live frogs, earthworms, dragonfly nymphs, mayfly nymphs, grasshoppers, crickets, cockroaches, catalpa worms and meal worms. The fish usually like a lively bait in the summer. You can still-fish with any of these baits. If I'm going to troll with live bait, I prefer a large gold spinner attached ahead of a hook baited with an earthworm, catalpa worm or meal worm.

During the winter months, the fish usually like a small mouthful. Small minnows or crawfish tails are still good, but the fish will also take prepared baits: cut up pieces of minnow, fish eyes, beefsteak (not as good as these others), shrimp or clams. The various larvae and worms will also be very effective through the ice. I don't feel that grasshoppers, crickets and cockroaches are as effective in the winter as in the summer.

FLIES AND LURES

The following flies or lures are suggested for yellow perch:

Nature Lures (either troll or cast)

  Crawfish (Burke)
  Flyrod (either Burke or Creme)
  Grasshopper (Weber)
  Minnows
    Life Like Lures, Minnow (3-L Products)
    Spinner Minnow (Weber)
    Tiny Flash Minnow (Delong)
    Panfish Worm Lure (Sportsman's Products)

Wet Flies (sometimes fished
      with a small spinner and
      pork rind)

  Cowdung
  Montreal
  McGinty
  Parmachene Belle
  Royal Coachman
  Western Bee
  Professor
  Wooly Worm (green,
      brown)
  Picket Pin
  Yellow/Red Tail or Black/
      Red Tail (Weber)

Nymphs (Weighted)

  Tan Shrimp
  Mayfly Nymph (Black, Brown, Yellow)
  Gray Nymph
  Ted Stonefly Nymph, Black and Orange (Orvis)

Streamer Flies

  Gray Ghost

Red and White Bucktail
Mickey Finn
Blacknosed Dace
Nine-Three
Yellow Marabou

Terrestrials

Worth Special Hornberg Fly (Worth)

Fly Rod Lures

Flatfish, 1¾″ (Helin)
Flicker-Spinner (Hildebrandt)
Harrison's Rocky Lure, Junior, ⅟₁₆ oz. (Harrison-Hoge)
Inch Minnow, ⅟₁₆ oz. (Falls)
L & S Mirrolures, Jointed, ⅟₁₆ oz. (L & S Bait Co.)
Dardevle, Skeeter Plus, ²⁄₃₂ oz. (Lou Eppinger)
Feathered Shad-King, #2 (Hildebrandt)
Pork Rind, Fly Strip, White (Uncle Josh)

Because yellow perch are a deep-water fish, and you have to fish over the bottom, spinning lures are usually more effective than flies. I would suggest the following spinning lures for yellow perch.

Floating-Diving Plugs

Flatfish, 2½″ (Helin)
Rebel, Deep-Runner Minnow (Plastic Research and Development Corp.)
Tiny River Runt Spook (Daisy-Heddon)

Sinking Lures

Deep Inch (Falls Bait Co.)
L & S Spinmaster (L & S)
Rapala (Normark)
Ultra-Sonic (Daisy-Heddon)

Spoons

Al's Goldfish (Al's Goldfish Lure Co.)

Marathon Dictator (Marathon)
Feathered Shad King (Hildebrandt)
Little Bantam (Southern Tool and Die Co.)
Williams' Nymph (Williams)
Super Duper (Gladding-South Bend)
Midge (Glen Evans)

Jigging Spoons

Select from Mitzi Series, Russian Hooks, Tear Drop Series (Best
Tackle Mfg. Co.) May be used successfully through the ice,
with or without bait.

Weighted Spinners

Spinning Flicker (Hildebrandt)
Mepps Aglia (Sheldon's)
Hep (Daisy-Heddon)
Worden's Rooster Tail (Yakima)

Jigs (use with or without bait or pork rind)

Baby Lead Head Jig (Glen Evans)
BJ Bucktail Jig (Horrocks-Ibbotson)
Little Crappie Killer (Cordell)
Panfish Weighted Hair Fly (Glen Evans)

Nature Lures

Spinner Minnow (Weber)
Panfish Worm Lure (Sportsman's Products)

PERCH AS A FOOD FISH

It is strange that in some sections of the country yellow perch are
considered only a trash fish, but in other places they are considered
a delicacy. I fish every summer in the lakes of central Maine where
the natives will never keep or eat a yellow perch. Yet, yellow perch
are one of the most coveted fish in other sections of the country. I
caught them by the hundreds in North Dakota and considered them
a delicacy. Commercial fishermen harvested over 2 million pounds

of yellow perch in the waters of Lake Michigan and Green Bay, Wisconsin, in one year. The retail value of this catch was several million dollars.

Actually, yellow perch are one of the most palatable of the panfish, especially when caught in cool, clear waters. The flesh is firm and white, with a mild flavor. Because of its low fat content, the fish keeps very well when frozen. I stored over 30 pounds of yellow-perch fillets in our freezer last winter and they provided delicious meals throughout the winter.

Most fishermen who will not eat perch say the fish have worms. Actually, many of the common varieties of parasites afflict most game fish. I have caught lots of delicious brook trout which had tapeworms in their stomachs. The most common parasites inflicting yellow perch are the eye grub, yellow grub and black spot. These black spots or yellow cysts are commonly found in the flesh of the fish, particularly in areas where fisheating birds are common. Also, a large percentage of perch harbor flukes on their fins, gills or scales, plus bass tapeworms in their stomachs or intestines. None of these parasites affect in any way the eating qualities of these fish, however. Worms are only found in the intestine or stomach and are removed when the fish are cleaned. The spots or cysts which get into the muscle of the flesh are completely destroyed in cooking. It is a shame whenever yellow perch are not eaten. They are one of our most delicious panfish, and information on how to cook them can be found in Chapter 13.

6

WHITE AND YELLOW BASS

The white bass (*Roccus chrysops*) and the yellow bass (*Roccus mississippiensis*) are true bass, belonging to the sea-bass family Serranidae. As such, they are related to the striped bass which affords such sport for ocean fishermen, and to the white perch which is found in brackish and landlocked waters of the eastern seaboard. These fish are in no way related to the black bass, which are not really bass at all, but sunfish.

The white bass has an over-all color of silver with a golden cast on the lower sides. From the head to the tail along each side, narrow, dark lateral lines run the entire length of the fish. Usually four or five of these lines are above the lateral line and three to five are below it. The white bass has two distinct, separated dorsal fins; the posterior portion of the dorsal fin has one spine and thirteen or fourteen soft rays. The anal fin has three spines and twelve soft rays; the three spines are of different lengths: the second is twice as long as the first, and the third is twice as long as the second. This is a fairly deep-bodied fish with a medium-size mouth, and with teeth on the base of the tongue.

There are several positive ways of distinguishing the yellow from

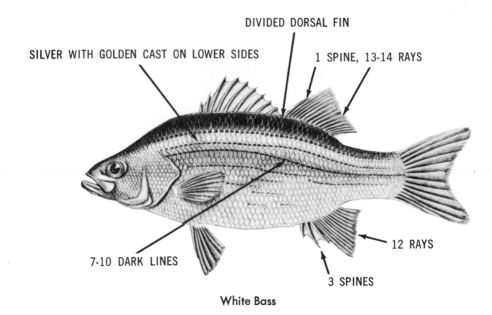

SILVER WITH GOLDEN CAST ON LOWER SIDES

DIVIDED DORSAL FIN

1 SPINE, 13-14 RAYS

12 RAYS

3 SPINES

7-10 DARK LINES

White Bass

the white bass. As the name implies, the yellow bass is more golden in hue; the lines on the sides below the lateral line are interrupted, with the back part of the stripes alternating with the front half. Furthermore, the yellow bass has the two parts of the dorsal fin

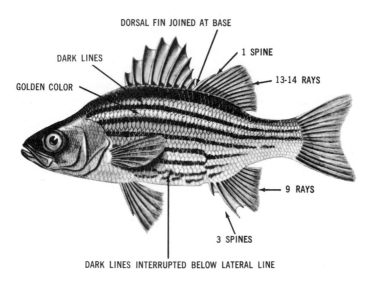

DORSAL FIN JOINED AT BASE

DARK LINES

1 SPINE

GOLDEN COLOR

13-14 RAYS

9 RAYS

3 SPINES

DARK LINES INTERRUPTED BELOW LATERAL LINE

Yellow Bass

Distribution of the white bass.

joined at the base; it has one spine and only twelve soft rays in the posterior portion of the dorsal fin. The second and third spines of the anal fin are nearly the same length, the first spine is shorter, and there are only nine soft rays in the anal fin.

Some years ago, the white and yellow basses were almost unheard of in sections of the country where they are now plentiful. The white bass was largely a fish of the northern part of the country, especially abundant around the Great Lakes region and Mississippi River. Because of widespread planting, it is also now numerous in the South. As can be seen from the map, the white bass is now found in thirty-three states; the boom is on and promises to continue in the years ahead.

Perhaps the main reason for the rapid expansion of white-bass distribution is that this fish seems ideally suited to the large artificial reservoirs and impoundments that are being constructed each year in many parts of the country. The fish will multiply at a phenomenal rate (a large female lays up to half a million eggs); it grows faster and larger than any other panfish (up to 5 or 6 pounds); it can stand

Distribution of the yellow bass.

the turbid water which is usually present in our reservoirs. It is a predator and lives off the gizzard shad in many reservoirs. Whenever the fish is planted in large lakes, the population fairly explodes, even in some waters where crappie, black bass and other game fish are only doing fairly well.

Furthermore, the fish is easily harvested; it can be caught by the ton by any angler of fair skill. Oklahoma fishermen alone catch 2½ million pounds a year in that state. Also, the fish is a real battler on light tackle.

I'll never forget my first experience with white bass; it was on Winona Lake in Indiana. I was fishing for black bass, but hooked a 2-pound white bass which fought very deep and hard. I had quite a time landing it on my light spinning tackle. Ever since that day I have certainly been sold on the gameness of these fine fish.

During the spring spawning periods, these bass swim up tributaries of rivers and streams to reproduce. They get so thick below the dams across some rivers that you can almost walk across on their backs. And, best of all, they can be caught by a variety of methods and with different types of tackle. They will hit many types of artificial plugs, spoons and spinners. They hit both surface and underwater lures; they can be taken readily by trolling, casting or still-fishing. They will gobble up live bait or viciously attack a streamer fly. They love artificial jigs or other bottom-bumping lures.

The only criticism of white bass I have ever heard is that they are not as tasty as many other kinds of fish. I find the meat to be somewhat strong-flavored, but not objectionable. Apparently thousands of fishermen eat them regularly because they are becoming more and more popular with anglers.

The yellow bass is not as widely distributed, being found in only fifteen states. The yellow bass is not quite as prolific as is the white, nor does it grow as fast or as large, which probably is the reason why fish and game departments are not introducing it in nearly as many new waters as they are the white bass. The record yellow bass weighed 2 pounds 4 ounces and was caught in Indiana.

The yellow bass is a true game fish, however, hitting lures viciously and putting up a hard, dogged fight when hooked. It seems to prefer more southern waters than does the white bass, and has a greater preference for deep, slow streams and rivers. It never runs up rapids or fast-water streams to spawn as does the white bass, preferring the more sluggish waters of rivers.

The growth rate of white bass is truly phenomenal. In a study made in Oklahoma, 3,430 bass from 33 bodies of water were studied over an 11-year period. On the basis of an average rate of growth, white bass in Oklahoma reach 7.5 inches at the end of the first year of life, and, during successive years, attain lengths of 12.2 inches (2nd year), 14.4 (3rd year), 16.1 (4th year), 17.1 (5th year) and 17.8 (6th year). The average white bass in this state weighs 2 pounds by the end of the 4th year; fast-growing individuals may weigh 2.5 pounds by the end of the third year. A female (6 years old), 19.4 inches in length and weighing 5 pounds was caught at Lake Clinton on April 15, 1954, and represents the state record. The record came from the Colorado River in Texas and weighed 5 pounds 9 ounces.

These figures reveal one of the reasons why these fish are becoming so popular: they attain a very respectable size in a short time. Furthermore, there has been found no clear-cut difference in the rate of growth under clear and turbid water conditions although excessive turbidity may curtail spawning somewhat.

One significant factor revealed by this Oklahoma study was the relationship between forage fish such as gizzard shad and white bass. Wherever the forage fish are available, the white bass can also be found in great numbers. Gizzard shad do best in large reservoirs; white bass thrive in the same type of water. The lakes in Oklahoma which contain significant numbers of white bass range in size from 800 to 93,000 acres and average 12,200 acres.

HABITS AND HABITAT

The white bass is a big-water fish, roving about open waters in large schools, foraging for food. It seldom remains around cover, but moves from place to place, feeding as it goes.

For this reason, it may be taken in the middle of a lake just as readily as along shore. One day it may be found in shallow water, playing around the surface, or chopping schools of shad or minnows to pieces. At another time, it may be found holed up in the depths around an underwater spring. A great traveler, it may be in one section of the lake one day and several miles away the next. Tagged fish have been reported to have traveled well over a hundred miles in a short time.

Because its habits are erratic, catching the white bass is unpredictable. If you can find it, it usually strikes willingly, but you have to find it first. At times, it just disappears, usually retiring to deep water. In Ohio waters of Lake Erie, the tagging of white bass has revealed that after spawning in shallow waters the fish move farther out into the lake, often reaching Canadian waters.

When the fish are deep, the preferred habitat is still water over sand or gravel bottoms. Sand bars and points projecting into deep water are preferred angling spots. I've also caught white bass near sharp drop-offs along deep-water shores. They seldom remain in any of these spots for very long, however.

It is generally agreed that in cloudy or rainy weather white bass lose some of their shyness and are most easily caught. On bright days the fish go deeper at midday so you have to fish for them very near the bottom. (The exceptions to this are during the spawning season, and sometimes very early and late in the day.) During the warm, sunny weather, though, the fish will many times begin their surface feeding early and late in the day. This is the time to break out the light tackle and cast into the school.

Studies on the Lake of the Ozarks in Missouri reveal some very interesting facts about the habits of white bass. During the spring and early summer, the fish did not seem to have any particular depth preferences. During this period, they were usually caught by trolling at various depths. As the summer progressed, the fish began an upstream movement in the lake during the time of the mayfly hatches (June 20 to July 10). Surface fishing was good during this period,

STEVE PRICE PHOTO

Because white bass are big-water fish, roving a lake in search of food, they're not easy to find. Here a fisherman prepares to drop a marker buoy near a school of white bass he spotted on a flasher-type depthfinder.

probably because the fish were feeding on these hatches. About July 7, the first schools of gizzard shad were observed on the surface. This good surface fishing continued, especially early and late in the day, as long as the schools of shad appeared.

At the time the fish stopped striking the surface plugs, fishermen began taking them on the bottom further upstream near the mouth of Ha-Ha-Tonka Spring. Netting showed that both white bass and gizzard shad were present in these bottom waters near the spring.

It is interesting to note, however, that in other areas of this particular lake, away from the spring, the white bass went no deeper than 10 to 14 feet during the months of July and August, avoiding deeper waters which had too low a level of dissolved oxygen to support them. As the season progressed, by late August the fish around Ha-Ha-Tonka Spring migrated slowly downstream as the dissolved oxygen increased.

There are some very valuable lessons to be learned from this study. You are certainly more likely to have surface fishing during the periods of spring and early summer when the fish are feeding on mayflies or on schools of gizzard shad which are roaming the surface. Then, as the heat of summer progresses, the fish go to the cooler depths, but never in water so deep that it is devoid of oxygen. In the Lake of the Ozarks, the white bass avoided the very deep water in July and August, going no deeper than 10 to 14 feet. The reason for this was that the deeper water was stagnant and contained only a small amount of dissolved oxygen. Instead, the fish migrated toward an underwater spring which gave a continuous stream of cold, aerated water. During the month of September, however, the white bass moved slowly to the deeper water again as it cooled and absorbed more oxygen.

Of course, each lake has its own temperature and oxygen patterns. You may find white bass in deep water in midsummer in your favorite lake, but only if the oxygen content is sufficient.

In the majority of the reservoirs of the South, the gizzard shad is the principal forage species of the white and yellow bass. In Lake Erie, the emerald shiner is the principal forage fish. Crawfish, mollusks and larger insects and their larvae are eaten to a certain extent. The smaller fish eat microscopic crustaceans, aquatic insects and worms.

Any artificial lures or flies which represent shad or minnows are good ones to use. I have never found that these bass take ordinary flies well. Flies and spinners, streamer flies, spoons, spinners or small plugs are better lures, probably because they represent small fish. ·

These fish are nocturnal as well as daytime feeders. They move into the shallow waters early in the morning and late in the evening to feed, as long as the forage fish are there. In the hottest weather,

White bass are aggressive fish and take a variety of lures and live baits. The fish are often found in large schools, frequently feeding on the surface in summer and early fall.

they may remain deep if the shad or minnows are also deep, so you can't always catch the bass in shallow water at night. So much depends upon the availability of feed.

As the water temperature approaches 60°, the bass leave the deeper waters of the lake and swim near shore or up the larger rivers to spawn. No nests are prepared; the eggs are deposited in a hit-or-miss fashion in mid-water, slowly sinking until coming into contact with some object to which they adhere. After the eggs are laid, the males deposit the milt; both parents then desert the eggs.

The exact spawning time depends on the temperature of the water. In Iowa and Ohio, the bass spawn between April and June, while in Kentucky the spawning period falls between March and May. If you happen to be in fishing country when the spring spawning runs occur, you can have some amazing angling. In migrating up available streams and rivers, the fish crowd together in tremendous numbers, especially below dams and other obstacles across the larger rivers. It's not too difficult to catch them by the hundreds during this time of the year.

FISHING TOP AND BOTTOM

Not too many years ago, fishermen knew very little about how to catch white or yellow bass, but with the rapid increase in the number of impoundments and the widespread transplanting of white bass, particularly, fishermen have developed many different techniques for catching these fish.

My favorite method is jump-fishing. This technique can be used only during the period of summer when the bass are feeding on the surface on flies or forage fish. Early morning and late afternoon or evening are the best times. The procedure is to row or motor quietly around your favorite bass lake, staying in those bays and areas where the fish are likely to feed. The action usually begins suddenly with the bass coming to the surface after their prey. They will slash viciously into the schools of small fish, splashing the water violently and causing quite a commotion.

Once a school is located, approach very carefully so as not to put the fish down. I prefer drifting up to the school or rowing quietly. If a number of schools are feeding around you, it's better to stay put and wait until a school begins feeding within casting distance. Then cast right in the middle of the school and you'll have action as long as the school remains on the surface. Then suddenly the fish just seem to disappear, perhaps to resurface some distance away.

For this kind of jump-fishing, I prefer surface or floating-diving lures. A plunker-type plug to which a small white or yellow jig has been attached with about 15 inches of nylon line is a wonderful lure. Small floating-diving plugs which closely resemble shad or minnows are excellent. Small spoons with gold, red and white, or nickel finishes are very successful. Other specific recommendations will be made a little later on in this chapter.

If you are using small plugs or spoons, many times a very fast retrieve, imitating a small fish trying to get away, brings the best results. Sometimes you can even run the lure along the surface of the water right through the school. The bass will hit your lure so hard you'll find your heart in your mouth.

Another good method is to fish jigs along the bottom. This method is effective during spawning time or in late summer and fall after the surface fishing is over. White or yellow are productive colors.

The technique here is to cast the jig, let it sink to the bottom and retrieve very slowly so it bumps along the bottom. Reel a few inches or a foot, then stop, letting the jig sink, then retrieve another short distance. Strike as soon as you feel a hit. If your line is kept tight, the bass strike will come as a hard, quick pull.

If you are using sinking plugs, spoons or spinners to fish deep, then be certain to let your lures sink to the bottom before beginning a slow, erratic retrieve. Bass prefer cool waters during the heat of the summer, so if you're going to catch them when they are near the bottom, you'll have to keep your lures deep. This means you should retrieve a short distance, then let your lure sink, then retrieve some more, and so on.

If you prefer live-bait fishing with your spinning outfit, then use minnows (the favorite bait) or crawfish. If you have to fish deep, use a sliding bobber that will enable you to reel in most of your line. Tight-line fishing just off the bottom is also effective.

The hardest task in live-bait fishing is to locate the fish. Many anglers prefer trolling until a school is located, but you can also drift-fish, casting ahead of you as your boat drifts slowly along, or letting your bait drag along near the bottom behind your boat. Don't waste too much time in one spot. Bass are a school fish and you have to locate the schools to catch them.

During the heat of the summer when the fish are deep, or at other times when you cannot locate the schools, trolling is an effective method. You can use your fly-fishing equipment, spinning outfit or special deep-water trolling equipment. When the fish are shallow, troll a streamer fly, small spoon, plug or spinner 10 or 12 feet behind your boat in the wake of the motor. The bubbles and commotion from the propeller seem to attract the fish. Keep moving along at a good clip, say 5 to 7 miles an hour. The bass hit with quite a jolt.

If the fish are in medium-depth water, 10 to 20 feet, put a dipsey sinker or other weight on your spinning line and troll slowly, keeping your lure just off the bottom. If you have much trouble getting hung up, put the sinker on the end of your line or on the bottom attachment of a triangular trolling rig; then place a floating plug above it. If the sinker gets hung up, you can break it off and attach another without losing your floating lure. The nylon leader to your sinker should be of slightly weaker test than your trolling line, however, so when you try to pull free your sinker line breaks before your trolling line.

Sometimes the only way you can catch white bass is by getting down very deep for them: perhaps 30 to 50 feet. You have two choices in lines: either a wire (usually Monel metal) line, or a lead-core line. You can reel the Monel wire line on a fairly large fly reel and use it with a stiff fly rod or trolling rod. The lead-core line requires a large casting or trolling reel, sometimes of the salt-water type, and a fairly stiff trolling rod. To get down 40 feet deep with lead-core line will usually require at least 250 feet of line out. Such a line is extremely heavy and requires a heavy rod to hold it. You will scarcely be able to feel the fight of the fish with such heavy gear, so this method is usually used by the meat fisherman who is interested only in bringing back a string of fish to eat. Certainly, there is not much sport involved in catching the fish. You feel only a slight wiggle along with the heavy drag of the line. If you have to go deep in trolling, then I would prefer the Monel line. It's more sporting and allows for more action in fighting your fish.

When you do get a strike while trolling, fish back and forth over that area and you'll usually be able to pick up other fish of the school. When the fish are deep, they are not as easily spooked as when shallow, so you can run your motor right over the desired spots without scaring the fish.

One of the principal considerations in trolling is to know the depth of water over which you are fishing. This way you can let out and take in line as you move along, thus keeping your bait near the bottom but without getting hung up. If you are using a marked line (one that is dyed with different colors to designate the length that is out) you can more easily know how much line you need to let out or reel in to be at the proper depth. All lead-core lines are marked with different colors; you can also get marked nylon trolling line to use with your spinning gear. It's a big help in trolling; once you get a strike, you can know how much line you had out and can duplicate that amount exactly. If you troll at the same speed with the same weight and lure, you can then be sure your lure is traveling exactly at the depth at which you got the strike.

You can also use live minnows while trolling by using a minnow harness or by sewing the bait on your hook. Put enough weight on your line to get down to the desired depth.

RECOMMENDED LURES

Actually, white and yellow bass are not fussy about artificials. Many times you can catch them on most any lure, especially when jump-fishing. Small plugs, spoons, weighted spinners and jigs are all good lures. As these fish do not have very large mouths, the main thing is to get lures small enough so the fish will take them readily. In order to do this and still be able to cast, many fishermen use trailer flies, jigs or very small plugs behind larger lures. These make excellent attractors.

I'm certain I have not tried out all of the good lures that are used for these bass, but I guarantee the ones listed below will catch fish when used properly. You probably have some other favorites to add to this list.

Surface Lures

   Whopper Stopper Pop 'n' Jig (Whopper Stopper, Inc.)
   Creek Chub Injured Minnow (Creek Chub)
   Rebel Popper (Plastic Research and Development Corp.)

Floating-Diving Lures

   Creek Chub Pikie Minnow (Creek Chub)

Flatfish, 2½″ (Helin)
Rainbow Runner (Phillips)
Rapala (Normark)
Rascal (Gladding-South Bend)
Thin-Fin Super Shiner Minnow (Storm Manufacturing Corp.)
Tiny River Runt Spook (Daisy-Heddon)

Sinking Lures

Deep Inch (Falls Bait Co.)
Harrison's Rocky Lure, Senior (Harrison-Hoge)
L & S Spin-Master (L & S)
L & S Trail-O-Lure (L & S) Can be attached to a larger plug.
Rapala (Normark)
Tiny Ike (Daisy-Heddon)

Spoons

Al's Goldfish (Al's Goldfish Lure Co.)
Dardevle Midget (Lou Eppinger)
Feathered Shad King (Hildebrandt)
Little Cleo (Seneca)
Phantom Wobbler (H & J)

Weighted Spinners

Abu-Reflex (Garcia)
Spinning-Flicker (Hildebrandt)
Hep (Daisy-Heddon)
Little Fooler (Hildebrandt)
Mepps Aglia (Sheldon's)
Panther Martin (Harrison-Hoge)
Worth Pearlie (Worth)

Jigs

Baby Lead Head Jig (Glen Evans)
Little Doggie Marabou (Glen Evans)

Crappie Killer (Weber)
Li'l Crappie Killer (Cordell)
Little-Hornet Jig Fly (Arndt and Sons)
Pinkie Jig (Marathon)
Plan Jig Head (Assassinator Lures) Use with bait or pork rind.

Nature Lures

Panfish Worm Lure (Sportsman's Products)
Flash Minnow (DeLong Lures)

FLY FISHING

Many fishermen will be surprised to learn that both white and
yellow bass take flies. This statement ought to be qualified, however.
They take flies when they are feeding shallow enough to see them.
Fly fishing is strictly a shallow-water technique, so you have to pick
those times when the bass are not too deep: in the spring during
the spawning runs, and in early summer after the water has warmed
sufficiently for the fish to surface feed on shad, minnows and insects.

The best technique is to find a school feeding, then cast into the
school. When you can't find the fish, you can troll with flies and
spinners or with streamer flies. Or you can cast areas where you
know the fish are spawning or feeding. The most likely spot in
rivers is below the dams or in other areas where the fish congregate
to spawn. In lakes, try the shallow, sandy or gravelly bays and tributaries near drop-offs, ledges or bars. It's hard to guarantee success
since the fish move around a great deal, so you'll just have to move
until you find the fish.

The following flies and fly-rod lures are recommended:

Fly Rod Lures

Flatfish, 1¾" (Helin)
Dardevle, Skeeter Plus (Lou Eppinger)
Williams Nymphs (Williams)
Uncle Josh Fly Rod Strip. Pork Rind, White (Uncle Josh)

Floating Bugs

   Band-It Popper (Glen Evans)
   Fire Fly Shimmy (Falls Bait Co.)
   Mountain (deer hear) Hopper (Phillips)

Dry Flies

   Grizzly Bivisible
   Royal Coachman
   Gauze Wing Drake (blue
      dun, yellow)
   Wulff Blonde

Wet Flies (use with spinners)

   Coachman
   Cowdung
   Professor

Streamer Flies

   Blacknosed Dace
   Black Ghost
   Gray Ghost
   Muddler
   Professor
   White Marabou

7

WHITE PERCH

Unless you fish along the Atlantic seaboard, you would not have much occasion to get acquainted with the white perch. Even fishermen in the sixteen states where it is found have a sketchy knowledge of its habits. William Tompkins, aquatic biologist for the Division of Fisheries and Game of Massachusetts, writes:

Although widespread on the North Atlantic coast and well-known as a game species to generations of New England anglers, its [the white perch's] biography is extremely sketchy. The paucity of information on this species, especially published materials, necessitated the omission of many points and left unanswered many questions. The white perch is an enigma to anglers and biologists alike. To the fisherman, it is capricious and temperamental; to the fishing manager, it is unpredictable and mystifying, capable of supplying excellent sport fishing in one instance, and in the next, of reducing sport fishing to a mere pittance.

Perhaps one of the reasons for the above statement is that the fishermen of Massachusetts have a great deal of trouble catching white perch. Jack Woolner, writing in a pamphlet published by the Division of Fisheries and Game of Massachusetts, says: "The white perch may be one of the smartest freshwater fish in existence.

He's certainly the prince of the panfish and would probably give any trout a run for his money in the matter of intelligence. This species is a problem in Massachusetts. White perch are grand fighters on light tackle. They're excellent in the frying pan, but are generally hard to catch."

This fact is borne out in Massachusetts where statewide tagging studies have revealed that in many ponds white perch outnumber other fish, but account for only a fraction of the creel count. In some ponds, harvests of other types of fish were very high: for example, largemouth bass—28 percent; smallmouth bass—61 percent; chain pickerel—64 percent; bullheads—16 percent; and yellow perch—36 percent, but the total harvest of the white perch never seemed to exceed 1 percent.

Lest these figures discourage you from fishing for these fish if and when you have a chance, let me add a more encouraging note. Though not much has been written about white perch, they are not hard to catch, if you know where and how. I've fished for them in Maine for the last thirty years. At times, they have been capricious, temperamental, exasperating, but I can truthfully say that on most occasions I have, or could have, caught my limit of twenty-five fish. It was just a question of fishing long enough to find the fish and discover the proper technique for the time. One day white perch will hit any plug or spoon thrown at them; the next day you'll catch your limit while fly fishing; the next day you'll have to troll deep. One day you'll find the fish congregated in one area; the next day they will be all over the lake or in another isolated area.

It is my purpose here to try to remove the so-called mystery which surrounds these fish. They are one of the finest of our game fish, hard fighters and excellent as a food fish. And they can be caught by every conceivable angling technique.

The white perch, like the white and yellow bass, belongs to the sea bass family Serranidae. It is of the same genus as the yellow bass (*Roccus*); the Latin name for its species is *americanus*. Thus, the white perch is called *Roccus americanus*. It is therefore a relative of the striped bass of the ocean and of the white and yellow bass of freshwater lakes and rivers. Undoubtedly, sometime in the past it became landlocked and developed its own version of the sea bass, evolving much smaller, but with the same unpredictability.

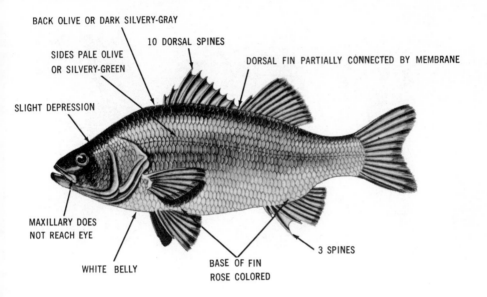

BACK OLIVE OR DARK SILVERY-GRAY

10 DORSAL SPINES

SIDES PALE OLIVE
OR SILVERY-GREEN

DORSAL FIN PARTIALLY CONNECTED BY MEMBRANE

SLIGHT DEPRESSION

MAXILLARY DOES
NOT REACH EYE

WHITE BELLY

BASE OF FIN
ROSE COLORED

3 SPINES

White Perch

There are several ways of distinguishing this fish. The upper surface is olive, dark grayish-green, or dark silvery-gray, shading to paler olive or silvery-green on the sides and to silvery-white on the belly. The ventral and anal fins are sometimes rose-colored at the base. Young fish have pale longitudinal stripes which usually fade out with growth.

The body of this fish is short and deep. It has no canine teeth; only the edge of the tongue has some semblance of linear patches of very tiny teeth. The head is depressed above the eyes; the snout is rather pointed; the lower jaw slightly projects; the mouth is small, somewhat oblique, with the maxillary not reaching the middle of the eye.

The anterior and posterior parts of the dorsal fin are partly connected with a membrane near the base of the fin. The ten dorsal spines are very strong; there are three spines in the anal fin and eight or nine soft rays. The second and third anal spines are about the same length and much longer than the first.

The scales of the fish are rather large, ctenoid-type scales. There are eight scale rows between the base of the dorsal fin and the

Distribution of the white perch.

lateral line, fifty to fifty-five scale rows crossing the lateral line, and twelve scale rows between the lateral line and the base of the anal or vent. The lateral line itself is slightly arched to follow the contour of the fish's back. The only noticeable difference between the male and female is that the female has a prominent abdomen just prior to spawning.

DISTRIBUTION

The white perch is now found in fresh, salt and brackish waters along the Atlantic coast of the United States from Nova Scotia to Georgetown, South Carolina. It is especially abundant in Chesapeake Bay and its tributaries, in the lakes and streams of the St. John River, New Brunswick, and in the vicinity of Halifax, Nova Scotia. Recently, the fish seems to be making its way through Lake Ontario as far west as Lake Erie. Only sixteen states report white perch in their waters.

White perch are caught commercially in some tidal waters. Over

2 million pounds are taken along the Atlantic coast each year. Over 1 million of these pounds are caught in Chesapeake Bay. In the northern half of its range, however, white perch are found mainly in freshwater ponds and streams; they are not usually fished for the market.

SPAWNING AND GROWTH

White perch generally mature during the second year of life and spawn for the first time during the spring of the third year of life. The fish is a very prolific breeder; a 1-pound female will release as many as 150,000 eggs in one spawning season. The males release millions of sperm. The sperm are attracted to the eggs and fertilize a large percentage of them.

Large schools of perch seek a tributary stream, a shallow cove or a section of a river estuary to release their eggs and milt. The perch do not "pair off" nor do they build nests; they simply swim about, causing quite a commotion. After the females release their tiny eggs, the males immediately gather around to release the milt. The method of spawning is careless, but the eggs and sperm are released in such numbers that there is little chance for failure, even though the adults scatter their eggs and then abandon them.

The eggs are heavier than water and sink rapidly, fastening to rocks, plants or anything they chance to touch. They adhere to objects by means of a sticky disk. The eggs are very sensitive to temperature changes and a sudden drop of 4 or 5 degrees can destroy them. However, since the school of perch spawns over a period of about two weeks, reproduction is seldom a complete failure in any one year.

Within a few days, depending upon water temperature, tiny fry less than ⅛ inch long and almost invisible to the naked eye hatch from the egg and are on their own. If they are in a current of water, they are helpless against it and drift down to quiet water.

The exact time of spawning depends upon the water temperature. The fish usually spawn when the water is between 58° and 60°. This is sometime during the period from May to July in Maine. When the water is kept at 58°, the fry hatch in four or four and a half days. At a temperature of 68° F. the eggs hatch in thirty hours. If the water is as low as 45°, the eggs do not develop at all.

It is difficult, at times, to determine why white perch reproduce successfully in some waters and not in others. Certainly, water levels should be kept constant during May and June so that the eggs will not be left on dry land. Tributary streams should be kept open for spawning; either man-made or beaver dams prevent these fish from reaching their normal spawning areas. When placed in some waters the fish never seem to reproduce; in contrast to this, the fish have reproduced successfully in a 1/5-acre farm pond with a maximum depth of 5 feet and a clay bottom. Following spawning, the fish seek deeper water to recuperate.

Like most other fish, the growth rate of white perch depends mostly upon the habitat and the food supply available. Water temperature, food supply and the length of the growing season are all important factors, along with sex, since the female is slightly larger than the male. Studies have shown that most of the growth takes place during the warm summer months with little or no growth during the winter.

The following table shows the average growth (in inches) and weight (in ounces) of the white perch from three states.

AGE GROUP	MAINE		NEW YORK		MASSACHUSETTS	
	Length	*Weight*	*Length*	*Weight*	*Length*	*Weight*
2	6.9	3.0	5.7	1.3	5.4	1.5
3	6.7	2.4	7.5	3.5	7.1	3.0
4	7.8	4.3	8.4	5.6	8.3	4.3
5	8.1	4.7	9.3	7.4	9.5	7.3
6	8.6	6.0	9.6	9.0	10.1	9.3
7	9.2	7.3	11.1	13.0	–	–
8	9.7	7.6	11.6	14.8	11.4	13.1
9	10.0	8.5	12.1	17.4	12.2	14.9
10	10.5	9.6	12.6	17.6	–	–

Shallow, warmwater ponds are usually more fertile, and perch living in these waters grow very fast if not overcrowded. If, however, the perch are not continuously thinned out by predators or heavy fishing pressure, the populations increase until there is not enough food available to maintain a good growth rate. The result is a population of stunted fish. A few large fish may remain until caught or until they die, but the new, over-crowded populations remain small.

You can have some idea of the terrific reproductive potential of these fish from a netting operation which was conducted in Indian Lake, Worcester, Massachusetts, This lake is 172 acres and is a shallow, artificial lake with a maximum depth of 15 feet. For some twenty years this lake was used as a source of white perch for stocking other waters. During this time, approximately 47,000 pounds of perch (338,000 individuals) were removed prior to intensive thinning operations. These operations were then conducted to reduce the fish populations. The first year, over 10,000 pounds of white perch were destroyed, the second year about 1500 pounds. Before the netting, the fish averaged 6 inches in length with a mean age of five years. Two years after the thinning operation had begun, the average length had increased to almost 8 inches and the mean age to less that three years.

Other states have also substantiated the fact that the chief problem in management of white perch is over-population and stunting and that thinning operations are needed to keep the fish under control. For this reason, there should be no limit on the size or number of white perch caught. In most cases, even heavy fishing pressure has no effect upon the numbers of perch.

The life span of the white perch is on the average about six or seven years. The fish lives much longer than trout or salmon, however, with twelve- or thirteen-year-old specimens not uncommon in Maine waters. The oldest recorded fish in Maine was in its seventeenth year, was 12.3 inches long and weighed 14.6 ounces. The world's record of 4¾ pounds was taken in Maine; the fish was 19 inches long.

HABITS

Like most fish, white perch will eat whatever food is available in large quantities. The fry feed mainly on plankton. In the evening, schools of young perch swim to beaches or other shoals where they feed on water insects and water fleas. By late evening, the feeding is over and the schools return to deeper water.

The adult perch change their feeding habits throughout the year.

In the winter and early spring, they feed mainly on the bottom on the larvae of insects. Small midge worms are consumed by the thousands as the burrowing mayfly nymphs emerge from the mud; the perch eat them and the adult insects which hatch. One of the best times to dry-fly fish for white perch is during the mayfly hatches in June. Caddis-fly larvae and dragonfly nymphs are other favorites.

One study in Maine of the stomach contents of 1,249 white perch showed that midges comprised 49 percent of the bottom organisms eaten. Freshwater shrimp made up 32 percent of the bottom organisms eaten. A selectivity for mayflies and caddis flies and an avoidance of mollusks was also noted.

Following the early-summer spawning periods, small fish of different species become available in large numbers so that the perch begin to feed more and more on fish up to 2 or 3 inches long. Smelt, yellow perch and white perch are favored prey.

By autumn, when the young fishes are too large for the perch to eat, they return to a diet of insects, water fleas and freshwater shrimp. Small minnows are seldom eaten since large perch do not venture into shallow enough water to catch them.

I have caught perch at all hours of the day and night, but they feed most readily, especially in shallow water, in the late evening. The best time to fish shallow for them is the several hours before and the hour or so after dark. During daylight, you will find them deeper or roaming the surface out in deep water.

White perch, along with bass, sunfish and other panfish, are an advanced fish; that is, they have evolved to a high level of intelligence to become very adaptable, aggressive and prolific. Perch could be compared to salmon or trout as modern man is compared to the Stone Age man. Salmon or trout have to be protected and coddled, and when placed in the same water with white perch, the perch will dominate every body of water they can get into.

White perch exhibit a wide tolerance of water temperatures. They will tolerate the water of both warmwater and cold-water lakes, but seem to prefer the same waters as bass and other warmwater fish. In the spring, summer, and fall, I have caught them in waters as warm as 80°, as cool as 45° and have caught many through the ice. But when the water gets over 70° the fish usually search out the cool depths, at least during the daylight hours.

Studies indicate that white perch move on to shoal areas at the approach of darkness and back to deeper waters after dawn, In the summer, look for them in the rocky shallows late in the day and after dark. Usually depths of from 1 to 8 feet deep are best during these evening and nighttime hours. They will be found in deeper waters during the day unless they are in fairly shallow water while spawning. When the water temperature is suitable (60° to 70°), they will occasionally feed up near rocky shorelines during the daytime hours.

Usually found in waters from about 10 to 30 feet deep, white perch have been discovered in waters as deep as 120 feet. I have caught them no deeper than 40 feet by trolling with lead lines, but this is about as deep as one can conveniently troll with freshwater tackle. Generally, though, you can find them in most lakes in much shallower water.

White perch also have a wide tolerance of salinity. They will live in normal salt or brackish water as well as in freshwater ponds. This adaptability enables them to adjust to living in brackish waters along the coast or in the inland lakes. Marine white perch winter in the deeper bay areas in a state of semihibernation and ascend tidal freshwater streams in the spring to spawn. During these migrations, they can be caught by the thousands.

White perch are a schooling fish and are found in schools varying in size from a few to hundreds or even thousands of fish. This fish can often be seen moving in schools very close to the surface, many times in the middle of the lake. As your boat approaches, the fish fairly splash the water in their efforts to dart down to the depths. When the perch are on the surface, however, is a wonderful time to catch them. If you're trolling, look for the schools and troll back and forth through them. If you're casting, try to approach a school quietly and cast into the middle. If many schools are breaking the surface, sit quietly and let them rise around you and cast to rising fish.

FLY FISHING FOR PERCH

As far as I am concerned, white perch are one of the most wonderful fish to take on ultra-light fly tackle. They hit flies and lures hard; they fight continuously and with great strength until brought in, they're also a superb eating fish. Taking them consistently on flies gets a little tricky, however, but if you follow these suggestions you will increase your chances.

When the fish are rising to the surface in late evening after mayflies and other insects, your best bet is to use fairly large dry flies or small popping bugs. Brown, black, gray or other somber colors are all good. Fish slowly, giving the fish plenty of time to take the fly. You need not cast to particular cover but only in the general area where fish are rising. Also, you can troll streamer flies along rocky shorelines with great effectiveness in the late evening.

When the fish are schooling at the surface in the daytime and in the middle of the lake, your best bet is to cast or troll for them with small streamer flies (about size 6 or 8). By far the best pattern under most conditions is a Gray Ghost. Other good patterns are the Mickey Finn and Black Ghost.

If the fish are down deep, you'll have to add sinkers to your leader and let the streamer or fly-rod lure or spoon sink after each cast or troll deep with weight added. Personally, if I have to go very deep for white perch, I prefer switching to spinning tackle: it's less bothersome and more effective.

If you want to fish for white perch at night, I feel your best bet on the fly rod is a small, black popping bug. You'll have great sport on this equipment.

I would recommend the following flies and lures for white perch.

Nature Lures

Tru-Life Cricket, Black (Weber)
Brown Grasshopper (Burke)
Floating Panfish Spider, Orange and Black (Burke)
Tru-Life May Nymph (Weber)
Stonefly Nymph (Burke)

Floating Bugs

Dylite Deluxe Creepy Popper (Weber)
Nitwit (Weber)
Marathon Grasshopper Fly (Marathon)

Mountain (deer hair) Hopper (Phillips)
Screwball (Glen Evans)

Dry Flies

Bivisible (black, brown,
    gray)
Adams
Black Gnat
Iron Blue Dun
March Brown
Mosquito
Royal Coachman
Gauze Wing Drake, Blue
    Dun, Yellow, Ginger
    (Phillips)
Gray Hackle Red
Wulff Flies (black, grizzly)

Streamer Flies

Black Ghost
Gray Ghost
Mickey Finn
Muddler Minnow

Fly Rod Lures

Dardevle, Skeeter Plus (Lou Eppinger)
Flatfish, 1¾" (Helin)

SPINNING

Spinning tackle is very suitable for fishing for white perch since these fish take all kinds of spinners, spoons, nature lures and small plugs regularly. Essentially, there are three ways to use this tackle: 1) casting, 2) trolling or 3) still-fishing with live bait. The type of fishing will be dictated by circumstances.

I prefer using artificial plugs, nature lures or spoons, so I try the artificials first and use live bait only if the lures do not work. The same suggestions for fly fishing apply to spinning. Cast the rocky shorelines during the spawning season, during cloudy, cool weather, or when the fish are rising to flies and insects, or late in the evening or night. Troll shallow with spoons or plugs when the schools are on the surface; troll deep during the day (particularly on sunny days and in warm weather) when the fish are on bottom. At these times, you will have to weight your lures to get down to the fish.

White perch are sometimes fussy as to what lures they will take so it's wise to have a good assortment. I would recommend the following lures for white perch.

Surface Lures

Jitterbug (Fred Arbogast)

Floating-Diving Lures

Flatfish, 2½″ (Helin)
Rapala, 2″ (Normark)
Rebel, Deep-Runner Minnow (Plastic Research and Development Corp.)
Tiny River Runt Spook (Daisy-Heddon)

Sinking Lures

Deep Inch (Falls Bait Co.)
Harrison's Rocky Lure, Junior (Harrison-Hoge)
Rapala (Normark)
Tiny Ike (Daisy-Heddon)

Spoons

Al's Goldfish (Al's Goldfish Lure Co.)
Lil Devle (Lou Eppinger)
Feathered Shad-King (Hildebrandt)
Marathon Dictator (Marathon)
Williams Nymphs (Williams)

Weighted Spinners (use with or without pork rind or worms)

Droppen (Garcia)

Hep (Heddon)
Marathon Bream Buster (Marathon)
Mepps Aglia (Sheldon's)
Spinning-Flicker (Hildebrandt)
Worden's Rooster Tail (Yakima)
Worth Pearlie (Worth)

Nature Lures

Panfish Worm Lure (Sportsman's Products)

LIVE-BAIT FISHING

White perch will bite on a variety of live bait, but the best all-around bait for them is worms. The most productive method is to put a large (about size 5) gold spinner or two about 2 feet ahead of a hook baited with worms and then to troll the bait very slowly at the proper depth. If the fish are shallow, you do not need to add extra weight, but if the fish are deep you'll have to get down to them. Actually, you can catch the perch on worms at any time during the day if you'll get down to their level. Usually, you should troll just fast enough to keep the spinner turning. Once you locate the school, you can anchor in that spot and still-fish, although I prefer trolling back and forth over the spot—it's not so monotonous.

Other good baits for white perch are small minnows, crawfish, dragonfly nymphs or mayfly nymphs. Unless you use a minnow rig or sew on your minnow, however, it is better to still-fish with these baits. The nymphs are too delicate for trolling.

During the winter months, you can catch white perch through the ice. Various larvae are effective: caddis worms, crane-fly larvae or meal worms. However, shiners remain the favorite bait, with angle-worms a second choice.

8

BULLHEADS

The fish with the whiskered face, the projecting barbels and the slick, scaleless body has been cussed and discussed by many generations of fishermen. However, most anglers seldom can distinguish between the different species of bullheads, nor do they know much about their habits.

Bullheads belong to the catfish family Ictaluridae. There are about twenty-four different species of catfish in the United States and many additional species in other countries. The family can be divided into three principal genera as follows:

1. Genus *Ictalurus*—channel catfish and bullheads.
2. Genus *Pylodictus*—flathead catfish (mudcat or yellow cat).
3. Genus *Noturus*—stonecat (madtom).

The general physical features of the catfish are well known. The head is wide and flat, the body is tapering and elongated. The dorsal fin is small and set far forward. There is a single tough spine at the anterior edge of the dorsal fin and the edge of each of the pectoral fins. These spines are sharp and stout and can inflict a poioned wound. There is a small adipose fin forward of the tail. On

112

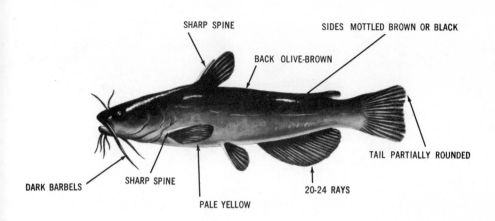

SHARP SPINE

BACK OLIVE-BROWN

SIDES MOTTLED BROWN OR BLACK

TAIL PARTIALLY ROUNDED

DARK BARBELS

SHARP SPINE

PALE YELLOW

20-24 RAYS

Brown Bullhead

the stonecat and madtoms this fin is long and low and connected with the tail or caudal fin. On the bullhead, however, there is a space separating the adipose fin from the tail.

The ventral fins of the catfish are placed midway on the belly; the anal fin is placed far back on the fish and is wider, or broader, than the dorsal.

Of the three genera of catfish, the channel catfish is probably the most important since it is the only catfish often classified as a game fish. Maximum size is around 4 feet long and 50 to 60 pounds, but it usually runs not much bigger than 4 or 5 pounds. The large blue catfish, which grows over 100 pounds in weight, the white catfish, which reaches about 2 feet in length, and the bullhead are also of this same genus.

The flathead catfish is another large specimen and may weigh up to 100 pounds. The stonecat is a member of the group of madtoms which are the smallest catfish; some species do not grow over 2 or 3 inches in length.

The bullheads are of medium size; most do not grow over 4 or 5 pounds and these would be very large specimens. There are three principal species of bullheads:

The black bullhead *(Ictalurus melas)* is the largest. The record is 8 pounds, although the usual size is much smaller. It will thrive in very small ponds and creeks and in muddy reservoirs where other

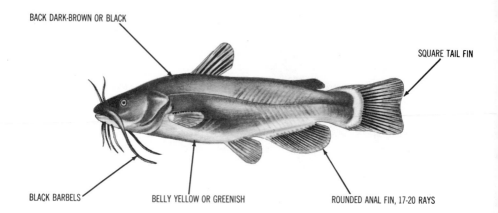

BACK DARK-BROWN OR BLACK

SQUARE TAIL FIN

BLACK BARBELS

BELLY YELLOW OR GREENISH

ROUNDED ANAL FIN, 17-20 RAYS

Black Bullhead

bullheads do not do well. It makes an excellent fish to stock in small farm ponds.

The record brown bullhead *(Ictalurus nebulosus)* is 5 pounds, 8 ounces. It is limited in distribution since it prefers clearer waters than do the other bullheads.

The record yellow bullhead *(Ictalurus natalis)* is 3 pounds.

All of these fish are bottom dwellers, swimming lazily along the mud bottoms of ponds, lakes and sluggish rivers. They are practically blind, with very small eyes, but with a keen sense of smell and touch. The barbels are used as feelers. Since the bullheads feed partially by smell, stink baits of various kinds are highly successful. All catfish are primarily nocturnal feeders; they occasionally feed during the day, but you will have far faster action late in the evening and at night.

Bullheads, especially black bullheads, are known as extremely hardy fish. When waters recede, the fish will bury in the mud, staying alive until the rains fill up the pond again. Bullheads will come to the surface breathing air directly when oxygen supplies are depleted; during winter when other fish are suffocated from lack of oxygen the bullhead will bury itself in the mud in semihibernation and emerge unharmed after the ice is out in the spring. I have kept bullheads in damp sacks for several days, only to find

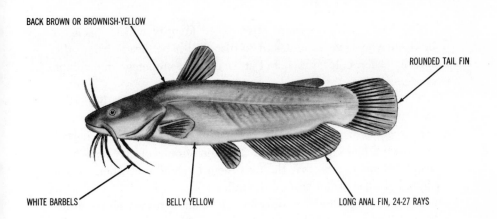

BACK BROWN OR BROWNISH-YELLOW

ROUNDED TAIL FIN

WHITE BARBELS   BELLY YELLOW   LONG ANAL FIN, 24-27 RAYS

Yellow Bullhead

them completely alive at the end of that period.

Bullheads are not extremely prolific since they lay only a couple of thousand eggs, but they care for their young carefully and have such a low mortality rate that they soon will populate a new body of water. They will find their way up irrigation ditches and remote tributaries, so it is almost impossible to keep them out of particular waters if these are connected in any way with other waters which hold them.

Since bullheads have large mouths, they like a good hunk of bait. They will toy with the bait for some time before swallowing it enough for the angler to set the hook. Their bite is therefore gentle and deliberate; you should never be in a hurry to strike back, but let the fish run with the bait. Once the fish has his mouth clamped over your bait, however, you will seldom lose him, even when the hook is not caught in his jaw, since he does not like to let go. Once hooked, the fish fights by just hanging back; it never gives much of a struggle, certainly with no swift runs or surface acrobatics.

This fish usually teams up with other bullheads, so where you catch one, you may catch others. It eats all manner of animal and vegetable matter, algae, plant remains and aquatic insects. Rarely can it ever be caught on artificials (channel catfish can, however) so it should be fished for entirely with natural bait.

HOW TO TELL THEM APART

You have to be a careful observer to identify which species of bullhead you have caught and to distinguish bullheads from other catfish. Color helps some, but it is not a completely dependable guide.

The black bullhead is usually the darkest of the three bullheads. It is usually very dark with a blue-black, dark-brown or black back and a yellow or greenish belly, never a white one. The chin barbels are always black or dark gray. The membrane of the anal fin is deeply pigmented so that the rays seem to stand out. There is usually a light bar at the base of the tail.

The brown bullhead is olive-brown or dark brown above and a pale yellow on the belly. The back and sides are usually mottled with a darker brown or black. The coloring of the sides and belly becomes lighter. This fish prefers clearer waters more than any of the others.

The yellow bullhead is usually the lightest in color with a brown or brownish-yellow back and a yellow belly. The yellow bullhead is the only species to have white or cream-colored barbels under the chin.

Another way to identify these fish is by the number of rays in the anal fin and the shape of the fin. The black bullhead has 17-20 rays and a rounded anal fin; the brown bullhead has 20-24 with a medium-elongated fin; and the yellow bullhead has 24-27 rays with a longer anal fin. Since the count of rays sometimes overlaps from one species to another, this method can be used only as a general guide.

The most positive means of identificaton is by the shape of the tail or caudal fin. The black bullhead has a tail that is very nearly square; the brown bullhead has a tail which is partially rounded, and the yellow bullhead's tail is very rounded and has no fork.

These fish can be distinguished from the channel cats by the fact that all of the channel cats have deeply forked tails, spots on the body and 24-29 rays in the anal fin. The bullheads cannot be mistaken for any of the madtoms since the adipose fin of the madtom is not free at the posterior end but is attached to the tail fin with only a notch between them. The blue catfish (a member of the channel cat genus) has a deeply forked tail and 30-36 rays in the anal fin. It

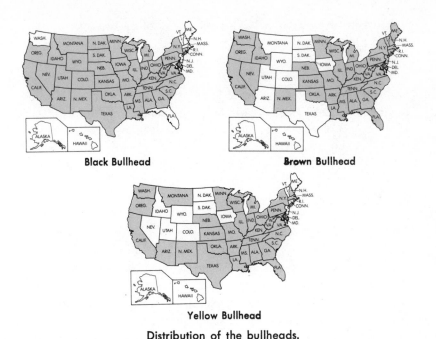

Black Bullhead   Brown Bullhead

Yellow Bullhead

Distribution of the bullheads.

does not have spines.

The flathead catfish, mudcat or yellow cat, as it is sometimes called, is sometimes mistaken for a brown bullhead since both are mottled. The flathead catfish, however, has a large adipose fin, a short anal fin with only 15 to 17 rays and a flattened or shovel-like head. The tail of the flathead is not forked.

DISTRIBUTION

As can be seen from the maps, black bullheads are found in thirty-eight states, brown bullheads in thirty-nine, and yellow bull- heads in thirty-six states.

Reference has already been made to the fact that black bullheads are the most hardy and can live in extremely turbid, even polluted, water of small ponds and streams as well as large lakes. Wherever the black bullhead is present with other bullheads, it will soon be- come the dominant species. Since it is also the smallest, however, it is less desirable than the brown or yellow, so the black should never be stocked in waters that will support the other two species. The brown bullhead is the best tasting, primarily because it requires the clearest water. Yellow and brown bullheads do not do well in the turbid waters of reservoirs. When the Black River in Missouri was impounded to form Clearwater Lake, the yellow bullhead was the dominant catfish species with only one black bullhead captured in two years of collecting. Despite this small brood stock, however, the black bullhead became the dominant species, outnumbering the yellow by 12 to 1 only a year and a half after impoundment.

SPAWNING

In spite of their barbaric appearance, bullheads are really very gentle and attentive parents. After the warm weather of spring arouses the spark of romance under its ugly hide, the fish begins to move into shallow water to spawn. When the water temperature is between 65° and 80°, the female lays her eggs, usually in water from one-half to 4 feet deep. If some sort of cavity or impression is present in the mud, sand or other cover, the female will deposit her gelatinous masses of cream-colored eggs there, the eggs numbering from 2,000 to 6,000. Nests have been found in cattle tracks in the mud, in old field tiles, under submerged logs, in hollow logs, under old stumps, under the roots of cattails, in old rusty buckets or in large tin cans.

If natural nests are not available, the male and female may prepare a nest together, using their pectoral spines as picks and their mouths as shovels. After the eggs are fertilized, both the male and female will guard the nest for a time; then the female leaves, or is driven away by the male. The male will work his fins and tail to keep the eggs clean; at other times, he will inhale the eggs in his mouth, rinsing them around as he would mouthwash, and then exhale them.

The incubation period depends upon the water temperature. The average incubation period of brown bullheads in the state of Maine is three to five days. After hatching, the male will patrol the school of fish, herding them together in the shallows and keeping them out of danger until they are almost 2 inches in length. In the face of danger, papa will stir up mud, laying a dense "mud screen" to shut out the getaway route while he and the kids beat a hasty retreat.

Occasionally, the dutiful father will forget himself and swallow one of his brood that wanders away from home. Those that survive his tender-loving care usually remain together in relatively shallow water sheltered among the aquatic vegetation.

BAIT FOR BULLHEADS

Bullheads are omnivorous feeders, eating many kinds of plant, animal and insect material. Included in their natural diet are algae, pond weeds of various kinds, plant remains, seeds from water lilies and other plants, fish and fish remains, crawfish, frogs, mollusks (clams and snails), microscopic crustaceans, aquatic insect larvae, nymphs and adult insects. Stomachs examined from forty-four bullheads taken from Maine waters contained mostly algae and other plant remains, fish and aquatic insects. Fifty-one percent of 143 bullheads examined during the spawning period of lake trout in one lake contained lake-trout eggs in their stomachs.

Beside these natural foods, bullheads can be taken on an almost infinite variety of other natural and prepared baits. Bullhead fishermen each have their own special formulae for baits; the outdoor magazines practically always have ads selling secret catfish bait formulae. Catfish aren't fussy, so you can select from among the following:

Earthworms. These have always been a standard bait for bullheads and are extremely effective. You can use common angleworms, nightcrawlers or manure worms; it doesn't seem to matter. I prefer angleworms, however, since they stay on the hook better without breaking. Be certain to place three or four on the hook, however, since bullheads like a large mouthful.

Crawfish or crawfish tails. These will work, although I don't consider them as good as earthworms and they are usually more expensive.

Frogs, dead or alive. I have caught numerous bullheads when frog fishing for bass. Other baits are far more effective and easier to obtain.

Clams. Take pieces of either freshwater or ocean clams and use these. Some anglers like to let them ripen in the sun to give them a foul odor. Any spoiled meat will attract bullheads by its smell.

Fish. You can use live minnows, but pieces of smelly fish, such as smelt, are really more effective. Put generous portions on your hook.

Shrimp, either fresh or frozen, is a favorite of fishermen in many parts of the country. It is always possible to obtain frozen shrimp in stores.

Liver was always a favorite of mine when I was a boy. Any kind of liver works, the bloodier and smellier the better. Cut into cubes about ¾ of an inch square.

Chicken entrails. This is another standard bait in many sections of the country. Ask your butcher to save you some bait next time he draws chickens.

Beef. Use cut pieces, either fresh or partially ripened.

Soap. Believe it or not, this is a favorite in a few small sections of the country. Bury the hook in the soap so the fish will swallow the whole thing readily. It takes a very long time for the soap to dissolve in the water.

Blood bait is one of the unusual baits sometimes used for catfish. It works, but is not especially superior to many others. To make blood bait, place chicken or animal blood in a cloth sack which is hung up to let the plasma drip out. Then mix the blood with pieces of cotton and let harden.

Doughballs. Use ground rancid meat or strong cheese, mix with flour, cotton wool and water to make a very thick dough.

Paste cheese bait. Add 1 quart of boiling water to 1 pint of corn meal and heat. Stir to keep the meal from sticking, adding small chunks of rancid cheese. Keep mixing until the mush has the consistency of rubber and will roll around the pan. Remove, place on a board sprinkled with corn meal, and knead the dough, putting in small pieces of cotton until the dough is very tough and rubbery. Pinch off pieces and roll into small balls. You can keep the bait fresh by keeping rolled in a damp cloth.

Peanut butter bait. Mix equal parts of peanut butter and flour moistened with hot water. Divide into balls. This is an excellent bait and it stays on the hook better than some others.

Sponge-rubber bait. Cut suitable sizes of sponge rubber, soak in rancid mixtures of cheese, ground beef or fish and use for bait.

As you can see, there are an infinite variety of bullhead baits, so use whatever seems easiest for you to obtain.

HOW TO CATCH THEM

Two factors that play an important part in whether bullheads bite are the time of day and the water temperature. No matter what season of the year you are fishing for them, from just before dark until about 12 p.m. is the best time for bullheading. As soon as the sun touches the horizon and the darkness begins to fall, Mr. Whiskers comes out of hiding and goes on a feeding spree. Ardent "hornpout" anglers in Maine wait until dusk to venture forth, then light their gasoline lanterns and anchor over their favorite bullhead feeding-grounds.

Bullheads definitely like warm water and become more sluggish as the water grows cold. Ice fishermen report seeing them moving freely about under the ice in the winter, but seldom catching them. I believe I have only caught two bullheads through the ice in all of the years I've been ice fishing. In general, as the waters warm up over 50°, you'll begin to have fair success, although temperatures over 60° are best. This means that late spring, summer and early fall are the best times for bullhead fishing. However, let water temperatures guide you rather than the season of the year, since the season may be either early or late in any one year in a certain section of the country.

When fishing for bullheads with a rod and reel, I prefer using light tackle the same as for other panfish. This tackle gives you far greater sport and also produces more fish. This means I use a 7½- or 9-foot leader when using my fly-rod outfit; also, I use a medium-size hook (about number 2 or 4) and a small bobber which is sensitive to the sometimes delicate bite of the bullhead. The bobber should be adjusted so the bait is only 2 or 3 inches off the bottom.

When using my spinning outfit I prefer to use about an 8-pound-test monofilament line with a dipsey sinker tied to the very end and one or two dropper loops tied about a foot or two up from the sinker. This rig allows for easy casting and for one to fish the bait right on the bottom. It's a good rig to use from a river or lake shore since you can cast a long distance from the shore if needed. In spite of all of the devotees that use them, I don't get much fun out of hoisting bullheads aboard with a long, stiff bamboo pole. Try light tackle and see if you don't agree that it's better sport.

If you want to fish for meat and have a lot of fun besides, then

Good rig for bullheads is a dipsey sinker on one end of line and a couple of dropper loops above for fishing bait on bottom. The angler lands a nice fish on an Alabama lake.

you can use set lines from the shore, or trot lines stretched out into the water for some distance. I've always thoroughly enjoyed running either set lines or trot lines; there is that element of suspense as one pulls up the line. Before you use these methods, however, check your state laws to be certain they are legal.

Set lines are best when used along undercut banks of rivers or creeks, or along deep shorelines of lakes. Put the baited hook end of the line in the water near the shore; the other end should be attached to a branch, tree or stake. Usually, a heavy sinker is used on the end of the line so the bait will stay on the bottom.

In using trotlines, one of the most important considerations is to have a properly constructed rig. The main line itself should be as long as needed; about 30 to 100 feet is most common. This line ought to be heavy and of a great tensile strength—at least 40 pounds. It can be made of white cotton or braided nylon. To this line is attached shorter pieces of line, to which the hooks are tied. These short lines are usually 15 to 20 inches long and are called "stagings." The stagings can also be of white cotton or nylon. I prefer nylon monofilament of about 20-pound test.

The stagings are detachable by means either of snap and ring sets or of blanket-type fasteners. If rings are used, they are slipped over the main line and tied to it about 3 to 4 feet apart by short pieces of ordinary casting line. One snap is tied on the end of each staging and it is a simple matter to unsnap the staging from the ring whenever you are tolling up the main line. Some fishermen have extra stagings and remove one that needs to be baited, replacing it with another which has the hook baited. The pieces of staging are then rebaited and used to replace others next time the line is checked for fish. If the blanket-type fasteners are used, they are snapped directly to the main line, thus eliminating the rings.

One secret of successful trotlining is to select a good location. Moving your line several hundred yards up or down stream can be the means of filling the stringer, so if you are not having any luck in one location, move to another.

In putting out the line, stretch it across the stream, tying one end to each shore, or tie it to one shore and anchor the other end with a float. Sometimes you will have the best success with your trotline parallel to the shore, often right by the deep river bank; at other times you'll do better with it in the middle of the stream or lake. Deep, quiet pools below dams and riffles are often likely spots. Once the line is set, you ought to check it at least every two hours to keep losses to a minimum.

Another lazy man's way of catching bullheads is to use set lines to which a medium-size jar or can is attached. The jar or can floats and serves as an indicator when a fish is hooked. The fisherman will then run down the float as it moves off, landing the fish. A boat is needed for this kind of fishing in order to chase the floats when they are pulled downstream by hooked fish.

One way to locate bullheads is to throw decaying meat, fish or meal into one area over a period of several days. The bullheads will begin to flock around this area of concentrated food and can be caught easily.

BULLHEAD FISHING SIMPLIFIED

One of the most amusing essays on bullhead fishing was written by Al Bromley, Assistant Superintendent of the Bureau of Inland Fisheries of New York State. This essay was originally published in the New York State Conservationist, the official magazine of the conservation department. A short excerpt follows.

If you haven't already met this chap on the end of your fish line (and the chances are extremely remote that you haven't) there are a few pointers to be observed for a proper introduction. For your contemplated call select a warm spring night along in May. A fine drizzle with a gentle south breeze is prescribed. Shortly after dark be on your way equipped as follows: One bamboo pole (anything over ten feet preferred) with 30 to 50 feet of heavy line attached to the far end and wrapped spirally down the pole in such manner as to place the hook in position to pierce your pants as you walk. For bait nightwalkers are prescribed with the No. 2 tomato can being the preferred carrier. Nevertheless there is a small group which leans to the Prince Albert tobacco can, several of which can be stowed on the person. This has disadvantages in the dark, however, if you are a pipe smoker. Other essentials are a kerosene lantern (the smoky variety is the most common) and a jug of tea or something for the marsh chill. A poll on the refreshment problem among bullhead fishermen in upper New York State showed hard cider to have a commanding lead.

Thus prepared, proceed to a likely marsh, pond or river anywhere in the neighborhood. Having arrived (a triumph in itself), deposit your gear, unroll your line, get out your jacknife and cut the hook out of your pant leg, attach a large cork bobber and a four to six-ounce sinker. Such a sinker may outweigh any fish caught but it's essential in securing a satisfactory splash following a full swinging overhead cast. Bait up. No need to hold the bamboo schooner; stick the butt in the mud.

You should soon have your first bite. Walk purposely to the pole and grasp firmly, right hand near the butt and left as far out as possible. Place left foot in front with knee bent. Now spring back, lifting mightily at the same time and follow through with a complete over-head maneuver.

If this technique is fully mastered your horned pout will be securely grounded some 50 feet to the rear where, with aid of lantern and matches, he can be located eventually.

There's no hurry; time means nothing to bullheads.

9

SPINNING
FOR PANFISH

Each method of fishing has its own boosters who claim that method to be superior to all others, and spinning is not without its ardent followers. Perhaps no other method has enjoyed such rapid acceptance and fast-growing popularity. The method was almost unknown in the United States until after World War II, but since that time millions of Americans have purchased equipment and taken up the sport so that today more fishermen use spinning equipment than any other type.

There are good reasons for the popularity of spinning. Thousands of fishermen who were never able to develop sufficient skill to be expert bait casters waited for years to be freed of the curse of backlashes. Spinning offered this redemption, since these fishermen could now cast all day without ever getting a snarl in their spinning lines. Freedom from backlashes thus enabled the mediocre caster to get out and really enjoy his fishing without wasting half his time unsnarling his line.

Furthermore, the advent of spinning enabled the fishermen to use very small, light lures, which they were never able to do with bait-casting tackle. The small lures were more sporting, and they caught a greater variety of fish. Fishermen who were never able to catch

126

much on large bass or pike lures were now able to catch at least a few panfish. Those who could never fish for trout with anything besides a worm, because they were never able to fly fish, were now bringing home strings of good-size trout caught on spinning lures. And even the bass fishermen caught more fish on the small lures. The result of this success was that the good news spread across the country and people turned to spinning by the millions.

When they did, they also discovered that catching fish on light, limber rods and small-diameter, invisible lines was more sporting. Sometimes the fish even had a fighting chance. A pound crappie or a large yellow perch exhibited surprising fighting abilities, something never realized in the days of the long, heavy bamboo pole.

Spinning was also adaptable to fishing in inaccessible places. One could cast from the shore of a pond or lake without having room behind him. If there was enough space to get a rod and lure through a hole in the brush, there was room enough to cast. Spinning made possible long casts to deep holes without using a boat. It was also much easier to use spinning tackle on brush-covered streams or rivers than to use fly-fishing equipment. When all of these advantages are taken into consideration, it is not hard to see why spinning became such a popular method of fishing.

What about spinning for panfish? It is an excellent method, especially for those panfish which feed on minnows and small fish. These include crappie, white and yellow bass, white perch and yellow perch. The smaller lures, spoons and spinners that can be used with the spinning rod are excellent for these species of panfish. I feel the fly rod is the most sporting and productive weapon to use for all species of panfish, particularly when the fish are in shallow water, but when it is necessary to fish quite deep, either by casting or trolling, then the spinning outfit is superior.

SPINNING OR SPINCASTING?

So far I have used the general term "spinning" to refer to any type of fishing using a fixed-spool reel. Since the wide acceptance of spinning in the United States, a number of changes have taken place in spinning rods and reels to necessitate differentiating between spinning and spincasting.

Open-face spinning reels are available in ultralight models that cast lures
$\frac{1}{32}$ ounce on 2- to 4-pound-test line. These are ideal for panfishing.

When spinning was first introduced from Europe, all spinning reels
were of the open-face type, mounted underneath the rod with reel
handle on the left (for right-handed casters). Now, however, two
additional types of fixed-spool reels have been developed in America.
One is the closed-face spinning reel, mounted like the conventional
spinning reel underneath the rod handle but with a cover over the
spool of the reel. This type is still a "spinning" reel. (I would not
recommend a reel of this type, however, since I feel both the open-
face and spincast reels are superior.) The second type of reel is the
spincasting reel (some call it a spin bait-casting reel). This reel is
a closed-face spinning reel, but it mounts on top of the rod like a
conventional bait-casting reel and has a pushbutton device to control the line. A standard, offset-handle, bait-casting rod is used
with the spincasting reel.

Which type of equipment should you buy and use? If you can
afford it, you should certainly buy both, but if you can afford only
one outfit, then I would select spincasting equipment. There are
several reasons for my selection.

1. Spincasting equipment is the most foolproof ever invented. Bill

Spincasting reel is mounted on top of the rod handle like a bait casting reel. Pushbutton controls the line.

Carter, of Dallas, Texas, established an uncontested record in 1956 by making 3,453 consecutive casts with spincasting equipment without a single backlash or line tangle of any kind. He began at sunrise and quit at sunset; he could have continued his trouble-free casting for hours, but it seemed pointless to do so. Even the most expert caster would have to admit that he gets an occasional tangle with the conventional, open-face spinning reel.

2. Even the worst beginner can learn to cast successfully in a very short time with spincasting gear. Anyone who is willing to practice a little can use a conventional spinning reel, but since most fishermen will never practice their casting until they get on the lake, they better select what they can use successfully without any practice. The equipment coming closest to this requirement is spincasting.

3. Spincasting equipment is suitable for all-around fishing when you want to cast lures of from ⅛ to ½ ounce. I am assuming now that you will use one rod and reel for all types of fish: pike, bass, trout, panfish and others. You can use spincasting equipment for all if you select a rod limber enough to cast very light lures, and if you use very light line when casting the smallest lures. When using the heavier lures, you can change to a heavier line. The simplest way is

to keep a spare spool with the heavier line mounted.

Please note, however, if you want the best possible outfit for casting only small lures, $\frac{1}{32}$ to $\frac{1}{4}$ ounce, then buy an ultra light, open-face spinning reel and an ultra-light rod. This equipment is really much better suited to panfishing, trout fishing and other small-lure fishing than is spincasting. For this reason, I am recommending two basic outfits in this chapter: one, a light spincasting outfit for all-around fishing which can also be used for panfish, and the other an ultra-light spinning outfit which is the best for panfish. Take your choice.

THE LIGHT SPINCASTING ROD

What rod should you buy? The best rods now come in three basic materials: boron, graphite, and tubular fiberglass. There are also combinations: boron-graphite, and graphite-fiberglass are the two most popular. You can also get solid fiberglass rods, but I would not recommend one of these for panfishing.

Each material or combination has its advantages and disadvantages. Boron is lighter in weight than a comparable graphite rod, but with more sensitivity and superior strength. This sensitivity allows you to feel the lure action, the strike, and even the softest pickups. Graphite is lighter than fiberglass, can be made in smaller diameter for less air resistance and casting fatigue, is two to seven times stiffer than fiberglass, and has a faster action which transmits energy efficiently for distance, accuracy, and a flat trajectory. It also allows you to set the hook more easily. Fiberglass is the toughest, strongest material available, although heavier, and with a somewhat slower action. Boron-graphite combinations combine some of the advantages of each material: the light weight, sensitivity, and superior strength of boron, and the power and fast action of graphite. Graphite-fiberglass combinations combine the light weight, small diameter, and fast action of graphite, and the toughness of fiberglass. One rod manufacturer told me they had to add fiberglass to their graphite rods to prevent them from breaking so easily.

Spincasting rods come in a wide variety of lengths: 5 to 6 feet are most common in the light rods. I feel that 5½ feet is about the right all-'round length. The action of the rod is even more important than length. Pay special attention to the manufacturer's recommendations regarding the weight of the lures the rod will handle. Light action rods ought to be able to cast lures from ⅛ to ½ ounce. Some will handle lures as light as $\frac{1}{16}$ ounce when a small enough line is used. You can't expect a light rod to handle ⅝-ounce lures or larger, so don't use these bigger lures with it or you'll strain or break it.

The only way you can really tell the action of a rod is to try it out. Use a line no heavier than 4-pound test for the ⅛-ounce lures to give the rod a fair trial. You would not be able to get long distances with such a light lure, but you ought to be able to cast far enough to catch fish, anyhow.

Spincast rods come with a variety of handles. Try different ones out to see which are most comfortable in your hand. Make certain that the spincast reel you select will fit snugly and securely on the reel seat, and that the rod has proper guides and tip-top. The most expensive and hardest guide material is silicon carbide, which is sometimes used for all guides, or at least for the tip-top, on the best rods. Silicon carbide is twice as hard as aluminum oxide. Less expensive materials, but still adequate, are aluminum oxide, ceramic, and stainless steel guides. Ceramic or aluminum oxide are often used as inserts in stainless steel or chrome-plated steel guide frames. Aluminum oxide and stainless steel are also used alone. Chrome-plated guides are the softest and wear most easily.

Your rod will usually be two-piece, disconnected from the handle. If it has a ferrule in the center of the tip, make certain the ferrule pieces fit snugly together.

If you are to get a satisfactory spincast reel to use with your rod, there are several things you ought to watch for.

1. *Ease of operation.* Does the reel feel comfortable in your hand? Can you reach the line-control level or "push button" easily? Is it easy to control the line? Can the drag be set easily? Is there a convenient click and anti-reverse adjustment?

2. *Smoothly operating drag.* Can the drag be set both light and heavy enough and, most important, does it operate smoothly without catching as the line is pulled out?

3. *Ease of take-down and maintenance.* Is it possible to get to the vital parts easily so that the reel can be serviced, oiled, greased or cleaned? Is it possible to change spools easily?

4. *Necessary features.* Does the reel have all of the features that

are considered essential on this type of reel? These include: a safe, sure, easily operated method of line control, a drag-tension adjustment, an anti-reverse adjustment, a click, an automatic line pick-up arrangement, an interchangeable spool and a level wind to spool the line evenly. The level wind might be considered optional, but it is a helpful feature. Less than half of the reels have this feature.

ULTRA-LIGHT SPINNING TACKLE

If you want to have the very maximum of sport in panfishing, then by all means get a really ultra-light spinning outfit. Rods in this category range from 4½ to 7 feet in length and from 2 to 4½ ounces in weight. Reels to match weigh from 5 to 9 ounces in weight. With such hairline spinning equipment you can use monofilament line ranging from 2- to 4-pound test.

There are several advantages to this type of equipment:

1. This ultra-light spinning gear will allow you to cast the lightest spinning lures considerable distances and with accuracy. Some lures that are as large as ¼ ounce are too heavy for panfish. The best sizes and weights usually range from $\frac{1}{32}$ to ⅛ ounce. These sizes are easily cast with ultra-light gear if a very light line is employed.

2. This equipment enables you to get the maximum sport out of catching small fish. A 10-inch bluegill seems like a monster on this equipment. You really have to play such a fish to land it on 2-pound test line! And you will enjoy it just as much as catching a 5-pound bass on heavy tackle.

3. The short rod and light reel are very pleasant to use, allowing you to fish the cramped places in the brush on small streams and creeks and to cast all day without tiring. Handling a 2- or 3-ounce rod is like using a fairy wand.

There are fishermen who try to get the shortest and lightest rod available (4½ feet and about 2 ounces in weight). Other equally as competent fishermen prefer a very long, limber rod (7 feet long and about 4 ounces). Both will cast very light lures effectively if small line is used. I prefer a compromise: a rod of 5 to 6 feet in length weighing around 3 ounces. Total rod weight is not as important as action, however. The important thing is to get a rod of good action with enough backbone in the butt section to set the hook in the fish and play it, yet limber enough to cast the very lightest lures. The best way to tell is try the rod out, using different weight lures, from about ⅟₃₂ to ⅛ ounces. See the previous section on spincast rods for a discussion of rod materials and action.

When buying an ultra-light reel, it is wise to choose one of good quality that is as light and strong as possible, and that has all of the features of a heavier reel: smoothly operating drag, automatic (internal) bail closing and pickup, anti-reverse, and automatic positioning bail. The newest Japanese reels (Shimano, Daiwa, and Ryobi) and some by Abu Garcia also have a trigger-operated bail opener, so that when you pick up the line, your finger presses a lever which opens the bail automatically in preparation for your cast. I also prefer open-faced reels with skirted spools, which prevent the line from coming off the end in tangles.

There is a considerable variation in the types of drag arrangements. The most common is a spool-controlled drag, adjusted on the front of the spool. Properly designed, with enough discs, such a drag can operate smoothly without sticking. Make certain the drag can be adjusted both light enough and heavy enough for the lines you will be using. Some reels have rear-mounted drag adjustments. I have no special preference as long as they work properly. A few reels have drag adjustments on the side, at the base of the handle.

THE SPINNING AND SPINCASTING LINE

What line should you use? A good line should fulfill the following requirements.

1. *Maximum and uniform strength per diameter.* Some lines are stronger than others, so try to select those with the greatest tensile strength for the smallest diameter. Two lines deserve special mention here: Stren by DuPont and Platyl by Gladding. Both have a greater strength per diameter than do ordinary nylon lines. They are also more expensive.

2. *Ease of casting.* The line should be flexible enough to spool easily and to go off the spool without kinking or tangling. The smaller the lures you are going to use, the lighter will have to be your line. Also, if you will fill the reel spool to within ⅛ inch of the lip, your line will go out easier.

3. *Maximum invisibility.* Undyed monofilament that is of a natural clear color seems to meet this requirement the best. Monofilament

also comes in many so-called invisible, dyed shades. None of the dyed lines are as invisible as the natural, clear color.

4. *Long wearing.* Buy the very best grades of monofilament line and periodically cut off the frayed and weakened end, which loses its strength in use. Never buy line because it is the least expensive; it usually is of inferior quality and wears quickly.

The best all-around line for both spincasting and spinning is a good grade of monofilament. Some anglers use braided monofilament but, since it is not invisible and requires the use of a leader with it, I would not recommend it.

What pound test should you use? This depends upon the type of fishing you are doing, whether trolling or casting, the weight of lures you are casting and the abundance of brush, weed beds and other cover in the water you are fishing. Use about 6- or 8-pound-test line when trolling so that if you are hung up you can free your lure. If you are spinning with ultra-light lures (⅛ ounce or below), you will have to use a line of from 2- to 4-pound test. I would use about a 4- to 6-pound test for casting light lures (⅛ to ½ ounce).

In order to be able to get the maximum strength from your line, be certain to use the proper knots. A small ball-bearing snap swivel ought to be tied to the end of your line to facilitate changing lures. Use the improved clinch knot (described in Chapter 10) for this purpose. In tying the ends of two pieces of monofilament together, use the 5-turn blood knot (which is also described in Chapter 10).

THE ART OF SPINCASTING

It should not take the average person very long to learn to cast with spincasting gear. It will take considerable practice to develop real accuracy, but you can learn to cast well enough to catch panfish in an afternoon's practice. You therefore can have fun and produce results in a short time.

You can practice on either land or water. The first step is to make certain your equipment is properly rigged. Use about a 4-pound-test monofilament line, making certain to fill the reel spool to within about ⅛ inch of the lip of the spool. Pass the line through the rod guides and tie on a very small ball-bearing snap swivel. Use a ¼-ounce practice plug.

In making the overhead cast, hold the rod in your right hand (assuming you are right-handed) with your forefinger extended and wrapped comfortably around the rod trigger and your other fingers around and under the handle. Your thumb should be on the push-button (line control) device. Turn your hand to your left so that your palm faces down and the reel handle up.

Raise your forearm, bending at the elbow, bringing your rod up quickly to your right shoulder to the vertical. (Accuracy is improved if you minimize your wrist bend on this "backstroke.") Stop the rod at the vertical, quickly, allowing the plug to bend the rod tip back. As the rod bends back, begin the forward stroke of your arm. When the rod is at about a 45° angle on the downstroke, release the push-button, allowing the weight of the plug to take out line. While the plug is in flight, you can feather the line by reapplying very light pressure upon the line-control lever. Stop the rod at its original position and, as the lure nears the target, increase the thumb pressure. Just before the lure hits the water, stop the line completely by pushing all of the way down on the pushbutton, line-control lever. The cast should end with the rod tip pointing directly toward the target. The retrieve is then made by switching the rod to your left hand, holding it by the shaft just above the reel, and cranking in line with your right hand. As you reel in, let the line slide between the thumb and forefinger of your left hand, keeping the line taut as it is wound on the spool.

Several minor points ought to be mentioned.

1. Let the rod do the work when you cast. Never move your whole arm, only your forearm, in order to put a bend in the rod to give you power.

2. Always move the rod in a vertical plane both on the back and forward stroke and never bring the rod back farther than just beyond the vertical on the back stroke.

3. If your lure is cast too high, then you are releasing the line too quickly. If the lure bangs down in front, you have released the line too late on the forward cast. A little practice will enable you to cast the lure directly to the target without making too much or too little of an arc.

4. Always try to stop your lure just before it hits the water; this allows for a smooth, quiet, natural-looking entry.

5. For most ordinary fishing, use this overhead cast. It is the safest

when you are with companions in the boat, particularly if you cast only perpendicular to the center line of the boat. This cast is also the most accurate.

At certain times, particularly when there are obstructions above or behind you, you may want to use the side cast. Hold the rod as in the overhead cast except with the pushbutton up and the reel handle on the right side. With a quick movement, bring your rod back to the right in a horizontal plane and stop it at a right-angle position to your body. As in the overhead cast, pivot your forearm at the elbow, keeping your wrist fairly stiff. At the instant the rod is bending the maximum amount, move the rod forward, rolling and turning your wrist to the left until the reel handle is up, also releasing your thumb pressure from the pushbutton at the forward impulse. If you release the line too early, the lure will land to your right; if you release it too late, the lure will swing to the left. Practice will enable you to cast directly to the target in front of you. Try to feather the line as it goes out, stopping the flight of the lure just before it hits the water.

CASTING WITH THE OPEN-FACE SPINNING REEL

Casting with an open-face reel is similar to bait casting or spincasting, as far as the basic arm movements are concerned. The chief difference is in the control of the line and the way the hand is used for this purpose.

The spinning rod is held with the reel under the rod and with the reel base between the index and the third finger of your right hand (for right-hand casters). The thumb is extended along the top of the rod, the index finger is held on the lip of the spool and used to feather or stop the line as needed.

To begin the cast, back up the reel handle with your left hand until the handle stops and the bail is positioned. (If your reel does not have a self-positioning bail, you will have to stop the reel handle at the proper place to permit you to open the bail for the cast.) Open the bail with your left hand and push it down until it clicks into place, while you hold the line against the rod with the index finger of your right hand.

Cast as described in the previous section on spincasting, releasing

the line at the proper moment of the forward stroke by letting go
with your right index finger. Use this same finger to feather the
line as it goes out, stopping the lure just before it hits the water by
touching your finger to the lip of the spool. The retrieve is made

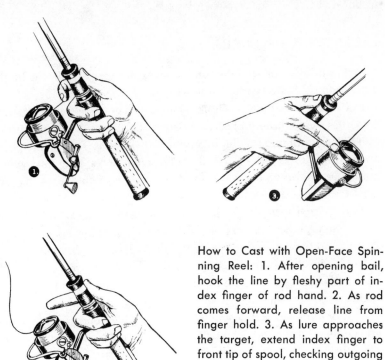

How to Cast with Open-Face Spinning Reel: 1. After opening bail,
hook the line by fleshy part of index finger of rod hand. 2. As rod
comes forward, release line from
finger hold. 3. As lure approaches
the target, extend index finger to
front tip of spool, checking outgoing
line so lure drops where you want it.

with your left hand on the reel handle, continuing to hold the rod
with your right hand. The bail will automatically close and catch the
line and wind it on the spool as you begin the retrieve.

By the way, the correct procedure in setting the drag on both
spincast and spinning reels is to play out about 50 feet of line, with
the lure tied to an object or held by your fishing partner. As you
try to reel in, set the drag to the proper tension for the line you are
using. Obviously, this should be at a loose enough setting so the line
cannot be broken by a running fish but not so loose that you cannot

maintain enough tension to set the hook or play the fish. I try to
set the drag as tightly as possible, making certain it is loose enough
to allow the fish to take out line if it pulls hard enough. In playing
a fish do not reel in line when the fish is taking it out; this will result
in line twist.

BASIC TYPES OF LURES

Artificial lures for spinning and spincasting for panfish can be divided into six basic types as follows:

1. *Plugs.* Usually ultra-light versions of bait-casting models, they
come in a wide variety of sizes, actions and colors, but can be sub-
divided according to the depth at which they work. Thus, some plugs
are surface lures; others are floating-diving lures that float when
motionless, but dive when retrieved; others are sinking lures that are
used for deep-water fishing.

2. *Weighted spinners.* These come in various sizes, weights and
colors. Some have feathers or hair covering a treble hook, or a fly
attached to the spinner and weight. Others have a weighted spinner
in gold, nickel, copper, brass or a painted finish with a bare treble
hook attached. At other times, live bait is put on a hook and used
with a single or double spinner in casting or trolling.

3. *Wobbling or darting spoons* are available in brass, nickel, gold
and copper finishes or with painted colors. Some have a decided wiggle; others wobble, while still others dart to and fro. The smaller spinning sizes are best for panfish.

4. *Nature lures* are plastic imitations of frogs, worms, minnows,
tadpoles, crickets, various larvae and grubs.

5. *Jigs* are available in feathers, hair or marabou with weighted
heads. The small sizes can be used in jigging for panfish in the spring,
fall or summer or through the ice in the winter. They are especially
good for deep-water fishing.

6. *Pork Rind.* I have listed this separately although it is usually
used in conjunction with a spinner and hook, a fly or a spoon. Comes
in various sizes and shapes of strips, chunks, skirts, pills and "flicks"
and in various colors: red, black, green, white and yellow.

Sometimes, combinations of lures can also be used. Thus, the fisherman may use a plastic bubble to give weight and buoyancy and cast
ordinary dry or wet flies on his spinning outfit. Or panfish bugs or

jigs can be attached to larger surface or underwater plugs with a short line of monofilament. Pork rind can be put on flies, spinners, plugs or spoons to give added attraction.

With so many effective lures on the market, it is difficult for the fisherman to know which to select so I am recommending some particular lures after trying out hundreds of different ones. Of course, there are still many others which I have not tried and which will undoubtedly catch fish, so please forgive me if I have omitted your favorite. Also, I have tried to suggest a varied enough assortment to meet most conditions encountered in different parts of the country, and when fishing for different panfish. Furthermore, just because I suggest only specific finishes or colors does not mean that the others in that lure are not suitable. Rather, the lures are suggested to give you a variety of colors. Don't hesitate to experiment on your own, however.

Plugs are most suitable for those panfish which eat quantities of small fish. This group includes crappie, rock and warmouth bass, white and yellow bass, white perch, and yellow perch.

A good assortment should include plugs of a variety of actions, sizes, and colors, and which run at various depths. Most should be small because the size of the fish caught is small.

Surface Lures

Baby Crippled Killer, ⅛ oz., Yellow Perch (Phillips)

Creek Chub Injured Minnow, ⅛ oz., Red and White (Creek Chub)

Creek Chub Plunker, ⅛ oz., Pikie (Creek Chub)

Jitterbug, ⅛ oz., Frog/White Belly (Fred Arbogast)

Rebel Poppers, ⅛ oz., Silver (Plastic Research and Development Corp.)

Weighted Spin Popper, ⅛ oz., Black Belly/Yellow stripes (Glen Evans)

Whopper Stopper Pop 'n' Jig, ½ oz., plunker trailed by a baby jig on a 15-inch leader, White (Whopper Stopper)

The addition of a small dry fly, panfish bug, or wet fly, attached with a nylon trailer to the plug, will catch fish with small mouths that are striking but not getting hooked.

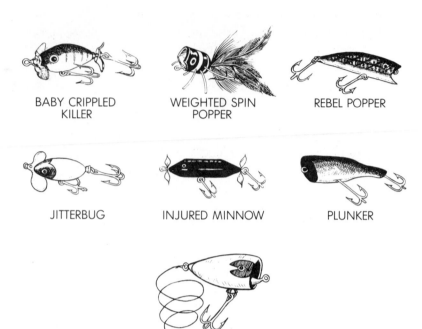

BABY CRIPPLED KILLER   WEIGHTED SPIN POPPER   REBEL POPPER

JITTERBUG   INJURED MINNOW   PLUNKER

POP 'N' JIG

SURFACE LURES

Floating-Diving Lures (Darters, Wobblers, Deep Divers)

Creek Chub Darter, ⅛ oz., Frog (Creek Chub)
Creek Chub Pikie Minnow, ⅛ oz., Perch (Creek Chub)
Finn-Oreno, ³⁄₁₆ oz. (3½″), Silver Back (Gladding-South Bend)
Flatfish, 1¾″ and 2½″, Frog or White/Assorted spots (Helin)
Rainbow Runner, ⅛ oz., Gold fish (Phillips)
Rapala, 2″, Blue (Normark)
Rascal ¼ oz. (1¾″), Yellow (Gladding-South Bend)
Rebel, Deep-Runner Minnow, ⅛ oz., Red Back (Plastic Research and Development Corp.)
Rebel, Shiner Minnow, ¹⁄₁₆ oz., Fluor. Red (Plastic Research and Development Corp.)

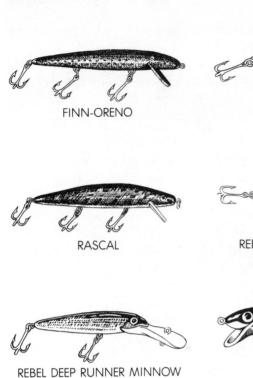
FINN-ORENO

RAPALA

RASCAL

REBEL SHINER MINNOW

REBEL DEEP RUNNER MINNOW

THINFIN SUPER
SHINER MINNOW

RAINBOW RUNNER

FLATFISH

ULTRA-LIGHT PIKIE

TINY FLOATING
RUNT

TINY LUCKY 13

DARTER

FLOATING-DIVING LURES

ThinFin Supper Shiner Minnow, ⅛ oz. (2½″), Green (Storm
Manufacturing Corp.)
Tiny Lucky 13, ¼ oz., Golden Shiner (Heddon)
Tiny River Runt Spook, ¼ oz., Red Head/Flitter (Heddon)

Sinking Lures (Deep Divers, Vibrators, Wobblers)

Deep Inch, ¼ oz., Black Dace (Falls Bait Co.)
Harrison's Rocky Lure: Junior—1/16 oz. (1″), Red and White;
Senior—⅛ oz. (1½″), Yellow/Black Dots (Harrison-Hoge)
Inch Minnow, 1/16 oz., Orange Tiger, or Pearl Spot (Falls)
L & S Mirrolures (Jointed), 1/16 oz., Green back-white belly-
silver scale (L & S Bait Co.)
L & S Spin-Master, 1/16 oz., Yellow body/brown bars (L & S)
L & S Mirrolure (Trail-O-Lure), 1/16 oz., Silver (L & S)
Rapala, 2″, Silver (Normark)
Tiny Ike, ¼ oz., Black-White Shore (Heddon)
Ultra-Sonic, ⅛ oz., Coach Dog (Heddon)

TRAIL-O-LURE

ULTRA SONIC

RAPALA

INCH MINNOW
AND DEEP INCH

HARRISON'S
ROCKY LURE

L & S MIRROLURE
OR SPIN-MASTER

TINY IKE

SINKING LURES

DEMON SPOON

GEMINI SPOON

PHANTOM
WOBBLER

FEATHERED
SHAD KING

JOHNSON'S SPRITE

LITTLE BANTAM

JOHNSON
BUCKTAIL SPOON

MARATHON
DICTATOR

DAREDEVLE MIDGET

SPOONS

SPOONS FOR PANFISH

Spoons are primarily for fish-eating panfish.

Al's Goldfish, $3/16$ oz., Gold (Al's Goldfish Lure Co.)

Dardevle, Skeeter Plus: $2/32$ oz. Red and White/Nickel

 Lil' Devle: $1/8$ oz.

 Midget: $3/16$ oz. (Lou Eppinger)

Demon Spoon, $1/32$ oz., Nickel (Worth)

Feathered Shad-King, #2, White Hackle (Hildebrandt)

Gemini Spoon, $1/30$ oz., Gold (Al's Goldfish)

Johnson's Bucktail Spoon, $1/2$ oz., Black Nickel/Black and white

 Bucktail (Louis Johnson)

Johnson's Sprite, $1/8$ oz., Blue Mullet (Louis Johnson)

K-B Spoon, $1/16$ oz., Copper (Prescott)

Little Bantam, $1/4$ oz., Hammered Brass (Southern Tool & Die Co.)

Little Cleo, $1/8$ oz., Black and Yellow (Seneca)

Marathon Dictator, $1/8$ oz., Black and White Stripe/Nickel

 (Marathon)

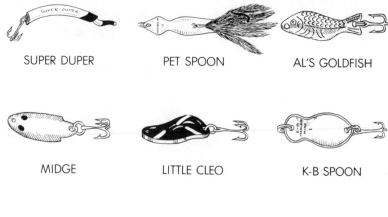

SUPER DUPER   PET SPOON   AL'S GOLDFISH

MIDGE   LITTLE CLEO   K-B SPOON

SLIM SPOON   WILLIAMS NYMPH

SPOONS

Midge, $\frac{1}{24}$ oz., Brass (Glen Evans)
Phantom Wobbler, Baby, Pearl/copper (H & J)
Slim Spoon, $\frac{1}{8}$ oz., Hammered Nickel (Weber)
Super Duper, $\frac{1}{6}$ oz., Red Head (Gladding-South Bend)
Tony Accetta Pet Spoon, $\frac{1}{16}$ oz., Standard Model, Feathered,
    Gold/Red Feather (Tony Accetta)
Williams Nymphs, $\frac{1}{40}$ oz. (1¼″), Silver Mirror (Williams)

Jigging Spoons

Select from Mitzi Series, Russian Hooks (Jig Spoons), Tear Drop
Series (Best Tackle Mfg. Co.) described in chapter on Spoons.
For use in ice fishing.

SPINNERS FOR PANFISH

For all kinds of panfish. Any type of spinner with a snelled hook
and bait makes an excellent casting or trolling lure for panfish. Use
larger spinners for trolling than casting. See the section on Spinners.

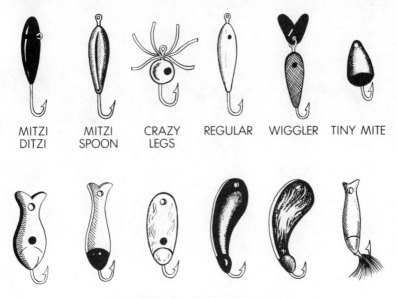

MITZI   MITZI   CRAZY   REGULAR   WIGGLER   TINY MITE
DITZI   SPOON   LEGS

JIG SPOONS — RUSSIAN HOOKS

JIGGING SPOONS

Spinner and fly, or spinner and pork rind are also excellent.

Weighted Spinners

    Abu-Reflex, $\frac{1}{16}$ oz., Yellow/Black Dots (Garcia)
    Colorado Spinner, 3/0 blade, Nickel (Glen Evans)
    Droppen, ⅛ oz., Gold (Garcia)
    Flicker-Spinner, #2, Nickel (Hildebrandt)
    Hep, ⅛ oz., Silver, Squirrel Tail (Daisy-Heddon)
    Little Fooler, $\frac{1}{12}$ oz., Red and White Skirt (Hildebrandt)
    Marathon Beam Buster, ⅛ oz., Black and Yellow (Marathon)
    Marathon Spin-O-Hawk, ⅛ oz., Black and Yellow (Marathon)
    Mepps Aglia, ⅛ oz., Red and White Spinner Blade, Bare Treble
        Hook (Sheldon's)
    Mepps Black Fury, ⅛ oz., Yellow hair (Sheldon's)
    Panther Martin, Regular, $\frac{1}{16}$ oz., Silver Blade/Yellow and Red
        Body (Harrison-Hoge)

MARATHON BREAM
BUSTER

WORDEN'S
ROOSTER TAIL

SPIN-O-HAWK

HEP SPINNER

WORTH SCAMP

ABU REFLEX

LITTLE
FOOLER

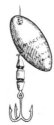
PANTHER
MARTIN

AGLIA

WORTH GOLDIE

DROPPEN

FLICKER-SPINNER

SPINNING-FLICKER

BLACK FURY

COLORADO SPINNER

WEIGHTED SPINNERS

146

Worden's Rooster Tail, $\frac{1}{16}$ oz., Flame (Yakima)
Worth Pearlie, $\frac{1}{6}$ oz. (Worth)
Worth Scamp, $\frac{1}{8}$ oz. White/Black Dots (Worth)
Spinning-Flicker, Gold, $\frac{1}{4}$ oz., #3 (Hildebrandt)

JIGS FOR PANFISH

Jigs are one of the finest lures for crappie. They are also excellent for white and yellow bass and are used to some extent on yellow perch. Get an assortment of types, sizes, and colors. White, yellow, pink are favorite colors. Blue, red, fluor. orange, red, or pink, black, and combinations of these (red and white, black and white, pink and white, blue and white, black and yellow, red and yellow, or white and yellow) are used to some extent. Buy sizes $\frac{1}{32}$–$\frac{1}{4}$ ounce. (The larger jigs are used on occasion with white and yellow bass particularly.) The following offers a good assortment:

Baby Lead Head Jig, #6 hook, Fluor. Red and White (Glen Evans)
BJ Bucktail Jig, $\frac{1}{8}$ oz., All White, Shaped Bucktail Jig (Banana Head), $\frac{1}{16}$ oz., All Yellow (Horrocks-Ibbotson)
Crappie Killer, #10 hook, Fluor. Red and White (Weber)
Fin-Nit, #8 hook, Black (Arndt & Sons)
Full Tail Jig, $\frac{1}{32}$ oz., White (Assassinator Lures)
Hot-Line, $\frac{1}{32}$ oz., Pearl (Arndt & Sons)
Jig Ike, $\frac{1}{16}$ oz., Black (Lazy Ike Corp.)
Li'l Crappie Killer, $\frac{1}{16}$ oz., Silver and Blue (Cordell)
Little Doggie Maribou Jig Fly, $\frac{1}{32}$ oz., Yellow/Black and Yellow (Glen Evans)
Little-Hornet Jig Fly, $\frac{1}{32}$ oz., Mud Dauber Finish (Arndt & Sons)
Marathon Canadian Minnow, $\frac{1}{16}$ oz., Black and White (Marathon)
Pinkie Jig, $\frac{1}{4}$ oz., White (Marathon)
Panfish Weighted Hair Fly, #8, Fluor. Pink/White Tail (Glen Evans)
Plain Jig Head, $\frac{1}{32}$ oz., $\frac{1}{16}$ oz., $\frac{1}{8}$ oz. Use with live bait, pork strip (Assassinator Lures)
Worth Ball Head Jig, $\frac{1}{8}$ oz., White and Yellow, or Black and White, or Yellow feather streamers (Worth)

Ice Fishing Jig Spoons, Flies

These are used for all types of panfish, especially with live bait. See the previous section on jigging spoons.

LITTLE-HORNET
JIG FLY

MARATHON
CANADIAN
MINNOW

WORTH BALL HEAD

BABY LEAD
HEAD JIG

LI'L CRAPPIE KILLER

PANFISH WEIGHTED
HAIR FLY

JIG IKE

.LITTLE DOGGIE
MARABOU

PINKIE JIG

CRAPPIE KILLER

FIN-NIT

PLAIN JIG HEAD

BJ BUCKTAIL JIG

FULL TAIL JIG

HOT-LINE

JIGS

FISH-GETTING TECHNIQUES

Certainly how the angler fishes his lure is more important than the lure he selects or the tackle he uses with which to fish it. It is my purpose, therefore, to give some definite suggestions on proper techniques to use with various types of lures.

There are different ways of fishing surface plugs for panfish. These lures are most effective when the fish are shallow or feeding on the surface itself. Usually you should let the lure lie motionless for a second or two before twitching it slightly. If the light twitches do not work, then try jerking the lure slightly to bring out its action. Some lures make a popping sound; others with propellers imitate wounded minnows swimming on the water surface; others, such as the small jitterbug, make a gurgling sound like a small creature struggling on the water surface. I have found these surface lures especially effective for white and yellow bass, crappie and white perch when they are feeding on or near the surface. Occasionally, but not very often, you will catch different kinds of common sunfish on surface plugs. These lures are simply too large for the sunfish to take in their mouths. The sunfish will strike but are rarely hooked. Yellow perch usually can be caught more readily on underwater lures. Bullheads, of course, being bottom feeders, cannot be caught on the surface with lures or bait.

One way of using your surface plug with all types of panfish, except bullheads, is to attach a panfish popping bug, wet fly or jig to the floating plug with about 15 inches of monofilament. The larger plug attracts the fish, and it will usually strike the smaller popper, fly or jig. This is an excellent method for white bass and crappie. Bluegills or other sunfish can also be caught in this manner if small flies or poppers are used.

Still another way of using spinning equipment to fish flies and panfish bugs is by use of the plastic bubble. Fill the bubble partly full of water, depending on the weight needed to cast it; attach the bubble to the line about 20 inches ahead of a wet fly, popper or rubber spider. In flowing streams, let the bubble and fly or lure float past likely spots, drifting naturally with the current, twitching or popping slightly as needed. In quiet creeks, rivers and lakes, cast and let the fly or popper rest quietly, twitching or popping occasionally to attract the fish. Plenty of time should be allowed for the panfish

Method of retrieving a typical surface plug

to discover and take the fly or bug.

Floating and diving plugs ought to be fished to resemble small fish and minnows. After casting, let the plug lie motionless for a second, then twitch it as in fishing a surface lure. Retrieve slowly and erratically, letting it float to the surface occasionally. Those plugs which float and then dive deep on being retrieved can be retrieved fairly rapidly to reach a maximum depth.

Floating-diving plugs are also excellent lures to use in trolling. They will float when not in motion so are not as likely to get foul-hooked. Furthermore, with proper rigs, the plug can be trolled just over the lake bottom. Three different ways of rigging your spinning outfit for trolling are shown in the accompanying diagrams. Such rigs are especially effective when the fish are lying deep, and can be used for white and yellow bass, crappie, white perch and yellow perch.

One further suggestion about trolling: always be certain you know the approximate depth of the water over which you are trolling. When the fish are deep, they will lie very near the bottom, along edges, bars, underwater cover and other hiding places. If your lures are running too shallow, they may never reach the fish. If you are fortunate enough to own a portable fishing fathometer, you can use it to tell instantly

1-2 SEC.
PAUSE

1-2 SEC.
PAUSE

Method of retrieving a floating-diving plug

1-2 SEC.
PAUSE

the depth over which you are passing, the type of bottom and the cover on that bottom.

Many states publish topographical maps on their various bodies of water; these maps are a real aid in helping you to select the right places and depths over which to troll. Lacking other means for obtaining information, you can always use a lead line to measure water depths where you are trolling. If you know the water depths, you can take in or let out line as needed, or subtract or add sinkers to adjust the depth at which your lure is passing.

Sinking plugs, weighted spinners and jigs ought usually to be fished slowly and near the bottom. After casting, allow the plug, spinner or jig to sink to the bottom before retrieving. At the instant your lure reaches the bottom, your line will go slack. Retrieve your sinking plug or spinner erratically, slow, then fast, then stop, allowing it to sink between retrieves. A jig ought to be allowed to bump along the bottom as you retrieve it. After casting, and after your jig has sunk to the bottom, reel in all slack line with your rod tip pointed in the direction of your lure. Then raise your rod about a foot; at the same time take in about 2 feet of line, then lower your rod tip and let the jig sink again.

If there are a lot of rocks, weeds, tree limbs or other obstructions

REPEAT

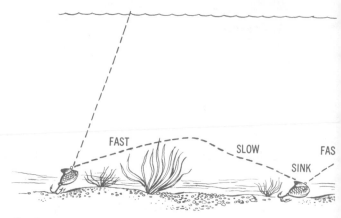

Most effective way to retrieve a sinking plug.

on the bottom, you can begin your retrieves just before your lure reaches them and avoid snagging. To tell how long to let your lure sink before retrieving, let out about 5 feet of line and drop your lure overboard, counting slowly to determine how long it takes it to sink the 5 feet. Then, after each cast, if you count at about the same rate, you can estimate how long to wait before your lure touches bottom or the underwater obstructions.

Wobbling and darting spoons can be fished at various depths. If you begin the retrieve the instant the spoon touches the water, you can make it travel just beneath the water surface. By waiting for various periods of time after casting, you can fish a spoon deep or at a medium depth. How deep to fish must be determined each time through experiment. I like to begin in fairly shallow water, especially during the early morning or late evening hours, then if such fishing has not produced after about a half hour at various spots, I move out to deep water.

It is important to remember that each spoon seems to have a best action at a certain definite speed of retrieve. If you retrieve your spoon too slowly, it may not wobble or dart at all, or you may continually get fouled up on the bottom. If you retrieve too fast, the spoon may skitter along the water surface, or run too shallow, or spin instead of wobble. You should therefore experiment with each

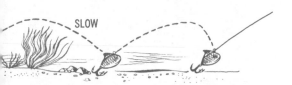

of your spoons to determine the proper retrieves to use with each.

Perhaps special mention ought to be made here of using both jigs and spoons in ice fishing. In this type of fishing, the jig or jigging spoon is lowered to the bottom, then pulled up gradually, jigging it by moving your hand up and down as the lure is pulled up very slowly. Usually, the fish are caught about a foot from the bottom of the lake or river, but occasionally you may take them from right beneath the ice, or anywhere between the ice and bottom. When you discover at what depth the fish seem to be located, then do most of your jigging at that depth.

All species of panfish except bullheads can be caught by jigging. Bluegills and other true sunfish are usually caught on ice flies; these are bright-colored flies with weighted heads. Usually marabou feathers are used so that they flutter as the fly is moved gently up and down. Bucktail or feathered jigs are excellent for crappie; occasionally they will work for yellow perch, white bass and white perch. Small spoons that are allowed to flutter down, then jerked up slowly, then allowed to sink again are excellent for all of the minnow-eating panfish. Small grubs can be added to the ice flies for bluegills; yellow perch eyes can be added to the jigs or spoons for yellow perch; worms or pieces of fish or pork rind can be added for crappie, white and yellow bass and white perch. However, when the fish are biting fast, then live-bait additions are not needed. The one advantage of some bait on the hook, however, is that the fish will continue to bite at the lure after the first strike, sometimes until hooked.

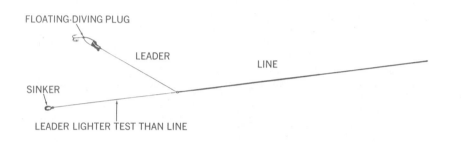

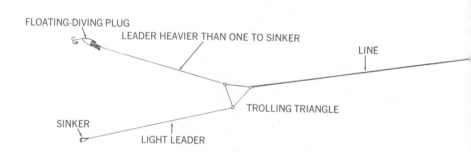

Three ways to rig a spinning outfit for trolling.

Nature lures are fished a variety of ways with spinning tackle. All types of nature lures can be fished by casting, with or without a spinner, or weighted spinner placed ahead of the plastic lure. Small grubs and other small lures that are too light to cast can be fished by

This nice haul of "stumpknockers" was taken from Florida's Dead Lakes.
Florida State News Bureau.

adding sinker or spinners as weight, or they can be used in still-fishing or jigging.

Plastic minnows and worms can be cast or trolled. By the way, try to get worms or minnows which have hooks very near the tails if you are going to try to set the hook as soon as you feel the strike, otherwise many fish will be missed. You can wait until the panfish swallows the bait before setting the hook, but sometimes the plastic lure is too large, or the fish is too shy, for this to happen. Personally, I prefer to have the hook right in the end which the fish will first bite. That way I miss fewer strikes.

Artificial frogs, tadpoles or eels can best be fished by casting. Yellow perch especially will bite readily on these artificials. The common sunfishes bite best on the artificial grubs; plastic worms are good for all types of panfish; minnows can be used for crappie, white and yellow bass, white perch and yellow perch.

Pork rind is a wonderful bait for all kinds of panfish. Use it with a small weighted spinner for crappie, white perch, yellow perch or white and yellow bass. Use a very small piece on a fly or tiny spinner for bluegill and other sunfish. Use a small frog pork chunk for yellow perch in the lily pads and weed beds. Fish it on a small weedless hook or together with a small spoon. Pork pills can be used in still-fishing or ice fishing, but ought to be jigged up and down to make them attractive.

10

FLY FISHING

If you are used to catching panfish on casting tackle or hoisting them aloft at the end of a long cane pole, then you have a thrill in store for you when you feel the remarkable fighting qualities of these fish on a light, limber fly rod. Not only will you derive far more pleasure from fly fishing, but you will catch more and bigger fish, particularly in shallow water. Those panfish that feed a great deal on insect and larval life (particularly the bluegill, pumpkinseed, rock bass and other true sunfish) will readily take artificial flies and bugs, both wet and dry. Those panfish that feed mostly on minnows and small fish (the crappie, yellow perch, white and yellow bass and white perch) will accept regular flies but will more readily bite on fly-rod imitations such as streamer flies, fly-rod spoons and lures. I would say, therefore, that the fly rod is the best and most versatile weapon for panfish. It can also be used effectively in trolling and as a live-bait rod, providing far greater sport than heavier or stiffer rods. If you want to learn to be an expert panfisherman, then you simply must learn to use the fly rod.

THE PROPER TACKLE

In no other kind of fishing is the right tackle so important as in fly fishing. By the right tackle I do not necessarily mean the most expensive. Money alone will not insure your having proper equipment; the only insurance is to select your tackle carefully. In doing so there are several principles to keep in mind:

1. The only purpose of the fly reel is to hold the line. The line is pulled from the reel by hand before the cast is executed so the line does not unwind as the cast is made. The reel, therefore, is the least important item of tackle. It can also be the least expensive, costing less than the line.

2. It is vitally necessary for the line to be the right size and weight for the rod you are using. In general, the heavier and stiffer the fly rod, the heavier must be your fly line; the lighter and more limber, the lighter the line. The secret of effective fly casting is to have exactly the right weight of fly line for your rod. If your line is too light, it will not flex your rod enough to insure easy casting. If your line is too heavy, it will strain your rod too much and perhaps even break it. This means that your line must be selected individually for each rod you use. This applies whether you are using a level line or tapered line, a floating or sinking line, of any material.

3. The size of the flies or lures you expect to cast determines the weight of the rod and line. The lighter and more limber the rod, the more fun it is to play the fish, but the more difficult it is to cast larger floating bugs, fly-rod plugs or spoons. If you will be using all types and sizes of flies and lures, then you will have to select an all-around outfit which will handle the heavy as well as the light attractors. This chapter contains recommendations for two basic outfits: one to use for all-around fishing which will cast panfish bugs, plugs and spoons, as well as small flies; and a second, ultra-light outfit to use exclusively for panfish flies and very small bugs. This second outfit will give the most sport since the rod is very light and limber, but it will not cast fly-rod plugs or spoons. If you can afford only one outfit, then by all means buy the all-around one, since it can be used for trout, bass, live-bait fishing and trolling, as well as for fly casting for panfish. The second, lighter, maximum-sport outfit can be purchased when you have the money and the inclination.

4. A tapered line and leader is easier to cast than a level line and leader, so if you can possibly afford them, buy the tapered ones. They cost three to four times more money, but they are certainly worth it since you can do a more delicate job of casting with them.

5. Rod manufacturers recommend proper line weights with each

rod, but sometimes they give you a range of weights rather than just one. In such cases, one sure way to tell if you have a properly balanced outfit is to try it out before you buy it. If you have never cast before, take along an experienced fly caster to help you. Experiment with different sizes and weights of lines and select the one that seems to be right for your rod. Then select a light, well-made fly reel which is large enough to spool the line. Your leaders should be purchased in accordance with recommendations given in a subsequent section of this chapter.

THE ROD

Fly rods are made of three different materials: boron, graphite, and tubular fiberglass. There are also combinations: boron-graphite and graphite-fiberglass are the most common. You can also still get split bamboo rods, but I would not recommend them for panfishing. You have to be willing to wipe off your rod each time it has been used and keep it varnished and in good repair. It has a tendency to develop a "set," is not as durable as other materials, and is too much trouble as far as I'm concerned.

Each material has its advantages and disadvantages. Tubular fiberglass is the toughest and heaviest, and the most durable, and is not as expensive as boron or graphite. It is a good recommendation for the all-around rod. Graphite is lighter than fiberglass, minimizes casting fatigue, and can be made in a smaller diameter for less air resistance. It is two to seven times stiffer than fiberglass, so produces a fast, "dry-fly" action, which is more suitable for small panfish flies than for fly-rod bugs or lures. Boron is even lighter in weight than graphite, but with more sensitivity and superior strength. Boron-graphite combinations combine some of the advantages of each material: the light weight, sensitivity, and superior strength of boron, and the power and fast-tip action of graphite—a happy combination. Graphite-fiberglass combinations produce the light weight, small diameter, and fast action of graphite, and the toughness of fiberglass. Such a rod will not break as easily as one made of graphite alone. Which type of rod you buy will depend largely on the amount of money you wish to spend, the use you give your rod, and your preferences.

What about length? For an all-around rod, I would select one 7½ to 8½ feet long, with the 8-foot length being a good compromise. A rod of this length should be two-piece, with only one, snugly fitting ferrule. (A three-piece rod is satisfactory, but has a slightly inferior action to the two-piece.) Guides are usually of silicon carbide, aluminum oxide, hard chrome-plated, or stainless steel. Stripper guides and tip top sometimes have ceramic inserts. Silicon carbide is the hardest material: twice as hard as aluminum oxide, which is harder than chrome-plated or stainless steel guides. The tip top and stripped guide get the most wear so should be of the hardest material. The best rods have a screw-lock reel seat which will secure the reel firmly.

THE FLY LINE

I have already mentioned how vitally necessary it is to select your fly line with the utmost care. Only by selecting a line the right weight for each rod can you cast properly. Also, you will need to select the type of line which is most appropriate for the kind of fishing you want to do.

First of all, lines can be divided into three major categories based upon their specific gravity (that is, their weight compared with an equal volume of water). Some lines are strictly of the floating type, because they weigh less than water. Others are of the sinking type, because they are heavier than water. Still a third group of lines are in an intermediate category, because they weigh approximately the same or a little less than water. Lines in this last group float when line dressing is applied but sink when they become soaked. There are still other lines that have a floating body and a sinking tip.

For most kinds of panfishing you will want a line that is strictly of the floating type. There are good reasons for selecting this type. If your line sinks when you are fishing with dry flies or small floating bugs, it will pull the fly or bug underwater with it. If it sinks while you are stream fishing, it will result in more drag on the fly and cause it to behave more unnaturally than will the high-floating line. Also, it is much harder to pick up your line in beginning the back cast if your line is underwater. It takes real skill to cast with a sinking line without causing so much disturbance that you scare all of the fish for some distance around. Furthermore, when your line is floating, it serves as an indicator when the fish bites. The slightest touch on your fly will cause a twitch of your line where it enters the water. And

finally, once a fish strikes, it is easier to set the hook when the line is
floating on the surface than when it is sinking. Your first choice, therefore, ought to be a floating line.

The best floating lines today are made of nylon with special lightweight finishes on them. The intermediate lines, those which either
float or sink, depending upon whether dressing is applied or not, are
usually of nylon or nylon-Dacron combinations. Most of the fast-
sinking lines are made of Dacron, a heavier material than nylon.
Some have special heavy finishes.

If you are going to buy several types of lines, then you might select
one of the fast-sinking type in addition to a floating one. A sinking
line is sometimes a real asset when fishing deep in large rivers, or in
lakes. I prefer using a sinking line whenever I cannot get down deep
enough even with a split shot added to a long leader. When panfish
are in holes 10 feet or more deep, sometimes the only way you can
get them to strike is by sinking your fly or line down to them. Such
deep fishing makes casting difficult, however, since it is hard to pick
up the line for the back cast. Also, since the line usually has a little
slack in it, you have to be very quick about setting the hook when a
strike is felt or you'll miss a lot of fish. At times, however, you may
have to resort to deep-water fishing or go fishless.

Fly lines can also be divided into three types according to the variation in diameter throughout their length. Some lines show no variation, that is, they are level lines. Other lines have double tapers,
that is, they have a large, level diameter in the middle but taper off
to a smaller point on each end. Still a third type of line is a three-
dimension line with the longest portion of small diameter, the belly
or shooting head of the line being heavy and of the largest diameter,
with the front portion tapering down from the large belly to the
medium-size tip which attaches to the leader. Lines in this third
category are called weight-forward, torpedo-head, rocket-head or
bug-tapered lines. Each type of line was designed for a specific sort
of fishing.

Level lines are the least expensive and the hardest type to use in
general casting. They do not provide enough delicacy either in dry-
fly or wet-fly fishing, nor do they provide enough weight to cast heavier lures, spoons or fly-rod plugs. They are strictly a compromise,
therefore. Like most beginners, I began using them at first because
they were cheaper, but since have realized that I could have learned

to cast easier with the proper tapered line.

What type of tapered line should you buy? For your all-around rod, which you will probably use for both wet- and dry-fly fishing and for lures and flies of a variety of sizes and weights, I would purchase a weight-forward, or three-dimension line. Such a line will enable you to cast panfish bugs, plugs and streamers and, by using a little longer tapered leader, you can also do a delicate job of casting small dry and wet flies and nymphs.

Let me add a word of caution, however. Some weight-forward tapered lines have long front tapers (10 to 12 feet or more) and are called rocket-tapered lines. Others have short front tapers (around 6 feet) and are called bug-tapered lines. The long front tapers are designed for distance casting with small flies. The bug tapers are the best all-around choice for casting all type of flies and lures. If you can afford a second fly line (and an extra spool or fly reel to keep it on), then I would buy a double-tapered line and use it exclusively for casting small flies and nymphs, saving the weight-forward line for use with floating bugs and heavier lures. For your ultra-light outfit, by all means get a double-tapered line of proper weight. It will enable you to cast delicately, and it is very economical since you can switch ends when one end is worn.

Both floating and sinking lines come in various diameters and tapers. If you want one basic line for your all-around outfit, then get a floating, weight-forward, short-tapered line. As a second line to use in addition to this one, I would buy a floating, double-tapered line. As a third line, I would buy a fast-sinking, weight-forward, short-tapered line. For the ultra-light outfit I would only buy the floating, double-tapered line. A sinking line would put too much strain on such a rod, and a weight-forward taper is unnecessary, since only small flies and bugs are ordinarily used.

Knowing what type of fly line you want to buy, your next task is to select one of the proper weight for your rod. This selection is by far the most crucial you will make because it is the weight of the line that determines how well it matches your rod and how well you will be able to cast with it.

Selecting the proper weight is usually an easy task, particularly since the fishing tackle manufacturers recommend a weight for each rod. Some recommend a range of weights, however, so that your best

bet is to try different weights in the type of line you are going to use
until you find the one that is ideally suited to your rod.

How do you tell what type and weight of line you are getting? The
Associated Fishing Tackle Manufacturers (AFTM) have agreed on a
system which designates fly lines according to weight rather than
size. In measuring the weight in grains, only the first 30 feet of line
is weighed (exclusive of any tip on the taper). The lines are designated
by numbers as shown in the chart below.

AFTM FLY LINE STANDARDS

No.	Weight (In Grains)	Range of Wt. Allowed	No.	Weight (In Grains)	Range of Weight Allowed
1	60	54-66	7	185	177-193
2	80	74-86	8	210	202-218
3	100	94-106	9	240	230-250
4	120	114-126	10	280	270-290
5	140	134-146	11	330	318-342
6	160	152-168	12	380	368-392

Thus, if you can discover what weight of line will fit your rod (as
designated by a certain number: 6, 7, 8, 9 and so forth on the chart),
you can be certain that your line will always balance your rod no
matter what manufacturer you purchase it from, no matter what type
of taper you use and no matter whether it is floating or sinking.

In addition to these simple numbers which are used to help you
select the right weight of line, certain letters indicate whether the
line is floating, sinking or intermediate, whether it is level or tapered
and, if tapered, the type of taper. The identification symbols are as
follows.

    L = Level
    DT = Double taper
    WF = Weight forward
    ST = Single taper or shooting taper
    F = Floating
    S = Sinking
    I = Intermediate (Floating or Sinking)

Thus, a DT6F line would be a double taper, weight 6 (approximately 160 grains as shown on the chart), floating. An L4I line would be level, weight 4 (approximately 120 grains), intermediate. A WF5S line would be a weight forward, weight 5 (approximately 140 grains), sinking.

For the 8-foot rod which I have recommended for your all-round outfit, you will probably need a number 6 or 7 line. The only way to tell is to try it, however. If your rod is especially limber, you might need a number 5 line. If your rod is stiffer than usual, you might need a number 8 line.

For the ultra-light outfit of from 7 to 7½ feet in length you will probably need a number 4 or 5 line. With extremely whippy rods you might need a line as light as number 3. A rod demanding a line heavier than 6 certainly cannot be classified as an ultra-light outfit. You will simply have to find the proper weight by trying different lines.

THE FLY REEL

As has been mentioned, the reel is the least important item of tackle in fly fishing. Its only purpose is to hold the line and to provide a means to wind and unwind the line from the spool. For this reason you need not spend a lot of money for a fly reel in order to be sure of having satisfactory equipment. Any light and durable fly reel is usually satisfactory.

However, you do have three basic types from which to choose: the single-action, the multiplying, and the automatic. Probably more anglers use the single-action than any other, but you will have to decide your own preference. The following general descriptions should help.

The single-action fly reel is so named because the spool makes one complete revolution for each turn of the handle. The spool, which revolves on a shaft, is deep and narrow and has a fairly large hub in the center to keep the line from winding on in too tight a coil. Line guards keep the line from wearing as it comes off the spool. One or two handles connect directly to the spool, and a foot plate fits the reel seat of the fly rod. Your reel should have a strong click and an adjustable drag for applying tension on the line.

The weight of your reel will depend upon its overall size. Light-weight reels for rods suggested in this chapter usually weigh from

Two types of fly reels. The single-action reel (left) holds line on a spool which makes one complete revolution for every turn of the handle. Automatic reel (right) has spring-operated spool which retrieves line when pressure is applied to trigger with little finger of rod hand.

2 to 6 ounces. Get the lightest which will hold 30 yards of line. The better single-action fly reels have interchangeable spools. This feature enables you to buy extra spools to hold different types and sizes of lines and to change them at will. The chief advantage of the single-action reel is that it will hold more line, or line backing, than the automatic reel. A long line or backing is never needed in casting for panfish, but might be used in trolling or in still-fishing. The lighter single-action reels also weigh less than the lightest automatics.

Multiplying fly reels have multiplying gears which turn the spool more than one revolution for each rotation of the handle. This gives greater speed in retrieving line, and is especially useful when a fish runs toward you, or when you need to retrieve slack line quickly. Gear ratios run from 1⅝:1 to 3:1, depending upon the make of the reel. These reels are heavier than single action reels. Reels which would be suitable for rods suggested in this chapter weigh from 4 to 7 pounds. Multiplying reels are also more expensive than single action ones.

The automatic fly reel has a spring-operated spool which retrieves line automatically whenever you press the spool-release lever. The spring is wound up by hand; line may be stripped off the reel by hand at any time, even when the spring is fully wound. The great advantage of the automatic reel is its ease in taking in or releasing the line. A touch of the little finger on the release lever will allow the spool to revolve. While the fish is never played from the reel, but by releasing or stripping in line with the left hand (assuming you cast with your right), nevertheless the automatic mechanism on the reel does allow you to let out or take in line as needed without ever changing your hand positions on the rod and line. With a single-action or multiplying reel, you also have to release or strip in line with your left hand, but if line is to be wound on the spool, you have to shift hand positions until you hold the rod with your left while your right hand is on the reel handle.

The automatic is convenient for all-around casting purposes when a long line is not needed. It is, however, slightly more tiring than the lighter, single-action reels, since it is usually heavier. Automatic reels weigh 8 or 9 ounces. Some are mounted horizontally on the rod (with the foot plate on the flat side of the reel). Others are mounted vertically (with the foot plate on one edge of the reel). Your selection is just a matter of preference.

If I could buy only one reel for all-around use on either the all-purpose fly rod or the ultra-light rod, I would buy a single-action reel with an extra spool so I could use two different types of line. My second reel then would certainly be an automatic.

THE FLY LEADER

The primary purpose of the fly leader is to keep the fish from detecting that the fly or lure is attached to a line. A secondary purpose is to enable the fly caster to present the lures or flies to the fish with delicacy and finesse. There is a need, therefore, to have the right combination of invisibility and casting qualities when selecting a leader.

On the one hand, the most invisible leader would be one with the smallest diameter. However, if a leader is too long and light, one will have trouble casting larger flies with it; casting fly-rod plugs or heavier lures would be impossible. Also, a leader which is too light is too easily broken. On the other hand, if a leader is too short and heavy it will not be invisible enough and it will not allow a delicate enough presentation of very small flies. Thus, the length and size of your leader will depend upon how much invisibility is required, the weight of the flies and lures you are going to use and the taper and weight of your line.

First, select a leader made of plain, undyed nylon. This is by far the best leader material available. The reason I suggest undyed material is that it is less visible than any color. Some leader material is dyed several colors; others are dyed in a single color: blue, mist, green, silver-gray and so forth. However, the undyed material is less visible than any other under a variety of water and light conditions and so will catch the most fish. I have had better luck with this type.

Second, use a tapered leader for casting all types of lures and flies. Level leaders are perfectly adequate and even preferred, because of their low cost, for trolling or still-fishing with the fly rod. But tapered leaders allow a smoother transference of power from line to fly and enable one to do a better job of casting. The degree and length of taper will depend upon the weight of your line and the weight of the fly or lure you are casting.

Third, select a leader with a large butt diameter (the end that attaches to the fly line), usually from .018 to .021 inches. The heavier your line, the larger should be the butt diameter. The reason for this is to allow the movement of the line to be transmitted smoothly to the leader so that the leader will straighten out easily during the cast. If the butt of the leader is too small, it is harder to make a good cast.

Fourth, the diameter of the leader at the tip end should be as small as possible and still allow enough weight to cast your fly or lure and enough strength to hold your fish.

Leader tip diameters are designated according to an established system of calibration as follows.

Gauge	Aver. Diameter (inch)
7x	.004
6x	.005
5x	.006
4x	.007

3x	.008
2x	.009
1x	.010
0x	.011
9/5	.012
8/5	.013
7/5	.014
6/5	.015
5/5	.016
4/5	.017
3/5	.018
2/5	.019
1/5	.020

Unfortunately, however, it is no longer possible to tell the tensile strength of a leader by knowing the gauge of the tip. The reason is that a variety of different types of nylon leaders are sold; they vary considerably in their strength for a given diameter.

The following table shows the pound test of some very excellent knotless tapered leaders (nylon) made by Berkley.

Tip Diameter	*Tip Size*	*Test* (lb.)
.015	6/5	14
.013	8/5	11
.011	0x	8½
.010	1x	7
.009	2x	4
.008	3x	3
.007	4x	2½
.006	5x	2
.005	6x	1¾

As can be noted, tip size is now meaningless in designating tensile strength, but it is a helpful designation of diameter (which relates to invisibility). Most leaders have the test in pounds printed on the package.

With your all-around outfit, I would use leaders with tips testing about 6 pounds in order to be able to cast fly-rod plugs, lures and larger flies. This gives enough weight on the end for the leader to turn over the lure or fly properly. If your lure will not cast properly, then you need a heavier fly line or leader, perhaps both. For casting the small panfish dry and wet flies and nymphs with my all-around outfit, I use a leader with a tip of about 2x (about 4-pound test). This is small enough for good invisibility, yet heavy enough to cast number 6, 8, 10 or 12 flies (the sizes most often used in panfishing).

For your ultra-light outfit, I would use leaders with tips varying from 3x to 4x (3 to 2½ pound). Ordinarily, only the smallest and lightest flies are cast with the very light leaders, and you will have to be careful in striking and playing your fish to keep from breaking the leader. If your fly flutters to the water without your leader ever straightening out, then your leader is probably too light or too long, or both (assuming you are using a line of the right weight for your rod). If your fly smacks the water too hard, then your leader is too short, or too heavy, or both. A little experimenting will show you what size leader works best for you with different size flies.

Fifth, for most panfishing your leaders should be 7½ or 9 feet in length. The shorter leader is easier to cast with larger flies or lures; the longer leader gives greater protection in very clear, quiet water. I have never used leaders longer than 9 feet when panfishing, although I know some anglers who use 12-foot leaders. Use the longer ones if you prefer, provided you are able to cast properly with them.

It is a good idea to keep your leader stretched out so that when you cast it won't bunch up. The leader can be stretched and straightened by pulling it between a piece of rubber inner tube held in the hand, or by fastening each end to a nail or hook and leaving it stretched until all loops and kinks are pulled out.

You may want to use tippets on the end of your tapered leader. A tippet is a short piece (usually about 1 foot) of level leader material of the desired diameter and test which is tied to the end of the leader and to which the flies or lures are tied. Tying the flies or lures to the tippet rather than to the leader prevents the more expensive tapered leader from being shortened each time you change your fly or lure.

Another excellent way to attach the fly or lure is to tie a large loop in the tip end of the leader. If the diameter of the tip is sufficiently small and the eye of the fly large enough, the loop can be pushed through the eye of the hook, then over and around the fly, and then tightened. If you want to change your fly, it is easy to pull the loop loose, slip the fly back through the hoop and then to pull the loop out of the

Two methods of rigging a fly line. Dropper loops allow you to fish more than one fly, try different patterns.

eye of the hook. When the hook eyes are too small, or the leader tips too large in diameter, the fly has to be tied directly to the tippet or to the leader.

You may want to use dropper loops on your leader so that two or more flies can be fished at once. I have found it very productive at times, especially when the fish are hungry and moving about in large schools. You can fish two patterns of wet flies or nymphs at once to determine which seems most appealing, or fish a panfish popper on the dropper loop and a wet fly on the end.

FLY-FISHING KNOTS

Tying the proper knots is very important, since some knots weaken leaders more than others and improper knots are inclined to slip and come loose. Nothing is more disconcerting than to discover you have lost a good fish only because a knot slipped or your leader broke at the knot. Use the knots on the opposite page for tying on flies and joining leader to line.

BASIC TYPES OF FLIES AND LURES

It is not my purpose in this section to recommend particular flies or fly-rod lures, but rather to introduce you to basic types before going on in the next section to make specific recommendations in selecting an assortment.

170

JAM KNOT

Use jam knot for tying fly line to leader. First tie overhand knot in tip of fly line, run it through leader loop as shown, and draw tight.

Improved end loop is for tying a loop in end of leader. Bending over about 4 inches of leader at the end, wrap the double strand around itself several times, and pull the end through the first loop.

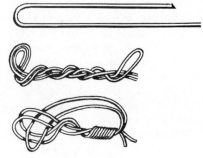

IMPROVED END LOOP

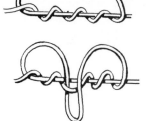

Dropper loop is started with a simple overhand knot which is continued for several turns. Tighten until you have about a 1-inch loop, then take the middle of the loop, pass it between one of the turns, and pull it tight.

DROPPER LOOP

For tying fly to leader end, use the clinch knot. Finish off the knot by passing end through big loop, as shown, and pull tight.

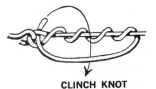

CLINCH KNOT

Blood knot is for joining two ends of a leader or a leader and line. Each end is twisted around the other, doubled back and pulled through center loop.

5-TURN BLOOD KNOT

BASIC TYPES OF DRY FLIES

Dry flies float on the surface of the water, simulating winged insects pausing in flight.

Spider: a hackle fly similar to the bivisible but tied with a much longer hackle for a given hook size.

Variant: Made with either hair or feather wings, with long hackles at the collar to cause it to float high and resemble an insect hovering over the water.

Hairbody: a fly with clipped deer hair body that floats like a cork.

Downwing: wings lie back flat along the body. Collar, head, tail and body of various materials.

Hairwing: wings of bucktail or similar hair tied to stand erect.

Bivisible: a fly with a hackle but no wings. Named for its visibility on the water—the result of using a lighter hackle in front.

Divided wing: the standard dry fly with two erect, separate wings, a collar of stiff hackle a body and a tail. It represents a mayfly.

Fanwing: large, flat wings protrude at an angle from the hook shank of this fly. It has a hackle collar, a body and a tail.

Spentwing: slender wings protrude horizontally from the body of the fly. Seldom used today.

SPIDER

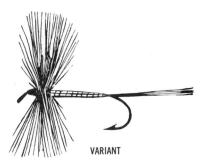

VARIANT

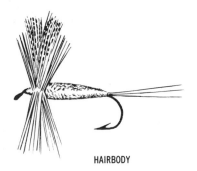

HAIRBODY

All artificial flies can be divided into two categories: those that float and those that sink. The floating—or dry flies—are in turn divided into eleven basic types: divided wing, fanwing, spentwing, downwing, hairwing, bivisible, spider, variant, midge, hair body and hackle. Sometimes these various types overlap; thus you may have a

DOWNWING

DIVIDED WING

HAIRWING

FANWING

BIVISIBLE

SPENTWING

hairwing variant or a hair-body spentwing, or a divided-wing midge fly, and so forth. Ten of the basic types of dry flies are shown on the following page. The midge, which is not shown, is merely an extremely small fly.

Three additional newer types of flies ought to be added to this list: *gauze wing, keel flies,* and *parachute flies.* The *gauze wing* is most often made of just that: gauze (sometimes plastic), while the *keel fly* is so named because it is tied on a special type of keel hook that rides upright, thus preventing snagging. The *parachute fly* is tied so the hackle rides horizontally in the plane of water. The wings are sometimes hair, at other times feathers.

Among the sinking flies we have three basic types: the *wet fly,* the *nymph* and the *streamer.* Wet flies represent drowned insects or flies, or hatched flies just rising from the bottom. They, in turn, come in four basic styles: the *divided-wing wet fly* with carefully paired quill feathers for wings (which are curved low over the body); the *hairwing* with wings made of bucktail or similar hair; the *feather wing* with wings made from speckled feathers from the flank, side or breast of ducks; and the *hackle* fly.

BASIC TYPES OF WET FLIES

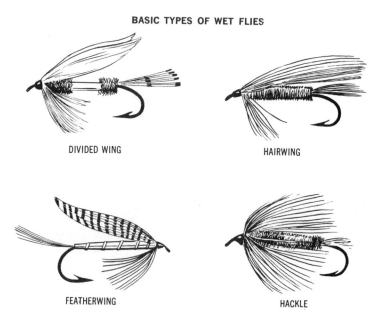

DIVIDED WING   HAIRWING

FEATHERWING   HACKLE

Wet flies imitate drowned insects or hatched flies rising from the bottom.

Today, there are other wet flies made of materials which make it hard to classify them into any of the above four categories. For example, some new types of flies have gauze wings, others have sponge-rubber bodies, others have rubber feelers for legs, or a combination of material. One new type of fly, the *keel fly,* is named because it is tied on a special hook which rides upright in the water. Therefore, the following categories of wet flies might be added to the traditional four groups: *gauze wing, rubber body or legs,* and *keel flies.*

What about flies which are designated panfish flies, "brim" flies, or crappie flies? Actually, these may be variations of flies in one or more of the four traditional wet trout fly groups, or they may be flies which do not at all fit into any of the traditional categories. For example, a panfish fly, or "brim" fly, usually is a hackle fly with a chenille body, or an all-hackle fly tied in colors that do not always follow traditional patterns.

NYMPHS

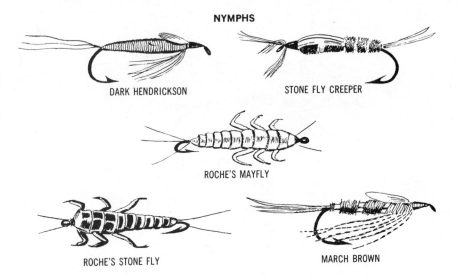

DARK HENDRICKSON   STONE FLY CREEPER

ROCHE'S MAYFLY

ROCHE'S STONE FLY   MARCH BROWN

Nymphs imitate the larval forms of various aquatic insects.

Nymphs are used to imitate the larvae of various forms of aquatic insects. They are made from a variety of materials: hair, feathers, fur, wool, yarn, floss, rubber, plastic, wire and lead. They come in different styles, colors and sizes; some are weighted to make them sink faster.

Streamer flies are tied usually to imitate minnows or small fish in the water. There are a variety of styles: some are called bucktails (those tied with deer hair); others are feather streamers; others are called marabou streamers (because of the type of marabou feather with which they are tied). Streamers are usually long and slender and tied on long-shanked hooks.

In addition to these standard types of dry and wet flies, a new category of flies has been developed called *terrestrials*. The term terrestrial refers to the whole group of artificials which imitate land

BASIC TYPES OF STREAMERS

BUCKTAIL

FEATHER STREAMER

MARIBOU

Streamers flies imitate minnows or other small fish.

insects which may fall, crawl, or jump in the water and provide food for fish. According to this definition, any imitation of a land bug, beetle, roach, cricket, hopper, or fly is a terrestrial. There are thousands of species of these in nature; artificials to represent them could go on without limit. Actually, there are only a few basic groups which have been developed.

Ants represent flying ants.
Beetles represent a whole group of natural beetles.
Crickets represent their counterpart in nature.

Grasshoppers, hopper flies, Hornberg flies all represent grasshoppers.

Inch worms represent their counterpart in nature.

Jassids are very small imitations which represent a variety of natural land insects.

There are also a number of basic types of fly-rod lures which are
effective for panfish; some of these are designed to float, others to
sink. The types are listed below.

1. *Floating bugs or "poppers."* Some of these bugs have faces which
are either sloped on concave so as to make a popping sound when
twitched or jerked slowly along the surface of the water. The bodies
are made of painted cork, plastic, or deer hair; some are dressed with
hackle; others have wings and tails; others have rubber legs that
"creep" when the bug is twitched. They come in various shapes and
sizes.

2. *Nature lures* are usually designed of rubber or plastic to represent grasshoppers, worms, crickets, spiders, salmon eggs, nymphs,
hellgrammites, frogs, minnows, crawfish, grubs, larvae, tadpoles or
eels.

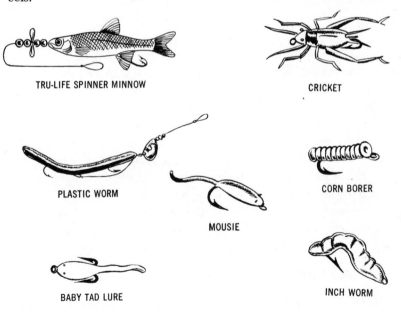

TRU-LIFE SPINNER MINNOW

CRICKET

PLASTIC WORM

CORN BORER

MOUSIE

BABY TAD LURE

INCH WORM

NATURE LURES

3. *Jigs* come in small, light sizes for the fly rod; they have weighted heads with bucktails, marabou, feather or nylon streamer or skirts. Sometimes feather hair trailers are attached to a metal jig spoon.

4. *Spoons* come in very small sizes for the fly rod. Some are designed to wobble, others to jig. They come with single, double or treble hooks, with or without hackle, hair or rubber skirts covering the hook. Spoons have a variety of finishes.

5. *Plugs* designed in very small sizes for the fly rod are usually patterned after larger plugs that are used in spinning or bait casting. Some fly-rod plugs are surface lures; others are floating-diving lures; others sink.

6. *Spinners* are usually used in conjunction with a fly or live bait, but are sometimes attached to bare hooks, as the double- or treble-hook Colorado spinners. Spinners may be obtained in a variety of finishes, shapes and sizes. All revolve around a fixed shaft when pulled through the water.

7. *Pork rind* now comes in pork pills, strips, skirts and other shapes and in a variety of colors. Used on either a bare hook, or with fly, spoon, jig or spinner.

SELECTING FLIES AND LURES

What flies or lures should you buy? Actually, you do not need a large assortment, nor do you need to spend a lot of money, since panfish often are not particular. But you ought to select what you do buy very carefully in order to get a variety of types, patterns, colors and sizes. Begin with only a few flies and lures, then add as you have the need and money, making certain you keep adding variety. Thus, before you get too many different types and patterns of dry flies, buy a few wet ones (including standard wet flies, nymphs and streamers), some terrestrials and a few lures: some popping bugs, some nature lures (plastic worms and sponge-rubber spiders are particularly effective), a couple of jigs, spoons, plugs, spinners and a jar of pork rind. You can select from the following assortment.

NATURE LURES FOR PANFISH

By far the best all-round nature lure for panfish is the plastic worm, trolled or cast, and used on a small, two-hook spinner rig. Use a worm, natural or red, 2 to 3 inches long. My favorite rig for trolling is the No. FR—432 Panfish Worm Lure, 2⅜-inch plastic worm, with two #7 hooks and Colorado Spinner, by Sportsman's Products. (The reason I like it is the trailer hook is right on the end of the worm, readily catching any panfish which bites the tail. If the fisherman threads his own, he should put the hook near the tail.) Burke Flexo-Products also sells a 2½-inch worm on a two-hook rig with nylon shaft and aerospinner. Delong sells a 1⅞-inch tiny plastic worm with two hooks molded into the worm (no spinner). Falls Bait Co. sells a 2- or 2½-inch worm and rig with two #10 gold hooks, nylon shaft and propeller spinner.

In addition to worms, I would buy the following nature lures.

Crawfish: Primarily for rock and warmouth bass, yellow perch.

    Flyrod Size, # 10 hook (Burke Flexo-Products Co.)
    Small, single hook (Creme Lure Co.)

Frogs: Primarily for rock and warmouth bass, yellow perch.

    Flyrod Frog, 1½″, Brown or Green (Burke)
    Brown Frog, or Green Frog, Small (#10) (Creme)

Insects: For most panfish, especially the insect eaters.

    Caddis Fly: #12, Brown or Yellow (Creme)
    Cricket: Black, #10 (Creme Lures)
       Black Floating Cricket, #8 (Burke)
       Tru-Life Cricket, #8, Black (Weber)
    Grasshopper: Green or Yellow Grasshopper, Small #10 (Creme)
       Brown (Burke)
       Tru-Life Grasshopper, #10 (Weber)
    Spider: Floating Panfish Spider, Orange and Black, #8 (Burke)
    Stone Fly: #10 (Creme)

Larvae: For most panfish, especially the insect eaters.

    Baby Hellgrammite, #10 (Burke)
    Caddis Worm, #12 (Creme Lure)
    Catalpa Worm, Small (Creme)
    Grub Worm (Midwest Tackle)

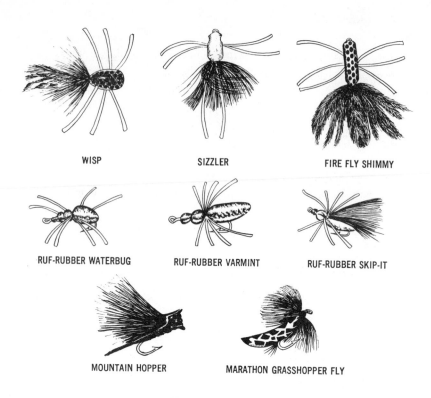

WISP SIZZLER FIRE FLY SHIMMY

RUF-RUBBER WATERBUG RUF-RUBBER VARMINT RUF-RUBBER SKIP-IT

MOUNTAIN HOPPER MARATHON GRASSHOPPER FLY

FLY ROD BUGS

Mayfly Nymph, #8 (Burke) Also, Tru-Life May Nymph (Weber) Stonefly Nymph, #10 (Burke)

Minnows: Especially for fish-eating panfish.

Life Like Lures, Minnows, 1¾″ or 2¾″, soft. Black and Silver, Gray (3-L Products)
Spinner Minnow, 2″ or 3″, Shiner (Weber)
Tiny Flash Minnow, (1¼″), or Jr. Flash Minnow (2″) with propeller spinner (Delong Lures)

ARTIFICIAL BUGS AND FLIES

Panfish Bugs (Floating)

Band-It Popper, #8, Yellow and Black (Glen Evans)
Dylite Deluxe Creepy Popper, #10 Black and White (Weber)

180

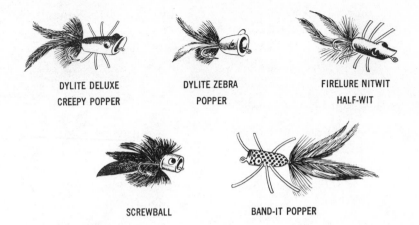

DYLITE DELUXE CREEPY POPPER

DYLITE ZEBRA POPPER

FIRELURE NITWIT HALF-WIT

SCREWBALL

BAND-IT POPPER

FLY ROD BUGS

Dylite Zebra Popper, #12, Black/Yellow Stripes (Weber)
Fire Fly Shimmy, #10, Fire Orange (Falls Bait Co.)
Firelure Nitwit, #12, Green Frog (Weber)
Half-Wit, #16, Black (Weber)
Marathon Grasshopper Fly, #8, 12, 16 (Marathon)
Mountain (deer hair) Hopper, #10 (Phillips)
Ruf-Rubber: Waterbug—#10, Varmint—#10, Skip-It—#10,
    Black, Yellow, Buff, Green colors (Glen Evans)
Screwball, #14, Red and White, or Yellow (Glen Evans)
Sizzler, #10, Yellow (Falls)
Water-Waif, #10, Black (Glen Evans)
Wisp, #8, Green-black-gray (Falls)

Dry Flies

Bivisible: black, brown,
    gray, grizzly
Adams
Black Gnat
Iron Blue Dun
Light Cahill
March Brown

Mosquito
Pink Lady
White Miller—#10, 12
Royal Coachman—#12
Gauze Wing Drake(Blue
    Dun, Yellow, Ginger),
    #12 (Phillips)

Brown Hackle Yellow,
  Gray Hackle Red—#10
Goofus Bug (#14—Yellow
  body) (Dan Bailey)

Irresistible, #10, Natural
  (Orvis)
Wulff Flies: Black, Blonde,
  Grizzly, Royal—#8, 14

Wet Flies

Black Gnat
Coachman
Cowdung
Gold Ribbed Hare's Ear
McGinty
Montreal
Parmacheene Belle
Royal Coachman
Western Bee—#8, 12
Professor—#10
Green, Brown—#8, 12
Picket Pin (Squirrel tail,
  yellow body—#10)
Fall's Spider, #10, Black,

Yellow, Green
Bream Wiggler, #8, Black
  (Falls)
Marathon Red Tail Crappie
  Fly, #8

(Select desired patterns
  from description in chapter on Wet Flies.)

Weber Brim-Fli, #10,
  Black/White or Red Tail,
  or Yellow/Red Tail, or
  Gray/Red Tail. For use
  with spinner. (Weber)

Nymphs (Weighted)

Black and Yellow (Worth)
Caddis Fly (Dan Bailey)
Tan Shrimp (Dan Bailey)
Gray Nymph (Orvis)
Mayfly Nymph, Black,
  Brown, Tan, Yellow
  (Dan Bailey)
Ted's Stonefly Nymph,
  Black and Orange (Orvis)
Tellico (Orvis)
Sizes #10–14

Streamer Flies

Black and White Bucktail
Blacknosed Dace
Black Ghost
Edson Tiger Dark
Gray Ghost
Mickey Finn
Muddler (Natural)
Nine-Three
Parmacheene Belle
Professor
Red and White Bucktail
White Marabou
Yellow Marabou #6–10

Terrestrials

Ants: Black, Red—#16
Grasshopper: Dan's Deer Hopper Fly—#12 (Dan Bailey)
Worth Special Hornberg Fly—#10 (Worth)
Jassid: Black, Orange, Yellow—#16 (Dan Bailey)

Select your jigs, spoon, plugs, and spinners for fly-rod use from the smaller sizes discussed in Chapter 9. Also, buy a jar of Uncle Josh's Fly Rod Strip, White, and cut in very small pieces to give added attraction. You will note in the above lists of flies that the sizes selected range from size 8 to 16. The larger sizes are for panfish that grow larger and have bigger mouths, such as the crappie, white and yellow bass, white perch and the yellow perch. Most of the small flies are for bluegill, pumpkinseed and other sunfish. Also, while any panfish may at some time or another take any one of these flies or lures, in general, the insect creations are for bluegill, pumpkinseed, rock bass and other sunfish, while the streamer flies and lures representing minnows or fish are more appealing to white perch, white and yellow bass, yellow perch and crappie. Also, some of the lures are used primarily for trolling (such as the fairly large plastic worm, minnow and spinner plugs, spoons and streamer flies). Obviously, it would be impossible to cast a good size spinner with a fly rod, but it is excellent for trolling ahead of a live worm.

There are literally hundreds of panfish flies and lures on the market; the ones that I have suggested here are only samples, but all are wonderful fish getters which I have thoroughly tested while actually fishing for many different kinds of panfish. You can't go very far wrong in following my suggestions, even though you will discover other favorites of your own as time goes by.

HOW TO FLY CAST

One of the reasons most fishermen never do any fly fishing is because they assume fly casting is too difficult, either because they have never done it or because they have tried it briefly—perhaps with an unbalanced outfit—and failed. If you have hesitated to learn how to fly cast, or if you would like to improve your casting, then this section is for you.

Before I describe how to cast, if you haven't already read the previous sections of this chapter on the proper tackle, fly rod, line, reel and leader then please do so before you read here. You can't do a good job of casting unless your tackle is balanced.

First of all, attach a 7½-foot tapered leader (well stretched so it will lay out straight) to your line (which also has been stretched and to which a little line dressing has been applied). Select a small, inexpensive fly (a number 10 will do), cut the hook off at the bend and tie it to your leader tip.

You can begin your casting lesson either on level land or on the water. If on land, select a wide expanse of lawn area away from trees, bushes and tall weeds. If on water, then find a place free from obstructions.

Now you are ready to learn the basic overhead cast. To execute this cast, strip about 20 feet of line from your reel, and work it through the rod guides so it lays out in front of you (either on the ground or floating on the water). If you have trouble getting the line out, just grab the end of the leader and walk it out straight on land the first few times. Hold your rod with your thumb extended along the top of the cork handle and the rest of your fingers clasped firmly around and under the rod handle. Keep the tip of your rod pointed toward the line so you do not pick up the line until ready to cast. Also, when first learning, keep the line under the forefinger of your rod hand so that more line will not come off the reel as you cast.

The cast is begun by lifting the rod sharply and forcefully, pulling the line off the water. Your forearm should pivot at your elbow and should be moved up and back in an arc until it reaches the vertical position. In executing the movement, keep your wrist absolutely stiff so that your rod becomes merely an extension of your forearm. This arm movement will lift your line into the air and will sweep it up and back of you for the backcast.

The backcast will throw the line into the air behind you, allowing you to cast it forward. Since the success of your forward cast depends to a large extent on a well-executed backcast, it is important that you try to cast the line high into the air so that it will straighten out behind you without touching the ground before you begin your forward cast.

It is important also to stop the movement of your forearm suddenly when the rod has reached the vertical position. This allows the line to continue going behind you and to bend your rod backward, thus providing real spring and power with which to cast the line forward.

When your rod reaches the vertical, you must also pause long enough to allow the line to straighten out behind before you begin the forward cast. The length of this pause depends on how much line is out: the shorter the line, the shorter time it takes for the backcast and the sooner you cast forward. With a very long line, the pause may seem longer than a second. When the line straightens out behind, you can actually feel a tug on the rod. When this is felt, you must then swing your forearm down forcefully and quickly, casting the line in front of you. If you "aim" at a point slightly above the water surface, your line and leader should be straight out ahead of you and fall gently to the water. At the completion of your cast, your rod should be pointed straight toward your lure and fly.

The secret of casting properly lies in a high and well-executed backcast, and just the right pause before you cast forward. The high backcast is accomplished by trying to throw your line into the air as you lift your forearm; this will keep the line high and off the water. Also, if you keep your wrist stiff and stop your backcast with the rod at the vertical, you will not slap the line on the water behind you before you begin the forward cast.

How long to pause before you begin the forward cast is a sixth sense which you will develop after some practice. Once you get the rhythm of "lift—stop—pause—down" with your forearm, your casts will be performed smoothly and effortlessly. Practice with various lengths of line until you can cast the fly smoothly and quietly.

After you have learned the rhythm of the cast, the next step is to learn to control the line. Line control involves letting out or taking in line as needed before or during the cast. In learning to let out line for longer casts, instead of holding the line under the fingers of your right hand (assuming you are casting right-handed) hold it between the thumb and finger of your left hand. Make several false casts. A false cast is one in which you begin another backcast before you allow the line from your forward cast to settle to the water. False casts are no different than regular ones except you continue to bring the rod back for the backcast, then forward for the forward cast, then back again, and so forth, for as long as you want to keep the line in the air.

While you are false casting, your left hand continues to hold the

HOW TO FLY CAST

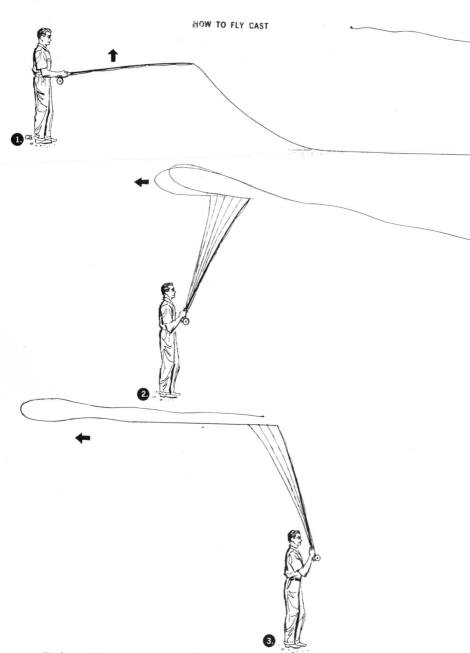

To learn the basic overhead cast, practice on land to acquire skill. First strip off about 20 feet of line and lay it out in front of you. 1. Begin the backcast by lifting the rod sharply and pulling the line into the air. 2. As the rod moves toward the vertical position, the line begins to travel backwards in a long loop. 3. Stop the rod at about vertical position, and allow

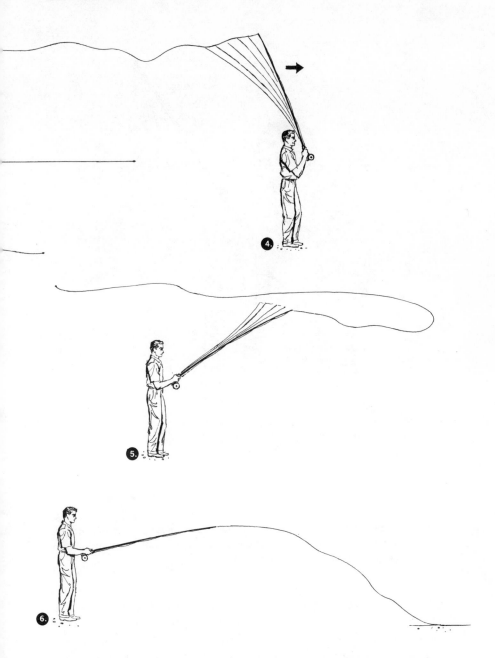

the line to continue its rearward travel. 4. At the instant the line straightens out (you'll feel a slight tug), swing your forearm down forcefully, bringing the rod forward sharply. 5. Further downward movement of the rod sends the line unfolding in a long, looping curve. 6. Point rod at target (a spot on ground you want fly to hit) and allow line to extend itself and flatten gently.

Line can be stripped from reel by left hand during false casts and held in coils. As rod comes forward for real cast, coils will shoot through rod guides, giving added distance to your cast.

line, but you strip a little more line from the reel while executing each backcast and allow the line to slip between the thumb and fingers of your left hand at the last moment. Continuing to do this will work out more and more line until it is of a desired longer length.

You can "shoot the line" to get more distance. This involves stripping off excess line from the reel and keeping the line hanging in loose coils from your left hand. As you make a powerful forward cast, allow some loops of line to pull from your left hand and to go out. It will shoot through the rod guides. As you develop skill, you will be able to shoot more and more line, thus extending each cast by many feet without a lot of false casting to work out the line.

In taking in line, simply loop the forefinger of your right hand loosely over the line, and pull it in with your left (letting it slide beneath the right forefinger), hanging it in coils over your right forefinger until the proper amount is in and you can switch the coils from your right to your left hand. If you want to wind excess line on your single-action reel, hold both the loose line coils and the rod in your left hand; keep the line tight as you turn the reel handle with your right. To take in line with an automatic reel, simply push the lever of the reel with the little finger of your right hand.

You must also learn to retrieve your fly or lure properly. To make your dry fly or panfish bug twitch or shimmy on the water surface, just quiver the rod tip gently, or pull lightly on the line with your left hand, being careful not to move the fly or bug from its position. At other times, you will want to retrieve slowly in little jerks, especially with wet flies, lures and streamers. This is done by pulling in line in jerks with your left hand and hanging the line over your right forefinger in loops. To retrieve steadily, just raise your rod slowly for a ways before snapping it up to make the backcast. Do not raise your rod tip too far before making the backcast, however, else you will not have enough power for the backcast.

ROLL CAST

Once you have mastered this basic overhead cast, after you can shoot the line to get additional distance, and have experimented with various retrieves, you are ready to learn other casts to be used in special situations. One you will need to know is the roll cast. This is used wherever there is not enough room behind you to allow a backcast. To begin the roll cast, work out about 15 feet of line on the water in front of you (you cannot practice this cast on land). Raise your rod tip up and slightly back of the vertical until your line sags to a point slightly behind your right elbow. Now bring your rod downward in a smooth, powerful stroke. This will provide power to cause your line to begin going away from you, pulling off of the water in a rolling loop. The downward stroke of your rod must be a strong and fast one, with enough force supplied to roll the line off of the water. During this cast, you should keep tension on your line with your rod hand; you can release some line for shooting at the end of your stroke, but only after the line is all in the air.

BACKHAND CAST

Sometimes you will need to employ a special cast when the wind is blowing. One of these special casts is the backhand cast, used when the wind is blowing across you from right to left (assuming you are casting with your right hand). Begin this cast by making a slight pull on the line with the left hand (this helps in sliding the line off the water). Pick up the line for the backcast by moving your forearm up, across in front of you and back over your left shoulder, letting your arm pivot at the elbow. The line will then travel to your left and behind you for the backcast. Start the forward cast with a slight left-hand pull on the line to take up tension, then bring your arm down and to your front, trying to keep your rod in a fairly vertical plane as it passes over your left shoulder.

BELGIAN CAST

Another cast to be used in the wind is the Belgian cast. This is used when casting with the wind. Here the problem is to get your line behind you far enough for the backcast, since the backcast is made against the wind and the forward cast with the wind. The backcast is begun by pulling on your line sharply with your left hand and then moving your rod in a horizontal plane, executing a side cast to throw the line behind you. Then as you bring your arm forward, bring the line forward in an upward circular motion so that the forward cast is made in a vertical plane. The line will go out easily for the forward cast as the wind blows it away from you.

SUPER WIND CAST

The last cast I will describe here is the super wind cast, used when casting against the wind. Here there is no trouble in executing the backcast since the wind blows the line behind you, but the problem is to get the line, leader and fly to turn over properly in front of you during the forward cast. This cast is performed by pulling the line hard with your left hand as you begin the forward cast and by putting emphasis on a wrist and thumb movement near the end of the forward cast, so that the line is given an extra snap near the end to turn it over. On this cast, always delay shooting the line until the very last moments. In strong winds you may have to use only small flies, short leaders and do very little shooting of the line.

TROLLING WITH THE FLY ROD

Wonderful fishing for panfish can be had by trolling with your fly rod. Why more fishermen do not employ this method I do not know, but it is a very productive way to catch white or yellow bass, crappie and white perch. All of these fish move about a great deal in large schools, usually following the forage fish. Trolling can be used to find the schools, or to fish in deep open water. Also you can use lures a little easier when trolling than when fly casting, since any fly-rod lure is bulky to cast. Small spoons, plastic worms, fly-rod plugs, streamer flies and natural bait with spinner attached are all effective when trolled.

When setting the hook, strike quickly, but not so violently as to yank the fly or lure away from the fish. If you missed the fish on the first strike, then leave the fly or lure within reach; the fish may strike again unless you so disturbed the water as to frighten the fish. Handle crappie gently since they have tender mouths and the hook is easily torn out.

In playing the fish, let out or take in line with your left hand, reeling in any access line whenever possible. With very light leaders you will have to avoid sudden and severe shock on the leader, so wear your fish out before bringing it in. Ultra-light tackle will double your enjoyment but must be handled carefully.

When landing a fish, always avoid lifting it out of the water with your rod as this may either strain or break the rod. Lead your fish up beside you and land it with a net or pull it in by the leader, or catch it with your hand, grasping the fish firmly over the back and squeezing it at a point just behind the gill covers as you lift it out of the water.

Really the best sport is to troll streamer flies. This is especially effective when schools of panfish are slashing the surface chasing minnows, shad, smelt or other forage fish. Once you find the fish, troll back and forth over the area and you will be able to get your limit in a very short time. Each strike will feel like a whale and each fish has a maximum opportunity to put up a good fight as you play him on the limber fly rod.

Yellow perch can also be caught by trolling, but usually by fishing in or around underwater weed beds. Yellow perch are not so much an open water fish (certainly they do not remain on the surface in open water) as are the white and yellow bass, crappie and white perch. Small lures, spoons, plastic worms or live bait seem best for these fish.

I've never had too much luck trolling for bluegills, pumpkinseed, rock bass or other common varieties of sunfish. These fish are caught more readily by casting with small flies.

When the panfish are deep, it's better to use your spinning or casting outfit for trolling, so that you can add enough weight to the line to get down to the fish.

FISH-GETTING TECHNIQUES

I want to include here a group of miscellaneous suggestions which will often make the difference between a full stringer and an empty one. Assuming that you have the right tackle, flies and lures and know how to cast fairly well, here are some points to remember:

Be careful to make quiet approaches and to avoid unnecessary noises which might scare the fish. The largest specimens of panfish are always easily spooked, so wade or row quietly, avoid scraping or thumping the bottom of the boat. When walking along the stream or creek bank, walk as lightly as possible. Keep your shadow off the hole where you intend to cast, particularly in shallow, clear water.

For many years, I used an inner-tube float for fishing creeks. It had a canvas cover with a seat across the middle and with spaces to put my two legs through the center. I paddled with my feet underwater as I cast. It was quiet, efficient and I caught hundreds of panfish from such a float. Also, I could reach many otherwise inaccessible places in creeks too deep to wade. I even used it to fish the shorelines of lakes. Such floats can be used with or without waders.

If you are going to anchor your boat, do so quietly, letting out and retrieving the anchor cord slowly. Soft talking is all right, but shouting or boisterous talking does carry into the water. Try to avoid being seen by the fish; you'll catch more and bigger ones if they do not know you are there.

When dry-fly fishing, put some dry-fly oil on your fly and line dressing on your line to keep both floating well. Usually, the leader can be allowed to sink, unless its weight continues to drown the fly; if that happens, you may have to dress your leader to make it float, even though the gleam from it on the water surface may scare some fish. Always use as fine a leader as you can cast easily and which will hold your fish. I have demonstrated dozens of times that panfish are line shy, especially the larger and wise ones.

Many strikes are missed in wet-fly fishing unless one watches the line carefully. If you see the slightest jerk on your line, strike quickly. If you feel nothing after striking, then let the fly stay longer and the fish may take it again.

When fishing a flowing stream, creek or river, wade upstream and fish by casting up and across the stream. This way you will be less likely to spook the fish, since the fish always turn their heads upstream.

Fish dry flies or bugs when the fish seem to be rising to the water surface to feed. Dry-fly fishing is especially good late in the evening. Use streamer flies or lures for fish that seem to be feeding on minnows or small fish. Streamers and lures can be fished down, across or upstream, retrieving erratically.

If you are missing too many strikes, you are probably using flies or lures which are too large for the fish to get in their mouths. Using flies which are too big is a common fault when fishing for bluegills or pumpkinseed, which have very small mouths. Usually size 10 flies are about right for bluegills; slightly larger ones can be used with yellow perch, white perch, white or yellow bass or crappie.

11

LIVE BAIT LORE

It takes just as much know-how, study and experience to be a proficient live-bait fisherman as it does to be a good fly fisherman or spincaster. Naturally, I do not believe it is very sporting to take panfish with heavy, stiff bamboo poles and crude lines and tackle, but, in the long run, neither do I believe it is very effective. However, the live-bait fisherman who can also use a light, limber fly rod with finesse, who uses small hooks and delicate leaders, and who studies the habits of his prey so that he may utilize all of his knowledge and skill to catch the largest and most wary specimens, is certainly to be admired. In live-bait fishing, as in other methods, 10 percent of the fishermen catch 90 percent of the fish. And, certainly, it is only the best fishermen who consistently catch the largest fish.

Also, there are certain times when I feel live-bait fishing is by far the most effective method for catching panfish. This is especially true when one must fish in very deep water, let's say over 20 to 25 feet. It is always hard to handle artificials, except jigs, under these conditions. At other times, of course, the fly- or spincaster using artificials will have far better results. In other words, I feel the best fisherman is one who can use the method appropriate to the conditions with which he is confronted.

194

The purpose of this chapter is to help you to become a better live-bait fisherman. I will include here a discussion of the most important live baits, along with many practical suggestions for fishing them.

EARTHWORMS

There are more than 2,000 species of earthworms found in the world but most of them are never used as bait. In the United States, the three species most commonly used are the common night crawler (*Lumbricus terrestris*), the manure worm (*Eisenia foetida*) and the ordinary earthworm (*Helodrilus caliginosus*).

By far the best way of obtaining earthworms, as far as I am concerned, is to buy them in quantity lots from wholesale bait dealers. Most local dealers that sell them by the dozen charge far more than do the wholesale dealers. All of the outdoor magazines run ads offering worms for sale. Prices usually range from $3 to $7 per 1,000, with most dealers charging between $4 and $5.

If you do want to gather your own earthworms, however, there are several methods. When the worms are near the surface (as they will be during periods of wet, mild weather), they can be easily obtained by using any one of a number of electric-shock devices. Or a metal stake can be driven into the ground and then pounded with a hammer to produce vibrations in the soil which send the worms in the surrounding area scurrying to the surface. Various chemical solutions can also be obtained to pour over the ground to chase worms from their burrows. You can make your own solution by dissolving one bichloride of mercury tablet per gallon of water or by mixing a strong solution of mustard and water. When such chemicals are used, the worms ought to be washed thoroughly after being captured. Please remember, however, that these methods are only appropriate when the worms are thickly distributed and near the surface of the ground. During very hot, cold or dry weather, these methods are fruitless.

The time-honored method of obtaining worms is by digging them with a spading fork. Try to select damp areas of rich soil such as along creeks or rivers, near drain-offs of septic tanks, in barn yards, or in moist, shaded areas in meadows. In dry weather you can make your job easier by watering a wormy section of land for several days before spading.

Another way of obtaining worms is by looking under boards or stones. If the soil is rich and damp, worms may be obtained easily from such places.

An easy way to have a constant supply of worms on hand is to raise your own. This is very easy to do provided the proper environment is provided for them. A bed can be prepared in a galvanized tub, wooden box or specially constructed worm box. A good size is about 4 feet long, 3 feet wide and 4 feet deep. Construct the box without any cracks through which the worms can escape but with screen-covered drain holes in the bottom. The box can be buried in a shaded, well-drained spot, leaving several inches extending above the ground. If the box is to be left outside during the winter, and if you live in a cold climate, you must cover the surface with manure to keep frost out.

Worms can be raised in any rich soil, but the process is speeded up if plenty of food is available. Garden humus in the form of leaves or grass clippings, plus other food such as peat moss, or manure mixed with soil and to which food is added periodically, makes an excellent bed. The worms can be fed almost anything: all kinds of table garbage, corn meal, chicken mash, grease drippings, bread crumbs, ground oats, cattle feed and other forms of animal or vegetable matter. The soil should be slightly moistened to keep the worms healthy.

After preparing the bed, I would then add several hundred worms, the exact number depending upon the size of the container. With proper care and enough feed you should breed enough worms to provide yourself with a good supply all the year round.

Worms that are to be kept for short periods of time may be kept in sphagnum moss, leaves or peat moss with a small amount of feed. Before being used, worms ought to be placed in your bait container with sphagnum moss (the kind obtained from a florist) to be scoured. This means the worms get rid of the earth inside of them while in the moss and become more transparent, and, at the same time, tougher and more lively.

The easiest and most common way of gathering night crawlers

is by searching for them on moist lawns after dark. If the evening is moderately cool, and the soil and lawn moist, the night crawlers will come to the surface and crawl out of their holes after dark. You must be careful in shining your light that the very bright beam does not hit the crawlers directly or they will retreat into their holes. Some people use a red beam, which does not frighten the worms. Care must also be taken in picking up the crawlers so that they will not be broken as they are pulled from their holes.

Manure worms can be found in any type of manure in barns and farm yards. These worms can even be gathered in winter since the manure usually does not freeze.

If you wade a stream or lake to fish, you will need a bait container in which to hold your worms. The standard bait container is a tin tobacco can with a hinged lid. If you want to get fancier, purchase a curved bait container which can be worn on your belt or get a fiber bait box to use in your boat. The worms ought to be kept moist and out of direct sunlight as much as possible.

There are several methods of putting your worm on the hook. Some anglers prefer to hook the worm only under the collar or ring or perhaps to put the hook through the collar and then through the worm one additional time. Such a method allows the worm a maximum amount of movement. For panfish, however, it is better to pass the hook back and forth through the worm several times until the hook shaft is covered. If too much bare hook shows, even panfish will not bite readily. If too much worm is left dangling, sunfish, yellow perch and other types of panfish will repeatedly steal your bait without getting hooked. Double- or triple-hook gangs, without spinners, can also be used.

Night crawlers are usually too large for many of the smaller species of panfish; also they break and come off the hook easily, so I prefer common earthworms or manure worms.

Worms will catch all of the species of panfish discussed in this book, but they are usually best for bluegills, common sunfishes and bullheads. Small minnows usually work better for crappie, white and yellow bass and yellow perch. White perch will sometimes prefer worms and at other times minnows. As the summer progresses, white perch usually feed more and more on small fish and minnows. Other baits, usually some types of larvae or gall worms, are substituted for angleworms when fishing for bluegills through the ice.

MINNOWS

"Minnow" is a general term used to designate any small fish which is used for bait. To be more precise, however, a minnow is any fish belonging to the family Cyprinidae, which includes the carp and gold-fish as well as the smaller and well-known minnows. All of these fish are spring or summer spawners. They have no scales on the head; they have a forked caudal fin and a toothless mouth. They chew with pharyngeal teeth which are located in the throat. Only a few species are vegetarians; the others eat both animal and vegetable substances. Carp root up vegetation from the bottom and keep the water continually discolored; this habit, along with their destruction of the spawn of other fish, makes them a highly undesirable species. The angler must be extremely careful, therefore, never to use carp minnows as bait or to introduce carp into any waters.

There are nearly 2,000 species of fish in the minnow family, of which 192 are found in the United States. The most common minnows in this country are shiners, chubs, daces and just "minnows." The more well-known ones are described below.

Shiners

1. **Golden shiner** (*Notemigonus crysoleucas*), a compressed, deep-bodied fish with large, regular, loose scales and a small, slanted, mouth. The maximum length is usually 10 to 12 inches. The color varies from silver to brass or gold. It is found from North and South Dakota, Nebraska and Oklahoma eastward to the Atlantic and south to the Gulf except most of Texas.

2. **Common shiner** (*Notropis cornutus*), a fairly long fish, sometimes called the redfin shiner because of the color of the fins of the males in the breeding season. The fish is found in most waters from Canada south to Oklahoma, Missouri and Alabama and east of the Rockies to the Atlantic. It reaches a maximum length of about 8 inches, is less hardy than many species, and cannot be successfully propagated in most ponds since it is a stream fish.

3. **Emerald shiner** (*Notropia atherinoides*), a forage fish of the open waters of the Great Lakes and larger rivers, widely distributed in the Mississippi Valley and north into Canada. It is silvery in color with a greenish back and is long and slender in shape. It cannot be propagated, or held too long during the summer without heavy loss. It spawns in early summer.

4. **Spottail shiner** (*Notropis hudsonius*). This fish derives its name from the dark spot found at the base of the caudal (tail) fin. Except for this spot, it is much like the emerald shiner in appearance and is frequently found with it in large lakes and rivers.

5. **Blacknose shiner** (*Notropis heterolepis*). This fish typically has eight anal rays with the dorsal fin usually closer to the caudal fin than to the snout.

6. **Bridled shiner** (*Notropis bifrenatus*), differs from the blacknose shiner in that the anal fin usually has seven rays; the fins are larger and the dorsal fin is usually nearer the tip of the snout than the base of the caudal.

Chubs

1. **Creek chub** (*Semotilus atromaculatus*). The chubs are rounded fish; they have olive-colored backs and white or silver bellies. They look very much like suckers except for the mouth, which is large and extends back to a line even with the eye. The most distinctive characteristic is a black spot on the dorsal fin near the front of the base; this is indistinct in the young. The fish is found in creeks and rivers over much of southern Canada and the whole United States except for the West Coast and west-central states. It is a large minnow, sometimes reaching 11 inches in length; it is very hardy and lively. During the spawning season in the spring, the males develop several large, horn-like structures on their heads, called breeding tubercles, which are used in nest building and in fighting other males. The male guards the nest until spawning is completed.

2. **Fallfish** (*Semotilus corporalis*). This fish is listed here since it is of the same genus as the creek chub; it is sometimes called the white chub and has the characteristic chub shape. It is a steel blue above with a silvery belly and red fins on the males during the

spawning season, which is in the spring. It can be distinguished from the creek chub by a flap-like, almost obsolescent, barbel on the lower edge of the upper jaw, located forward of the posterior end of the jaw and almost concealed in the groove between the pre-maxillary and maxillary bones. The fish usually grows to 18 inches or so, with the average about a foot. It is usually found in lakes and streams east of the Alleghenies.

3. **Lake chub** (*Hybopsis plumbea*), differs from the fallfish in that the barbel is located at, or near, the end of the upper jaw (maxillary). The barbel is small and often hidden in the groove above the upper jaw.

4. **Silver chub** (*Hybopsis storeriana*), a slim minnow with a greenish back and silvery belly. It lives well in captivity; it is active on a hook and may reach 8 or 10 inches in length. It is found from the Red River drainage in Canada to the southern shore of Lake Ontario and southward to Alabama and Oklahoma.

5. **Hornyhead chub** (*Hybopsis biguttata*), a heavy-bodied min-now with a large head and big, distinct scales. The color is generally olivacious with silver below. The fish has barbels at the corners of the mouth. The chief characteristic is a round, blackish spot at the base of the tail; the young have a red tail and fins; the males grow breeding tubercles on the top of the head during the spawning season (like the creek chub) and a red spot behind the eye. This fish prefers the larger creeks and smaller rivers with gravel bottoms. It reaches 8 to 10 inches in length, is a hardy bait which stands up well in a bait pail or on a hook, but it cannot be easily propagated. It is found from the Rocky Mountains east to the Hudson River.

6. **River chub** (*Hybopsis micropogon*), resembles hornyhead chub with its heavy body, blunt nose and large, distinct scales. The spot at the base of the tail, however, is not as clear or round as in the hornyhead chub. It prefers the larger rivers from the Rocky Mountains east to New England and south to Virginia and Alabama. It may reach 10 inches in length.

Daces

Pearl dace (*Semotilus margarita*), differs from the creek chub in having no black spot on the dorsal fin; the mouth is small with the upper jaw not extending to below the front of the eye. A distinguishing feature of this fish is also the silvery color of the sides, which are mottled by darker scales. There is a single, dusky lateral line with sixty-five to seventy-five scales along the line. The fish is a hardy bait minnow which prefers cool lakes, bogs and creeks east of the Rocky Mountains, particularly in Canada and our northern states.

2. **Blacknose dace** (*Rhinichthys atratulus*), a fairly small minnow found in cool, clear streams and brooks, seldom exceeding 2 or 3 inches in length. The snout scarcely projects beyond a somewhat oblique mouth. The fish gets its name from the fact that it has a dusky back, black spots all over and a dark streak on the side of the body from the tail to the snout. The western blacknose dace ranges from the Lake of the Woods region south to Nebraska and through most of the tributaries of the Great Lakes to the northern part of the Ohio River system. The eastern blacknose dace is found from Quebec southward, east to the coast.

3. **Longnose dace** (*Rhinichthys cataractae*). This fish is of the same genus as the blacknose dace but has a snout projecting far beyond the horizontal mouth.

4. **Redbelly dace.** There is a northern redbelly dace (*Chrosomus eos*) and a southern redbelly dace (*Chrosomus erythrogaster*). Both of these species are small minnows, usually reaching 3 inches in length; they are dark bronze in color, with two parallel, black, lateral bands along the side. The males are brightly colored with scarlet bellies during the spring spawning season. The northern species is found in bog ponds and sluggish creeks in many parts of Canada and most of the northeastern and north-central states while the southern species is found from southern Wisconsin and Michigan to Pennsylvania and south to Alabama and Oklahoma.

5. **Finescale dace** (*Chrosomus neogaeus*), similar to the redbelly dace, but has a single, incomplete lateral line.

Other Minnows

Included in this miscellaneous group ought to be listed at least three commonly found fish.

1. **Flathead minnow** (*Pimephales promelas*), a small, drably colored minnow (olive with brassy tinge below) except during its

breeding season when the male takes on brighter colors. Maximum size of the fish is about 3½ inches; spawning takes place from May to August with the eggs which are laid on the underside of objects guarded by the male. They are easily propagated in ponds.

2. **Bluntnose minnow** (*Hyborhynchus notatus*), a long, slim minnow, olivacious in color with a dark spot at the base of the tail. It reaches 4 inches in length and prefers clear lakes and streams from Winnipeg through the Great Lakes region to Quebec and southward to Virginia and the Gulf States. It can be raised artificially in ponds.

3. **Brassy minnow** (*Hybognathus hankinsoni*), a minnow with a blunt head, small mouth and short, rounded fins. The scales are large and brassy in color and come off the sides easily. It prefers small creeks, bog waters and occasionally is found in lakes through most of the Great Lakes region and from Montana to southern Ontario southward to Colorado, Nebraska and Iowa.

These are some of the principal species of bait fish found in the United States. Which ones you use are usually a matter of availability and of personal preference. In general, the shiners are the least hardy; they are harder to keep alive and they die sooner on the hook than any others. The chubs are the most hardy and stay lively on the hook for longer periods of time. The daces and common minnows rank somewhere in between.

Panfish seem to prefer shiners, and so I use them more often than any other bait. If you use chubs, be certain that they are small enough. Panfish bait ought to be from 1 inch to 2½ inches in size, depending on the type of fish caught. It is sometimes hard to find chubs small enough. The daces, fathead, bluntnose and other minnows are all good baits. It is more important that you have lively minnows of an appropriate size than that you use a particular species. If you cut the bottoms of the tails off your minnows, they have more trouble keeping upright and continue to struggle while on the hook, making a livelier bait.

The most efficient method of catching minnows is to use a large seine. Most states have laws governing the seining of bait, however, so check the regulations in your area. The length of the seine is usually governed by state law.

Usually, the best places to seine minnows are the small, shallow waters in creeks, streams or rivers below dams. A small pool formed below a rock wall or dam across a creek makes an excellent place, particularly if fresh water is continually pouring into it. Another good place is in shallow pools left by the receding waters of a river or creek. I used to seine minnows by the hundreds in such pools and they were easily caught since they could not escape.

In lakes try to locate the minnows before seining. They can be located usually in the shallow waters next to the shore, particularly in sandy, gravelly or rocky areas. The sandy bottoms of many populated bathing beaches seem to attract many minnows. After seining, those minnows or fish in the seine not utilized as bait should be carefully returned unharmed to the water.

Another way to obtain minnows is with a drop net or umbrella net. Lower the net to the bottom in a shallow spot where minnows congregate. Then throw cracker crumbs or other bait over the net. When the minnows congregate over the net, it can be lifted quickly to catch them. It is best to have a rope tied to the net and an overhanging branch so that you can pull the net up quickly. Or you can use the net from a bridge or the top of a dam.

Still another way to obtain minnows is with a trap. The traps come in a variety of sizes and types. Usually they are made of wire mesh or glass. I like the wire mesh ones since they permit the odor and "chum" from the bait inside the trap to leak into water and attract the minnows. If traps are set in streams, place them with the funnel entrance downstream. Fish swim upstream, and will therefore be more likely to enter the traps.

One of the problems of the minnow fisherman is to transport his minnows to the fishing spot without too many casualties. If the weather is cool and the distance short, an ordinary metal minnow bucket will suffice and the minnows will not need special care. After arriving at the lake or stream, the perforated inner lining, with the minnows inside, can be removed and put in the water.

Special buckets can be used if the weather is warm or one has a considerable distance to travel. The new pulp fiber buckets admit oxygen through the sides of the bucket and keep minnows alive longer. Also, when the outside of the bucket is kept moist, the evaporation cools the water.

Other tricks can be used to keep the minnows alive. One of the easiest and most effective is to put ice in the minnow pail. This cools the water and dissolves oxygen in it. Another trick is to buy a small, battery-operated pump which will pump air into the water through a tube. Some fishermen have even made a special rig on their car to utilize the vacuum pressure of the auto engine to draw air into the minnow water. Others take a tire pump along and pump air into the water by hand. Others prefer to stop periodically to change water in the bucket. Make certain, however, that any water you use for minnows is not too heavily treated with chlorine or other minerals or the fish will be killed.

The easiest way to keep a large number of minnows for long periods of time is to put a live box into your fishing lake or stream. If you return to fish frequently, but want to hide your bait, you can sink your live box in deep water, marking the spot carefully. If you want to keep your minnows at home, you can allow water to drip from the tap into your tank, but the tank ought to have an overflow outlet to drain off excess water, otherwise many of your minnows will flop onto the floor if the water rises to the top of the tank. Various kinds of aerating pumps can also be purchased to use in your minnow tank. They may be obtained from pet shops supplying fish and aquarium equipment.

How to hook minnows depends upon the type of fishing you are doing. For still-fishing, I prefer to place the hook just forward of the dorsal fin, being careful not to run the hook through the spinal column. Minnows hooked in this way live for a long time. Other fishermen prefer to hook their minnows through the lips or tail. If you hook through the tail, however, you have to be certain you allow ample time for the panfish to shallow the bait, since it swallows the minnow head first and will not be hooked unless the minnow is well down in its throat. If the minnow is hooked in the lips, the panfish are suspicious of the hook and have difficulty swallowing the bait.

If you are casting or trolling with live minnows, undoubtedly the best arrangement is to use a minnow harness or rig. There are a number of excellent ones on the market, among them the Weber Nev-R-Miss Minnow Rig; the Marathon Mino-Miser; and the Worth Sure-Take Spinner Hooks. This is a tandem hook with spinner.

Another way to cast or troll minnows is to sew them on your hook.

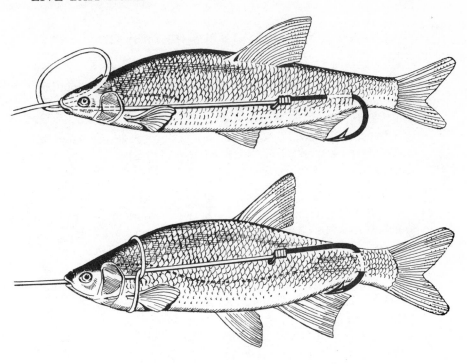

Two methods of sewing minnow on a hook for casting or trolling.

One method is to pass the whole hook in the minnow's mouth and out one gill, then back into the mouth out the other gill. The hook is then passed just under the skin at the base of the tail and out. The monofilament can then be tightened as needed.

Another method of sewing on the minnow is to pass the hook into the mouth, out one gill, around the minnow's body, under the leader (making a hitch around the minnow's body) and then back to the base of the tail where the hook is imbedded into the minnow's flesh.

With either of these methods of sewing, if the body of the minnow is bent when the hook is inserted at the base of the tail, the minnow will spin when cast or trolled. Usually you need to use swivels to keep the spinning minnow from twisting your line.

WATER INSECTS, THEIR NYMPHS OR LARVAE

Water insects and their nymphs or larvae are eaten at one time or another by most panfish. For this reason, they make excellent bait if they are the right size.

In the process of development from egg to adult, the insect goes through a series of stages. Some go through three stages: egg, nymph, adult; others develop in four: egg, larva, pupa and adult. The most commonly used baits are described below:

1. **Hellgrammite.**   This is the larval form of the big, winged insect known as the Dobson fly. The fly lays several thousand eggs on branches, rocks or other objects along a stream. After hatching, the tiny larvae drop into the water where they grow and develop (as hellgrammites) for nearly three years. At two years and eleven months the mature hellgrammite emerges, hides under a log or stone for about a month and changes into the adult Dobson fly.

Hellgrammites are most numerous in fast-water streams. They can be gathered by holding a wire screen or seine across a portion of the stream and turning over rocks immediately upstream of the screen so that the larvae wash into it. A rake or hoe is a helpful tool to use in overturning the rocks.

Hellgrammites range in size from about 1 to 3 inches; the smaller ones are better for panfish. Hellgrammites can be kept for a long time in running water, or they will live for weeks in a cool cellar. Put them in a box along with dampened leaves or moss. Keep them damp but not too wet. They can be transferred to your bait box to which some damp moss has been added at the time you go fishing. Feed the larvae small amounts of ground beef to prevent cannibalism.

Before you fish with a hellgrammite, break off the pincers on the end of the tail, to keep it from clinging to stones or sticks in the water.

HELLGRAMMITE

2. **Dragonfly nymphs** are often called "perch bugs" in many parts of the country. They live in ponds, lakes and the quieter sections of streams where they hide in the mud and vegetation. They live from one to more than three years in the water, then crawl onto a stem of a water plant, a branch or a stump, where the skin of the larva splits, allowing the adult insect to emerge.

DRAGONFLY NYMPH

These nymphs can be obtained by dragging a seine with a weighted bottom edge over the muddy bottom of stream or lake or through water plants. Or you can rake or shovel up the bottom muck and debris, carefully looking for these nymphs. Once obtained, they can be kept in tanks of water. They will live for short periods of time in your bait container to which moistened moss has been added.

3. **Damsel fly nymphs** are more delicate than the dragonfly nymphs, having longer, thinner bodies and legs. They are obtained and kept alive in the same way as dragonfly nymphs. They should not be stored with dragonfly nymphs, however, as both are cannibalistic.

DAMSEL FLY NYMPH

4. **Caddis worms** are the larvae of the caddis fly, which lays hundreds of eggs on submerged rocks or plants while flying over the water. After hatching, the larvae build portable, protective cases or sacks of sticks, leaves, stones, sand and other materials, cemented together with a special secretion. The larva lives in this case, dragging it around wherever it goes. Look for them moving around in the quieter waters of streams or shorelines of lakes where they can be seined or picked up by hand. The worm itself should be removed from the case before it is threaded on the fish hook.

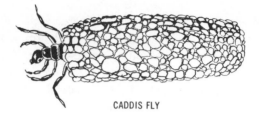

CADDIS FLY

Since there are over 200 species of these insects, ordinarily only those which produce the largest larvae can be used for bait. The larvae can be kept in tanks of cool water, although they are cannibalistic in captivity and will eat one another.

5. **Mayfly nymph.** These nymphs are the nymphal, or second stage of development of the familiar mayfly. There are many species, the nymphs varying greatly in size and shape. One of the largest is the nymph of the burrowing mayfly. The nymph may reach close to 2 inches in length. They live in mud in water depths of from a few inches to 40 feet. They can be scooped up with the mud in areas where they are plentiful and separated by washing the mud over a wire screen.

MAYFLY NYMPH

Other species of these nymphs prefer clear, rocky streams where they cling to stones in the riffles and from where they can be seined. Others swim around in the shallows of lakes or streams.

All species can be kept in tanks of cool, well-aerated water. The bottoms of the tanks should be covered with material similar to the stream or lake bottoms where found. Place the nymphs in a bait container filled with damp, cool moss. They can be kept in a minnow bucket of cold water for short periods of time.

6. **Stone-fly nymph.** These nymphs are sometimes mistaken for the mayfly nymphs, although the two are unrelated. However, the stone-fly nymphs prefer fast-running streams where they cling to the underside of stones. They can be caught by placing a wire screen

STONE FLY NYMPH   CRANE FLY LARVA

across streams, then lifting up stones upstream of the screen so that
the nymphs may be washed into it.

7. **Crane-fly larvae.** The adult crane fly is a "daddy-longlegs"
sort of insect, sometimes mistaken for a large mosquito. There are
about 300 species in the United States; the larvae of some live in
water, but most live on land in damp, decomposing earth. Those living in water can be obtained by shoveling or raking up material from
the stream or lake bottom and washing over a wire screen. The larvae
can be gathered off the screen. Commercial bait dealers handle a
larvae known as mousee. This is a species of crane-fly larvae. They
are excellent bait for ice fishing for bluegills.

All species of panfish can be caught on any of these larvae or
nymphs. In general, however, I prefer the larvae for bluegills, rock
and warmouth bass, common sunfish, yellow and white perch and
bullheads. I feel the nymphs are better for crappie, although minnows are better still. I have never fished for white and yellow bass
with these baits, but I do not see why they would not work, particularly the hellgrammites, although I could venture a guess that live
minnows are far better. The very small larvae are really suitable only
for those sunfish with small mouths.

A variety of methods must be used for hooking larvae and nymphs.
Some of these baits are quite soft and easily ruined if a hook is
passed completely through them. For these baits, use a small hook
(a number 10 is best for bluegills) to which two short pieces of wire
have been soldered. Put the larvae or nymph along the shank of the
hook and secure the bait by wrapping the flexible wire around it.
Other anglers tie the baits on with light thread.

An easier method is to use fine wire hooks and pass the hook
through the head of the bait. This can be done with caddis worms,
mayfly nymphs and crane-fly larvae. Stone-fly nymphs can be secured
by passing the hook through a collar just behind the head.

If the larvae or nymphs are big enough, some may be threaded on the hook by pushing the hook wire through the length of the body. In every method, try to cover as much of the hook as possible so the fish will not shy away.

LAND INSECTS AND THEIR LARVAE

Included under this heading are a variety of insects, many completely different and unrelated, but all commonly used as panfish baits. They are discussed below.

1. **Grasshoppers.** These insects are one of the most commonly used baits for bluegills, other common sunfishes and perch. There are many species; some seem better bait than others. The large, gray-brown, flying grasshoppers are too hard to catch and are too large for many panfish; others, like the very small, light-green ones, are too delicate to use as bait. Since grasshoppers are found throughout the United States, however, there will usually be more than enough of the right species in your vicinity to use for bait. They are especially numerous during the hot weather of late summer and early fall.

The big problem is to catch them. A small butterfly net or large fly swatter will help you to pin them to the ground to grab them. The best way to get them, however, is to collect them in the early morning when the grass is wet with dew and the air is cold; under these conditions, the insects can scarcely fly or jump at all.

Grasshoppers can be kept in any light, cheesecloth bag or insect box with a fine-mesh screen. Ordinary grass and leaves make good food for them. The insects should be kept dry and warm. Some fishermen use a small, light wooden box with screen wire over the ends to keep grasshoppers in. Put a piece of old rubber innertube over a large hole in the top with a 2-inch slit. The fisherman can reach down through the hole to get some bait without other insects escaping.

There are several methods of putting grasshoppers on a hook. One method is to tie them on with fine wire or thread or to attach them with a rubber band. Other fishermen put the hook under the hard skin of the shoulder or thread them right on the hook. If you want to use grasshoppers for bait all year round, gather them in season

AMERICAN GRASSHOPPER

CRICKET

and put them in your freezer until needed. They make excellent bait for ice fishing for bluegills and perch.

2. **Crickets.** There are two species of field crickets which are commonly used as bait: the gray and the dark-brown or black. The latter species (*Gryllus assimilis*) is one of the largest and is usually preferred.

Crickets can be found easiest late in the summer and in the fall under stones, hay piles and in wheat, corn or rye stacks. They can be baited and gathered more easily by scattering stale bread to lure them. Or take sheafs of oats or wheat and shake the crickets into a barrel or tub. They can be kept in the same type of containers used for grasshopers and fed grass, lettuce or chicken mash. If crickets are kept for very long, they can be supplied with water in shallow dishes which have been filled with cotton to keep the crickets from drowning.

If you prefer to raise your own crickets, obtain a garbage can, lard can or other metal drum which has had the top removed. Sandpaper the 12 inches of the inside next to the top until smooth, then wax and polish to keep the crickets from crawling out. Or cover the opening with window screen. Place 4 to 6 inches of fine, clean, damp sand in the bottom of the drum and over that 4 to 6 inches of excelsior or straw. Stock the can with an equal number of male and female crickets, about fifty in all. (The female can be distinguished by the long tube protruding at the tail, used to deposit eggs in the ground). Supply the crickets with chicken mash and water (the container filled with cotton to keep the young crickets from drowning).

The ideal temperature for crickets is about 80° F. If the barrel is too cold during the winter, an electric light bulb can be suspended to within 5 or 6 inches of the excelsior or straw. This will keep the crickets growing or reproducing. The cricket eggs hatch in fifteen to twenty-five days; the young crickets are large enough to use as bait in a month and the crickets fully mature in three months.

I think it's cheaper and easier to buy your crickets in quantity lots from wholesale bait dealers. Addresses of such dealers can always be found in the ads at the back of the better-known outdoor magazines.

Crickets can be attached to a fish hook by the same methods used for grasshoppers. Crickets are especially fine bait for bluegills, other true sunfish and perch.

3. **Cockroaches.**   There are four common species of cockroaches: German, Oriental, American and wood. The German or Croton bug (*Blattella germanica*) and American cockroach (*Periplaneta americana*) are most common and are easiest to raise. They can be found in barns, garbage dumps, warehouses and other places. They can be caught easiest in insect traps baited with raw or cooked vegetables, apples or moist bread. They prefer dark places and usually come out of hiding at night.

If you desire to raise your own, use metal containers with sand and excelsior or straw on the bottom like those described for crickets. Put oil or vaseline near the top of the container to keep the cockroaches from escaping. Feed them with lettuce, fruits and vegetables, or make a mixture of 50 percent whole ground wheat flour, 45 percent skim milk and 5 percent dried baker's yeast. Mix these with water and allow to dry. Keep plenty of water for the cockroaches to drink.

Thread the cockroach on the hook tail first with the hook running

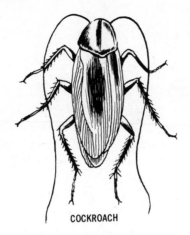

COCKROACH

SPHINX MOTH LARVA

the full length of the body and the point sticking out of the head. These insects are considered extremely fine bait for bluegills and other sunfishes.

4. **Catalpa worms.** This worm has been crowned by many fishermen, especially those of the Midwest and South, as the finest bluegill bait obtainable. The worm is the larva of the sphinx moth which lays its eggs on catalpa trees (these can be identified by their broad leaves and bean pods). When the larvae hatch, they feed on the leaves of the tree until about 3 inches long and too fat to hold on; they then drop to the ground where they burrow in, form pupae and eventually hatch into moths. The worms are dark brown in color, or black with green along the sides. They are smooth-skinned and very tough baits. You can often catch a half-dozen or more fish with one worm.

Some fishermen prefer to turn the worm inside out with a stick or nail, either using a half or all of the worm as bait. The worm can be kept for long periods of time if fed catalpa leaves. Or they can be placed in corn meal and put in your refrigerator and kept dormant for a few weeks until used. The worms can be placed on the hook by running the hook from behind the head down the length of the body about three-fourths the distance. Leave a small portion of the tail of the worm dangling.

5. **Meal worms.** These are another popular bait, especially for bluegills, common sunfish and perch. They are often used in the winter for ice fishing. They are the larvae of darkling beetles and mealworm beetles. A common species is the *Tenebrio obscurus*, which is known as the dark meal worm. Another species, the *Tenebrio molitor*, is known as the yellow meal worm. Both are excellent baits.

These larvae can be found wherever grain is stored: in granaries, feed stores, pet shops, poultry houses and other places. The beetles lay their eggs in the grain, hatch out as larvae and eventually grow into other beetles.

These worms are easily raised by the fisherman who wants a constant supply of bait. Use a large washtub or box over which a wire or cloth screen has been placed to keep the larvae and beetles from escaping. Put alternate layers of chicken mash and burlap sack in the tub or box, beginning with a ¼-inch layer of the mash. Build up about eight layers, four each of mash and sack. Sprinkle water in the container daily, and add some raw carrots or potatoes to provide the necessary moisture.

6. **Grubs.** There are over 100 American species of grubs, which are the larvae form of June bugs or May beetles. The beetles lay their white eggs in the ground, where they hatch and where the white grubs feed for two or three years. They pupate underground in the fall and adults appear the following spring. The adults feed on the leaves of many common trees. One species, commonly called the green June beetle, is most common in the South and Southeast where they do considerable damage to apricots, grapes, melons and other fruits. The grubs are delicate and need to be tied on a hook or impaled through the head. They can be kept in the same type of earth as that in which they were found.

7. **Gall worms.** This is the common name given to a variety of larvae of flies and wasps which grow inside the stems of various plants. Each insect selects a specific plant. The adults lay their eggs in the plant tissue. As the eggs hatch, the tissue swells and forms a hardened gall completely surrounding the larvae. The larvae form

MEAL WORM LARVA

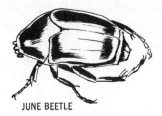

JUNE BEETLE   MAY BEETLE

pupae inside the gall and the adult emerges by burrowing through the side.

The most common galls are found on oak apples, on blackberry bushes and on goldenrod. Galls can be collected in the fall or early winter, kept in a cool, dry place until needed and then the galls split open when bait is required. The larvae make excellent bait for bluegills.

8. **Maggots.** Although many people are repelled at the thought of using maggots, these larvae make excellent panfish baits. The most common are maggots from the house fly, the black horse fly or stable fly, the greenbottle and bluebottle flies and the blowfly.

Blowfly larvae can be obtained by hanging a piece of meat or a small animal outdoors in warm weather. The blowflies lay their eggs on the meat; the larvae hatch out and, in about a week, mature, fattened maggots are available for bait. Place the maggots in corn meal where they will dry out, be scoured and become more pleasant to use for bait.

CRAWFISH

This crustacean is a favorite of many bass fishermen. In smaller sizes, however, it can also be used as an excellent panfish bait, especially for yellow perch and rock bass. Crawfish tails are also excellent bait for bullheads.

There are many species; some are found in swamps, small ponds and lakes; others live in fast-moving streams. I remember catching them by the hundreds in drainage ditches, culverts and stagnant ponds near my boyhood home. Use crawfish only about 1 or 1½ inches for rock bass or yellow perch and about 1½ or 2 inches for crappies. The tails from larger ones can be used for bullhead bait.

If you desire to collect your own, the best way is to seine them at night, since they come out of hiding then. Seine around shallow-water weed beds or in rocky areas. Have two people handle the seine and a third follow along, pointing the flashlight at the center of the net. After the crawfish are disturbed, they will travel toward the light. Another way to catch them is with a dip net and flashlight. Other fishermen prefer to use wire traps with funnel entrances, baiting the trap with dead fish or meat. Most of those caught in traps will be hard-shells.

All crawfish grow by moulting or shedding their skin. Right after the shell is cast off the crawfish is known as "soft-shell." When the new shell starts to harden a day or so later, it is called a "paper-shell." When this shell hardens, it is called a "hard-shell."

Most fishermen prefer soft-shells and so try to devise all sorts of ways to soften the shells. The best way, however, is to force-fatten the crawfish. Place them in a metal tank, or a screen-covered live box. The chief requirement is to have fresh, well-aerated water. A wooden box with a screen at each end, placed in a stream, is good. A tank into which air is pumped will work; or use one large enough to keep the crawfish fresh without the need for pumped air or running water. Feed them a diet of meat, dead fish or corn meal. They will grow fast and shed their shells quickly. The crawfish turn dark-colored just before the shells begin to peel. You can prevent the shells from hardening rapidly by putting the crawfish in moss and storing them for several days in your refrigerator. Try to keep the soft-shelled craw-fish, and the smaller ones, separated from the hard-shells and larger ones so that the latter won't kill the others.

You can hook crawfish under the shell at the back or through the tail. In the case of soft-shells, use a harness or tie them to the hook. A hook to which two pieces of flexible wire have been soldered will provide an easy means for attaching the crawfish to the hook. I prefer to remove the large pincers before using the crawfish as bait.

FROGS

If the very small ones are used, frogs make excellent bait for yellow perch or bullheads. The green frog (*Rana clamitans*), leopard frog (*Rana pipiens*), pickerel frog (*Rana palustris*) and other small species can be used.

Frogs can be found and caught along muddy, marshy ponds, streams and rivers. Small farm ponds provide a constant source of supply in some areas. Grassy fields and meadows adjacent to water often contain thousands of frogs. They can be caught fairly easily at night with the aid of flashlight. A small-meshed net helps in the daytime.

Frogs can be kept alive in a live box placed in the shallow water of a lake or stream. Place rocks in it on which the frogs can rest. I prefer putting them in a small nail keg turned on end. Put moss and about 1 inch of water in the bottom. A piece of screen wire placed over the top end will keep the frogs from jumping out. If kept reasonably cool, these frogs will live several weeks, even without food. They can be fed worms or insects that are alive and moving.

The preferred method of hooking a frog is through both lips. Small frog harnesses work reasonably well, especially for casting, and keep the frog alive longer. Some fishermen prefer to hook the frog through the hind leg. A small wooden and screen box with a hinged cover is the preferred bait box for frogs.

PREPARED BAITS

There are a number of other baits that are excellent for panfish. These baits are not alive when used and require some preparation. However, they can be good baits.

Yellow perch, for example will bite well on fish eyes, especially under the ice. After you catch several perch, pop their eyes out with your thumb nail by pressing just below the eye. Use one or two eyes on a small hook. Jiggle occasionally to attract the attention of the fish. Using fish eyes as bait, I once caught over 200 perch in two days, the fish averaging half a pound each. I have never found any better bait for ice fishing for yellow perch. These fish will also take cut bait. You can use beef steak, dead (but fresh) minnows cut into pieces, cut pieces of clams, mussels or shrimp.

Bluegills, rock bass, pumpkinseed, redear sunfish and bullheads will bite on freshwater clams and mussels, especially if the bait is jiggled occasionally. The clams are easily gathered by hand while you are swimming in shallow water over sandy bottoms. They can be kept alive in a box partly submerged in water, or, for short periods of time, in containers filled with water. Crack the shells with a hammer or open them with a knife. Use the clams raw, but cut into bite-size pieces. Snails (with shells removed) and slugs (found under damp boards or on decayed wood in cool gardens and forests) are also excellent bait for these common sunfishes.

There are a variety of prepared baits for bullheads: doughballs, meat baits, blood baits, cheese baits and various stink baits.

METHODS OF LIVE-BAIT FISHING

There are really six principal methods of live-bait fishing for panfish.

1. *Still-fishing with bobber, hook, line and sinker.* If the bobber does not have to be set for water over 10 feet deep, the fly rod is excellent for this type of fishing and will provide the maximum sport. If the water is deeper than 10 feet, use your spincast or spinning outfit with a sliding bobber. In this type of fishing, a knot is tied in your line at the point you want the bobber. A special sliding bobber permits you to reel in all but the last 2 feet of your line (when sinker and hook are attached). After casting, the sinker pulls the line through the hole in the bobber until the knot is reached. This method will allow you to fish very deep water and still be able to use a bobber and reel in your fish.

Several suggestions will help you catch more and bigger fish. Have a small enough bobber and a heavy enough sinker so that the bobber will dip under the water at the slightest touch. If the bobber is too buoyant, even with line, sinker and hook attached, the larger fish may be hesitant about biting because of the drag.

Use very small hooks. Sizes 10 or 12 are about right for bluegills and other true sunfish; size 6 or 8 is usually best for other panfish.

Some fishermen prefer long-shank hooks so that the hook can be removed easily from the fish's mouth. However, you will have far more bites from bigger fish if you use short-shank hooks of fine wire and try to cover the hook shank as much as possible with the bait to decrease visibility.

Always use a fine nylon leader if the line itself is not monofilament. The leader should be about 6 to 9 feet long and of about 6-pound test.

Set your depth so the bait is about a foot off the bottom (except for bullheads which feed right on the bottom). The easiest way to set the correct depth is to clamp a heavy sinker to your hook and lower to the bottom. Then attach your bobber so that it will be pulled a foot under with the heavy weight attached to the hook. After the bobber is set, remove the weight from the hook and bait up.

2. *Still-fishing without a bobber.* In this kind of fishing the line is let out until the bait touches bottom, then reeled in about a foot. You can feel the nibble of the fish through the sensitive rod tip. A little practice will show you when to set the hook.

3. *Tight-line fishing with the bait resting on bottom.* This is a common way of fishing for bullheads since they are bottom feeders. If you are using spinning or spincasting equipment, have the bail or pickup disengaged so the fish can take out line easily. If you are using a fly rod, keep some extra line pulled from the reel and coiled by your rod. Two or more hooks can be used in this type of fishing. Attach the sinker to the end of the monofilament or leader and attach dropper loops. Some fishermen use set lines from shore in fishing for bullheads with a tight line. Although not very sporting, this is a good way to take a lot of bullheads.

4. *Casting.* I really enjoy fly casting with live bait; if you are careful, this can be done without pulling the bait off the hook. Cast to likely cover, let the bait sink to the appropriate depth and retrieve very slowly. You can use many types of live bait and catch practically all types of panfish by this method.

5. *Drift fishing.* Use a bobber; set it so the bait will travel near the bottom and let the line out behind as the boat drifts along. If you hook a fish, anchor there to try to catch more fish from that school. Or, you can drift along with a gentle breeze and cast bobber and line ahead of you as you move ahead, stopping to anchor and still-fish only when schools of fish are located.

6. *Trolling.*   Attach enough weight on your line to get your bait down where the fish are and try to troll with your bait at that depth. Fairly large gold spinners used with worms, minnows, larvae or other baits give added attraction. I have had very excellent results trolling with spinner and live bait for crappie, white perch, yellow perch and white and yellow bass.

12

ICE FISHING

When ice fishing first became popular, the summer fishermen began to moan that taking so many fish through the ice in the winter would ruin their summer sport. This has simply not been true, at least with respect to panfish. In fact, because panfish are so prolific, the primary problem is to catch enough to keep the population down so that large fish can be harvested. Since ice fishermen began taking millions of yellow perch from Lake Mendota in Wisconsin, the fishing has improved tremendously because the numbers of fish are kept under control and the remainder now grow much larger. I can go out and catch a hundred panfish with a clear conscience, confident that I am actually improving the fishing in the lake. Only on small lakes which are subject to tremendous fishing pressure year round is this not true. The vast majority of panfish lakes need hundreds more ice fishermen. Why not join the gang?

ICE-FISHING TACKLE

One of the wonderful things about ice fishing is that you don't need a lot of expensive tackle to enjoy it and be proficient at it, since casting is never involved. All that you really need is some method of lowering a bait or artificial into the water at the end of a line. Certain refinements will enable you to catch more fish, but a line, sinker and hook alone will do an effective job.

Ice fishermen are encouraged to take as many panfish as possible on large lakes, to keep population down so large fish can be caught in the summer. This angler will stock his freezer with winter supply of yellow perch. *Michigan Conservation Dept.*

What about rod, reel and that sort of thing? You can use your standard bait-casting, spinning or spincasting outfit, but it is usually better not to, particularly in very cold weather, since your line and reel may freeze. If you want to use a pole, I would recommend a special ice-fishing rod. This is a very short, solid-glass rod with a wooden handle and a metal line holder on the handle. The line is wound around the line holder by hand. Such rods are very inexpensive.

I like these rods because they are short and light, yet flexible enough to give you plenty of fun in playing your fish. I always stick the rod handle in the ice so that the rod tip sticks out at a slant over the hole. I also put a piece of red cloth on the tip; this provides a very simple method of telling when I have a bite. Furthermore, I usually use a small bobber and leave enough slack line out so the fish can run with the bait a short distance before pulling on the rod tip. These small rods are also excellent jigging rods to use with ice flies, jigs and spoons.

Many fishermen prefer to use tip-ups in ice fishing. I think they're wonderful to use with larger game fish such as pike, pickerel or walleyes, but I don't like them too well for panfish. One reason is that some panfish (bluegills and other sunfish in particular) like to see the bait jiggled around frequently. Another reason is that panfish sometimes bite so lightly that it's hard to set a tip-up sensitive enough to record the bite. If you set your rig so the flag or other indicator will be tipped at the slightest bite, then the wind will too often release the tip-up. For this reason, I prefer the short ice-fishing rod.

What about line, bobbers, sinkers and hooks? I always use clear monofilament line; about 6- to 8-pound test is adequate unless you might hook a large northern, pickerel or walleye, in which case a 25-pound test is better. The smaller line will get you more bites, however, since it is less visible.

Your bobbers should be small: from about ½ to 1½ inches in diameter is usually best. The main thing is to have just the right amount of sinkers on your line so that the bobber will be pulled under at the slightest nibble. Split shot are usually best for sinkers. If your bobber is too small, it will not support enough sinker weight to enable the sinker to take your bait down in the water rapidly enough. Experiment to find the right combination of bobber and sinkers.

Your hooks should be small: size 10 or 12 for bluegills and other true sunfish; size 6 or 8 for other panfish. I prefer the short-shank hooks so I can cover up the hook shank with bait. The gold-colored hooks have always worked well for me. I prefer to tie my hooks directly to the monofilament line rather than use snelled hooks. Use the improved clinch knot for this purpose. (See Chapter 10).

It is helpful to have a small tackle box to hold extra supplies. Various companies make lightweight, unbreakable, plastic tackle boxes that are ideal for ice fishing. After trying these plastic boxes, I feel they are far superior to steel, wood or aluminum. They won't rust, dent or corrode and are not as cold to touch in winter as are metal boxes.

Inside my box I carry the following: extra monofilament line, sinkers, bobbers and hooks, pliers, compass, artificial ice-fishing lures, knife, flashlight, hook disgorger, matches, fish stringer, minnow scoop, ice skimmer, live bait (except minnows) and (if I have room) my lunch and a thermos jug of coffee. A 30-foot length of strong nylon rope is carried for emergencies. Such equipment will usually enable you to meet most situations you might encounter on the ice.

In addition to your tackle, there are several essentials which every ice fisherman needs, plus a good number of luxury items which can be obtained if desired.

First of all, you need an efficient tool for cutting a hole in the ice. You have several choices.

1. Ice chisel or spud. This is a steel chisel with a steel handle about 5 feet long. The best spuds are heavy, with a chisel blade about 1½ inches wide. You should keep a loop of rope tied to the upper end of the handle and keep the rope around your wrist in case you let the spud go into the water.

2. Ice auger. The Swedish ice auger has a shovel-like, sharpened blade which cuts the hole as you rotate the auger. The Lake Mille Lacs ice auger works on the same principle as an auger bit, cleaning the hole as you turn the bit. The Ice Master auger removes a solid, round core of ice. All are efficient ways of drilling holes.

3. If you want to invest a considerable amount of money, you can get power units for your ice auger—either electric motors which run off your car battery or gas-powered engines. These are a real pleasure to use, but they are expensive.

You need an ice skimmer to scoop the ice out of the hole. This is usually an aluminum scoop with holes in it.

If you are using minnows, you will need a minnow pail and a scoop to catch the minnows.

You will need a stringer, bucket or box to hold your fish.

If you will be fishing at night (bluegills and crappie both bite well at night) a gasoline lantern is a welcome addition.

There are many other items that will add to your comfort. The ice fishermen in Indiana all make wooden sleds with boxes mounted on top to store their gear in and to use as seats. They keep their fish in one section of the box, their tackle and extra clothing and miscellaneous gear in another and a gasoline lantern in another. By leaving one side of the lantern compartment open so air can get in and light can get out, these fishermen can have light and enough heat to keep warm when they are sitting on the box.

Another way to be more comfortable is to use a portable, canvas windbreak. These are lightweight affairs which are stretched over a metal frame and are open on one side. You can also buy portable, canvas fish houses which are completely enclosed.

Of course, if you want real luxury, then use a heated fish house. Most of the fishermen in North Dakota make theirs of plywood with four sides, floor and roof bolted together, allowing for dismantling and easy transport. Usually a small kerosene stove is set up inside with a metal stovepipe to take the fumes out through the roof. Some houses even come equipped with furniture, including bunks, chairs, tables and portable radios. Incidentally, if you shut out the light so that your house is dark, you can add to your fun by watching through the hole when you fish. If you are over water not over 10 to 15 feet deep, and if it is clear, place a bucket of white beans or stones on the bottom of the lake below your hole. This will help you to see your fish as it comes to bite. Also, if you can observe the fish, you'll learn much about how to get it to strike by watching the way it approaches the bait.

The fishermen of Oklahoma really have it soft. They now use floating, heated fish docks in which to do their winter fishing. The docks are built on pontoons, have enclosed sides and a roof, and are sometimes fixed up like luxury lounges with T.V., a lunch counter, easy chairs, lamps, radio and so forth. The dock is usually rectangular in shape with the open water in the center. The fishermen sit around the open water in easy chairs to do their fishing. Sometimes a smart dock owner will sink brush piles on the lake bottom under his dock to attract the school of fish.

HOW TO STAY WARM

Most of us are not so fortunate as to be able to fish from heated houses or docks so we have to learn how to keep warm in the open. This is not too difficult, even in very cold weather, if you know how to dress warm. I have spent many days ice fishing when the temperature was down to zero and have been snug and warm for six hours.

Let me give some specific suggestions which are based on many years of experience in cold-weather fishing. First of all, wear lightweight, insulated, loose-fitting but windproof clothing. This traps the warm, dead air next to your skin and keeps the wind from blowing your body heat away. This type of clothing is much warmer than the heavy, snugly fitting kind, provided there is enough insulation to keep your body heat from escaping.

The clothing which best fulfills this requirement is the quilted, insulated underwear worn under wind-resistant, outer garments. The best suits of underwear are filled with Dacron Fiber-Fill with nylon covering. You can get underwear filled with 5 ounces of Dacron per yard or with 3 ounces per yard. Obviously, the 5-ounce material is the warmest. Put the insulated underwear over your regular undergarments. If the weather is 10° or below, you may need two suits of insulated underwear, one 5 ounce and the other 3 ounce.

Over the underwear, wear one pair of windproof trousers; a finely woven wool is excellent. Or you can wear just any old cotton or rayon trousers and over them wear the trousers of a rubberized rain suit. The rubberized trousers give complete protection from the wind and any dampness. I put on a wool shirt over the top part of my underwear and then a lightweight, quilted, Dacron Fiber-Fill parka with an artificial fur-lined hood to go over my neck and head. The parka has a nylon cover and is windproof. If the weather is extremely cold, I may wear a wool headpiece under the parka hood. The headpiece completely covers my neck, head and the lower part of my face in front up to just below my nose.

For gloves, it is well to remember that loosely fitted, insulated mittens are warmer than any type of closely fitting gloves. My mittens are also of Dacron Fiber-Fill covered with nylon. They are a bit bulky so when the weather is not too cold I wear my leather pigskin gloves which are insulated inside with a layer of foam rubber covered with nylon cloth.

To keep my feet warm, I wear two pair of boot-high wool socks and my insulated, rubber Korean-type boots which fit loosely on my feet. These boots look like ordinary rubber boots which come up to the calf of the leg, except these have an inch of felt insulation between the outer and inner sole, and a layer of insulation, between two layers of rubber, in the foot and sides. The boots are waterproof and extremely warm. I can stand out on the ice all day in zero weather and my feet will never get cold. I prefer this type of boot to the insulated leather boot.

Sometimes fishermen will have trouble keeping their feet or hands warm. One way to prevent the extremities from getting cold is to make certain your head is warm. This sounds strange but it is true. There are many, many blood vessels in the head to insure proper circulation in this most exposed part of the body. If your head is chilled, much of your blood is pumped there to keep your head warm, depriving your limbs of the circulation they need. For this reason, always have your head well covered, including the lower part of your face when necessary.

WHEN AND WHERE TO FISH

Part of the secret of successful ice fishing is in knowing where to fish and when to catch them. Let's first discuss the subject of finding the fish.

Make your task of catching fish easier by selecting the best water available to you. In Chapter 14 I give a state-by-state list of best panfishing waters across the United States. These evaluations were made by the men who know best—the state game and fish biologists— so try some of the places.

After having selected a lake or river, how do you know where to fish? If you have never fished the water during the summer and do not know the contour of the bottom, you might try and get a topographical map which shows water depth. Most states have made some surveys of their lakes and can provide you with helpful maps.

I like to do my ice fishing in fairly deep water. Usually at the very beginning of the ice-fishing season the fish will be in medium-depth water; then, as the cold weather increases, they move to the depths.

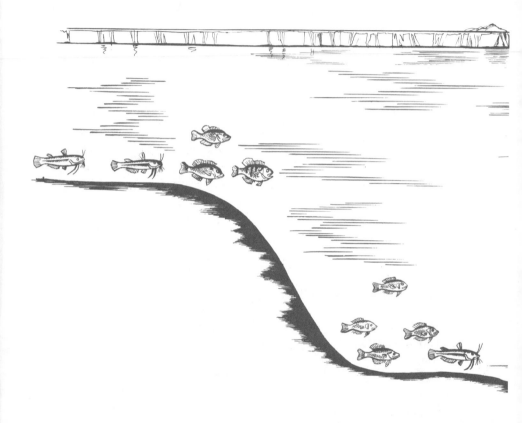

Panfish seek different depths under the ice. Knowing what fish a lake holds, the winter angler would do well to fish for them just off the bottom at the depths shown in the diagram.

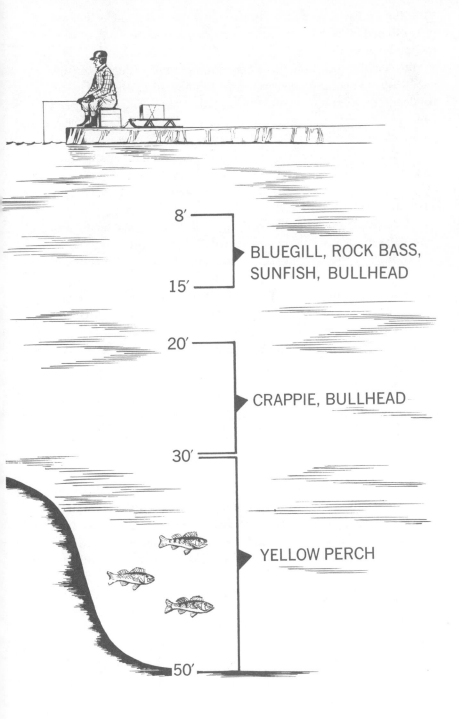

8'
15'

BLUEGILL, ROCK BASS,
SUNFISH, BULLHEAD

20'

CRAPPIE, BULLHEAD

30'

YELLOW PERCH

50'

After the ice has been on the lake for several months and as the oxygen is depleted in the very deep water, the fish move back again to the medium-depth water.

For bluegills, rock bass and other common sunfish, depths of from about 8 to 15 feet are about right. In shallow lakes, the fish are in the deepest water they can find. Bluegill like to hang out around weed beds, stumps, rocks and brush piles, but you may find them in comparatively open water in the winter. However, if you know of good cover in 8 to 15 feet of water, you might try those places first before moving on someplace else. Also, even in water 8 to 15 feet deep, try fishing at various depths. Sunfish sometimes swim around only a few inches below the ice.

Yellow perch generally like deep water, especially the larger fish, unless the oxygen has become depleted in the depths by the decay of vegetable matter. Extensive research studies in Lake Mendota in Wisconsin have shown that the greatest winter concentrations of perch are found in depths of from 30 to 50 feet. Perch were found from 10 to 50 feet below the ice, but ice fishing was most successful in the deeper water.

I have had excellent results in fishing over deep-water bars which are surrounded by still deeper water. Especially during warm sunshiny days, the perch come over the bars to feed. Usually about 15 feet of water or more over a bar is best. If this doesn't bring results, then try the deeper water around the edges of the bar. I have never had much success, at least with large perch, in the shallow water near shore. These fish seek out the depths so you had better, too.

Crappie seem to like the medium-deep water, usually from 20 to 30 feet, or, in shallow lakes, the deepest water they can find. Sometimes, especially early in the ice-fishing season, crappie will cruise around just below the ice, so try putting your bait only a few feet under if you do not have any luck near the bottom.

Try to look for weed-free depths. However, crappie will concentrate around underwater brush, so look for these places or for other cover such as old auto bodies. Deep holes bordered on all sides by shallow water are good spots as is the deeper water off bars and drop-offs. In deep lakes, don't waste much time in water less than 20 feet deep as the crappie will not usually be there.

I confess I do not hear very much about ice fishing for white and yellow bass. I've done a lot of ice fishing for white perch and find them most receptive to small minnows fished in medium-depth water. White and yellow bass are fish of the open water, moving about freely looking for schools of minnows, shad or smelt. Therefore, look for them in water 20 to 40 feet deep.

Bullheads will bite some in the winter, although these species are not usually sought after through the ice. If you do fish for them, then fish over the muddy-bottom areas of lakes and rivers. The depth may vary from 8 to about 30 feet.

Since all panfish swim in schools, and since the schools of fish are sometimes stationary, you will do well to change your location if you have not had a bite after thirty minutes or so in one spot. Probably you're in the wrong area and the panfish are not moving around enough to find your bait. If the fish are biting well and then suddenly cease, the school has probably moved off. You can either move or wait until another school swims along. If I am in an area where I have been catching fish, I am usually willing to wait.

Another excellent place to fish is near springs, streams or river inlets to a lake, or wherever warmer water may be flowing in. One lake I used to fish regularly had a spring of water running into it all year round. There were always concentrations of fish near or around that inlet. You do have to be extremely careful about walking on thin ice in such places, however.

You will also find that certain spots in any lake or river are usually good year after year, so try to keep the good ones in mind for another year. Also, if certain holes are productive, I usually try to mark them in some way so I can return to them on the next trip. One sand bar where I fished for yellow perch was good each winter for years; it will probably still produce hundreds of fish years from now.

I think it is important also that you fish at the right time of day. By far the best time for bluegills and other true sunfish is from late afternoon until dark. You may take them early in the morning, midday or midnight, but late afternoon is consistently the best time.

For yellow perch, you will usually have your best luck from midmorning to mid-afternoon. Perch may bite every hour of the day, but the middle of the day is usually best, especially on warm, sunny days. The schools of perch disband and settle quietly to the bottom in shallow water to rest at night; there is no use in fishing for yellow perch after dark.

Crappie, on the other hand, bite very well all night long. They will also bite at other times of the day, but late afternoon, evening and night are best for these fish.

Bullheads, of course, are notoriously nocturnal. Your best fishing for these fish will begin after the sun goes down.

White perch and white and yellow bass will feed early morning, during the day, in late afternoon, or at night. I have found early morning and late afternoon a little better than other times, but go fishing for these fish anytime.

BAITS FOR ICE FISHING

For bluegills, rock bass, pumpkinseeds and other true sunfish, small larvae are the best possible baits for ice fishing. The sunfish feed much more daintily in the winter and so they like small baits rather than the bigger mouthfuls which they will gobble up in the summer. The best baits to use when ice fishing for bluegills are caddis worms, crane-fly larvae or pupae, catalpa worms (use only part of the worm in winter), meal worms, gall worms and maggots.

Yellow perch are the least particular of all the panfish sought after through the ice. You can use any of the land or water insects or their larvae, small, live minnows or earthworms, or prepared baits, especially yellow-perch eyes or pieces of minnow. My two favorite baits for yellow perch are small minnows and yellow-perch eyes.

The best all-around winter bait for crappie is small minnows about 1 or 1½ inches long. The same larvae used to catch bluegill will also catch crappie, but I don't believe they are as effective as minnows.

The best winter baits for white and yellow bass are minnows. These can measure up to about 2½ inches, depending on how large the fish are running. White perch will take various larvae, earthworms and small, live minnows. Minnows, however, are the best bait.

Use some of your prepared baits for bullheads, or use earthworms, crawfish tails or any dead bait you may happen to have. All are good.

ARTIFICIALS

Many fishermen prefer to use artificial lures for ice fishing. When the fish are biting readily, artificials are cleaner and faster. There will be times, however, when the fish will not touch artificial lures and want only live bait. Sometimes using some live bait on artificials is just the right combination. Under different circumstances the fishermen must use different techniques and lures; the point is, learn to be flexible and to use whatever the situation demands.

There are three principal types of artificials used in ice fishing.

1. *Ice flies or jigs.* These come in a variety of materials, weights and colors. Use the very small sizes (about $\frac{1}{64}$ ounce with size 10 hooks) for bluegills and sunfish and a little larger ones (up to $\frac{1}{8}$ ounce with size 6 or 8 hook) for large crappie, yellow perch, white perch and white or yellow bass. Specific recommendations for ice flies and jigs are found in Chapter 9. The standard colors are white, black or yellow, although a variety of colors are also used: blue, orange, red, green and combinations. Some anglers prefer the waving motion of marabou or hackle feathers; others like the action of the bucktail jig. My advice is to get a variety.

In fishing an ice fly, lower the jig to the bottom and then wiggle it, jig it up and down slowly, give it all sorts of gentle action as you pull it very slowly to the surface. It is the movement of the lure which is so attractive to panfish.

Sometimes the fish will rush up to the lure and fail to strike. Try smaller sizes or change the color or basic type. If this doesn't work, put a small larva or some other bait on the hook with the fly.

2. *Jigging spoons.* These are good lures to use for crappie, yellow perch, white perch and white and yellow bass, although these fish will only take jigging spoons at certain times. However, the flashing, fluttering spoon will always attract the fish; if they refuse to take it, substitute an ice fly, or put a small piece of live bait on the spoon hook. You should purchase the jigging spoons in the smallest sizes available since you will not have to cast them.

Spoons are jigged up and down with an action similar to that used for ice flies. Lower the spoon to the bottom. Raise it slowly, jigging it up and down, sometimes letting it flutter slowly to the bottom again. A small piece of pork rind on the spoon gives it a nice action.

3. *Nature lures.* Plastic imitations of natural bait can be used in ice fishing. Such imitations include earthworms, plastic larvae such as the mousie, corn borer, inch worm or meal worm, and insects such as crickets, grasshoppers and cockroaches. In order to catch fish with these plastics, you have to jig them up and down slowly.

SAFETY ON ICE

There are several rules you ought to follow to avoid accidents while ice fishing.

1. Never go ice fishing alone. Always take a companion along so you will have help if something should go wrong. If you should travel to the lake or river alone, pick a spot near another fisherman to do your fishing. You may need help for any one of a number of good reasons. You might fall through the ice. Your car may get stuck in the snow or a bad fall on the ice may hurt you or knock you out. It's not hard to freeze to death if you fall in, or if your car won't start and you're miles from home, or if you should knock yourself out by hitting your head on the ice.

2. Make certain the ice is thick enough before you go fishing. Ordinarily, 4 to 6 inches of ice is about the minimum thickness to support, with complete safety, the weight of a grown man. Never drive on the ice with your car unless it is at least 18 inches thick. A few years ago I was ice fishing on a lake near our home and, after looking at the ice, which varied in depth from about 4 to 12 inches, decided definitely against driving my car on the lake, in spite of the fact that another car was already on it. Before the afternoon's fishing was over, however, the front end of this other car had fallen through a thin spot and the car was suspended at the edge of the hole. The two occupants ran for their lives, completely helpless to do anything to save their car. They let the car stay right there for several weeks until the ice was thicker and got a wrecker to pull it to safety.

3. Stay only on well-marked paths or roads, either walking or driving. On large lakes, the safe car roads are well-marked. If you drive off by yourself down a large and strange lake on unmarked ice, you're taking your life into your hands. Some lakes have underwater springs or currents which cause thin spots in the ice. Individuals have been known to get lost on large lakes in fog, blizzards or at night. It's wise to take a compass along when you go far from shore on a large lake.

4. Take a shovel, sand, chains or emergency equipment along in case your car gets stuck in the snow. A full tank of gas also comes in mighty handy if you have to keep your car and heater on for several hours to keep warm.

5. If you use a stove in your ice house, make certain it is adequately

vented so there is no danger from carbon monoxide poisoning.

6. Avoid prolonged exposure of bare skin to cold winds. You can freeze a spot before you realize it. Severe frostbite is a serious matter. If you take precautions, you can keep all parts of you warm in the coldest weather.

7. Don't chop your hole too near the other fellow's, or you may get killed. Don't make the hole too large; you may fall in.

8. Never let your retriever take more than the legal limit of fish from your neighbor's ice house. It's not sportsmanlike.

9. Never leave your fish house on the ice until the lilacs bloom or your may have to float it home.

10. And most important of all, never stay home in the winter and freeze in a drafty house, get out on the ice and fish. You might as well enjoy yourself, you're going to get the flu anyway.

13

CLEANING, PRESERVING AND COOKING PANFISH

The real proof of the panfishing is in the eating. Few fish surpass panfish for flavor and delicate meat texture. But as with all fish, if they are to taste their best they must be cleaned and cooked properly. I've tasted some bluegills that were as hard and dry as old shoe leather; others could have won a gourmet's prize. The same applies to preparing the other species of panfish—they can be tasteless or they can be delicious.

This chapter contains step-by-step instructions for the very best methods of cleaning, preserving and cooking your fish. I know some of you have been eating panfish for years, but I also know from experience that many of you have been partially ruining your fish by your methods of cleaning, freezing and cooking. All I ask is that you keep an open mind as you read this chapter.

CLEANING WHOLE FISH

Though most fishermen are used to cleaning and cooking panfish whole, large white or yellow bass, crappie, yellow or white perch are better filleted. This section then, applies just to the smaller species of panfish.

The cleaning procedure is simple, but is made easier if you proceed in the following order.

1. Bleed the fish by cutting their throats. This gives them a cleaner flavor. The fish, of course, will bleed more easily if still alive. (This is usually a more humane method of killing them than hitting them over the head several times.) The easiest way is to cut just behind the gills across the inverted V section. Cut deeply enough to sever the main artery behind the heart, or the heart itself, which is located just behind the gills.

2. Cut out the dorsal fin by running the blade of your knife next to the fin and parallel to it, cutting deeply enough to cut out the sharp spines from the flesh. Begin at the front of the fin and cut along one side, then turn the fish over and cut along the other side of the fin, until the fin is free from the back of the fish.

3. Cut out the anal fin by running your knife across and underneath the fin and perpendicular to the body of the fish, cutting from back to front along the fish. Be certain to cut deeply enough to remove the spines which are embedded in the flesh.

4. Cut off the tail or caudal fin next. However, you can remove this fin at any time you desire. I would advise leaving the two ventral fins and two pectoral fins until later, for reasons which will become more obvious.

5. Scale the fish. This is much easier to do before the entrails are removed. If your fish is fresh and not dried out, the scales will come off easily. If your fish has been dead for some time, all scales are harder to remove.

Several different scaling instruments can be used. For small, fresh panfish, I find a small knife as easy to use as anything. On a little larger fish, a regular fish scaler with a sawtooth edge is perhaps easier. Some fishermen's knives have a special scaling blade. These too are satisfactory. In scaling, scrape the knife along the skin of the fish from the tail to the head, applying just enough pressure to scrape the scales off.

6. Cut off the head of the fish, cutting just behind the gill cover and the pectoral fins, making certain that all gills are cut off along with the fish's head.

7. Remove the entrails. First, split open the fish's belly, beginning from the anal vent and cutting forward to the front. Then run your thumb along the body cavity from rear to front, pushing out all insides, breaking the air sac and removing the dark matter beneath the sac.

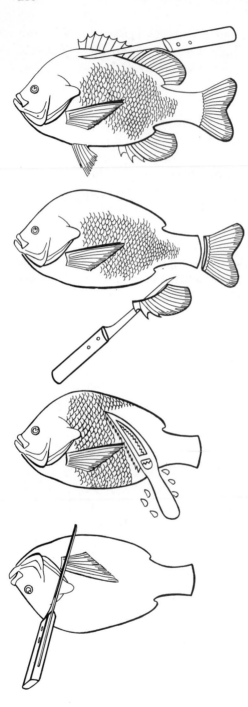

HOW TO CLEAN A WHOLE PANFISH

1. Cut out the dorsal fin by running the knife along each side of the fin, cutting out sharp spines.

2. Cut out anal fin by running the knife across and underneath the fin, cutting from back to front.

3. Scale the fish. Fish scaler with sawtooth edge does quickest job, although an ordinary knife will do.

4. Cut off the head by cutting just behind the gill cover. Then remove the entrails and cut out ventral fins.

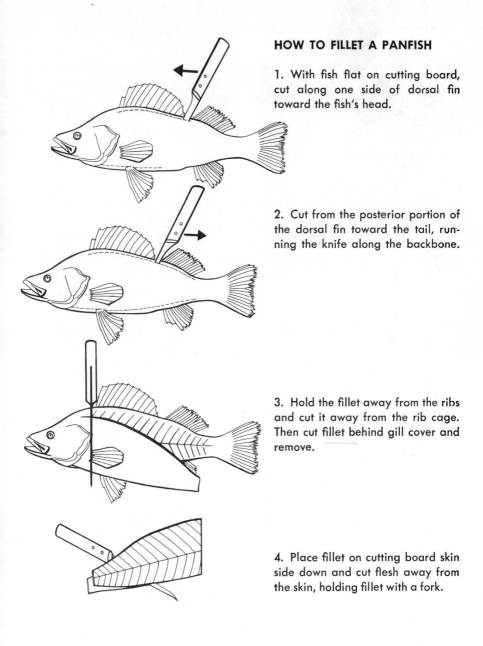

HOW TO FILLET A PANFISH

1. With fish flat on cutting board, cut along one side of dorsal fin toward the fish's head.

2. Cut from the posterior portion of the dorsal fin toward the tail, running the knife along the backbone.

3. Hold the fillet away from the ribs and cut it away from the rib cage. Then cut fillet behind gill cover and remove.

4. Place fillet on cutting board skin side down and cut flesh away from the skin, holding fillet with a fork.

8. Cut out the ventral fins which remain on the two sides of the split belly of the fish, being certain to cut out the bony spines which penetrate the fish.

9. Wash the fish in preparation for cooking.

The above procedure is one that I have found simplest and easiest after many years of cleaning fish whole and after trying a variety of methods.

FILLETING AND SKINNING

I prefer filleting panfish which are large enough. The reasons are simple: I can fillet a fish easier and quicker than I can clean it whole and the fillet makes for bone-free eating.

Whenever I suggest filleting panfish, someone always asks, "But doesn't filleting waste a lot of meat?" The answer is definitely no. When done properly, filleting recovers most of the edible portions of the fish. Furthermore, it enables you to really enjoy your eating or to use your fillets for chowder and in other ways requiring meat without bones. Unless the panfish is smaller than about 6 inches, I generally fillet it.

Filleting is not difficult. Lay the fish flat on the cutting board and cut along one side of the dorsal fin toward the fish's head, cutting deeply into the flesh and along the back bone, holding the fillet away from the bone as you are cutting. After this incision is made, then cut from the posterior portion of the dorsal fin, back toward the tail of the fish, by sticking the knife blade through the fish's side, along the backbone, with the knife edge facing the fish's tail. Move the blade back and forth, as you guide the blade along the backbone toward the fish's tail. After this is cut free, then hold the fillet away from the ribs and cut the fillet away from the rib cage until the only portion of the fillet attached to the fish is just behind the gill covers. Now cut the fillet behind the gill covers, removing the fillet entirely from the carcass of the fish.

Please note that you have not removed entrails, scales or fins before filleting. If you have filleted properly, the whole side of meat should be free of the fish with only skin and scales on the side (no fins). The entrails remain in the fish carcass as waste portion to be thrown away.

After this, turn the fish over and cut away the fillet from the other side by the same procedure. Throw the fish carcass away.

Last, skin the fish by placing the fillet on the cutting board *skin side down*. Begin at the tail end, holding the fillet with a fork, begin cutting the flesh away from the skin by passing the knife between the flesh and the skin. If you keep the knife slanted slightly toward the skin, the meat will be cut away easily, yet without cutting through the tough skin and scales of the fish, as you move the knife forward. After you have skinned two or three fillets, you will find you can cut the flesh free from the skin with one deft motion of the knife. The scales, of course, remain attached to the skin, which is thrown away.

If you have followed these directions properly, you will have two fillets of solid meat from each fish, completely free of bones, skin and scales. After you have practiced filleting your fish, you'll find this a much faster way than cleaning them whole, and more pleasant, as it is not necessary to clean out the entrails.

CLEANING BULLHEADS

Bullheads are in a special category all of their own when it comes to cleaning. Many people—even those who love to eat them—hate to clean bullheads. It is somewhat of a messy job, but it can be even messier if you do not know how.

Immediately after catching the bullheads, bleed and kill them by cutting their throat. The next step is to cut out all of the fins. Then cut the skin only around the head; grab the skin with pliers and pull back toward the tail. After the skin is off, slit open the belly and remove the entrails. Finally, remove the head and the tail. Wash the fish in cold water.

FREEZING METHODS

The principal problem in freezing fish is to keep them from drying out and free of freezer burn. All fish will become dehydrated over a period of time in a freezer, particularly if not tightly wrapped or otherwise protected from the cold air. The solution to this problem, therefore, is to properly protect the flesh before freezing. This protection can be provided in several ways.

One way, is to freeze the fish whole without cleaning or skinning. Actually, the skin and scales of fish provide excellent protection against dehydration, so I find it best to leave the fish intact, packing them tightly in packages of convenient size. They can be first wrapped in packages with cellophane paper, then with white freezer paper over that, making certain to squeeze out as much air as possible. Some people prefer packing them in empty, washed milk cartons, or in special freezer cartons, being certain to seal the cartons with freezer tape.

Another way to protect them from dehydration is to put them in waterproof containers, then fill the containers with water, freezing the fish in a solid block of ice. This method will preserve your fish almost indefinitely.

Be certain, however, that you freeze your fish immediately after catching. If the fish is not cleaned, it spoils readily in warm weather. Never thaw it out until just before you are ready to clean it.

In the winter, if you want to pack, freeze and preserve large quantities of panfish—perhaps up to hundreds of fish—pack them in empty cardboard cartons, alternating layers of fish and clean snow. Put a 3-inch layer of snow on the bottom of the carton, then one layer of fish, then 1 inch of snow, and so forth, topping off the box with another 3-inch layer of snow. Seal the box so that it is airtight. I've kept several hundred fish in my freezer all winter by this method. Sometimes I've kept them out of doors for over a month in freezing weather. You must be careful, however, not to let your fish thaw out until ready to use.

If you insist upon cleaning your fish whole, or filleting them before freezing, then be doubly certain to have your packages wrapped with moisture-proof cellophane paper and freezer paper or else to freeze the pieces in solid blocks of ice.

Fillets are the hardest to keep over long periods of time without dehydration, but they can be kept if packed tightly in moisture-proof packages from which all air has been removed, of if frozen in ice. I do feel, however, that in spite of all precautions, the fillets loose some juicyness and flavor when frozen for long periods of time. For this reason, I prefer freezing whole fish and thawing and filleting as needed.

FRIED PANFISH

There are a number of rules that should be followed when preparing panfish in the skillet.

If the fish is cleaned whole, with skin intact, simply rub it slightly with oleomargarine or butter, and season to taste with salt, pepper, or even onion or garlic salt if desired. Then fry in a hot skillet.

If the fish is filleted and skinless, always roll in canned milk, and/or beaten whole egg, and then in bread crumbs, cracker crumbs or corn meal before frying. This batter will keep the fillet from drying out and will make it a golden-brown color. I prefer a fairly thin batter in order not to hide the taste of the fish. If you like a lot of batter on your fillets, dip them in the liquid, and then in the crumbs or meal several times before frying.

Your fish can either be deep-fried (French fried) or pan fried. Generally, whole fish are pan fried. Fillets can either be pan fried or French fried. If you are French frying your catch, make certain the fat is fresh, never rancid, and fairly hot—about 375° F.—before frying. Fry quickly, and until the outside is a golden-brown color, making certain not to overcook the fish. If you fry the fillet too long, it will be dried out and tasteless, or the outside may be too dark a color. If the fat is too hot, the batter will get dark before the fish is cooked. The secret is to keep the fat at a proper temperature and to cook for a proper period of time. The mistake most cooks make is to overcook the fish.

In pan frying your fish, use plently of butter (my favorite), salt port, bacon fat or oleomargarine (it burns easily) in the skillet. Cook the fish enough on one side before turning it over and cooking on the other side. By turning the fish only once, you can keep it intact.

BAKED PANFISH

Practically all types of panfish can be baked whole or filleted. My favorite recipes are the following:

1. Place about 1 pound of fillets in a baking pan and add 1 can of undiluted mushroom soup, making certain the liquid just covers the fish. Preheat oven to 350° and then bake fillets until tender.

2. Rub each whole fish in butter or oleomargarine, season to taste, then wrap individually in aluminum foil. Bake at 350° until tender, making certain oven is preheated before putting in fish.

3. Put alternate layers of panfish fillets and American cheese in a casserole dish (using about three times as much fish as cheese), dusting each layer with flour. Then pour whole milk into dish until fillets are barely covered. Top with a layer of Parmesan cheese and

bake in oven at 350° until fillets are tender.

BROILED PANFISH

If you want to broil your fish, I would suggest that you do so only with whole fish, with the skin (not scales) on, otherwise the fish has a tendency to dry out in cooking. Rub the fish with butter or oleo-margarine, season to taste and broil until tender, turning once in the process of cooking. The fish are delicious served with a slice of lemon.

FISH CHOWDER

One of the most delicious fish dishes is chowder, prepared as follows:

Dice six medium-size potatoes and four medium-size onions, place in a large pan, cover with water and boil until done. Add approximately 1½ pounds of cut-up panfish fillets, cook until tender. Add two tablespoons of melted fat of salt pork and 1 cubic inch of butter. Add fresh or canned milk as desired, heat but be careful not to boil the milk. Add salt and pepper as desired.

For a thicker chowder, reduce the amount of water and milk, or add more fish. The more fish added per amount of potato and onion, the more tasty the chowder.

14

PANFISHING
ACROSS THE
UNITED STATES

In order to guide the reader to some of the best panfishing in the United States, a questionnaire was sent to the fish and game departments of each of the fifty states. The departments were each asked to name five bodies of water in their own state which they considered best for catching each of the species of fish which are discussed in this book.

Not all of the species of panfish are found in every state. Some of the departments were reluctant to choose the best water from hundreds or even thousands of lakes and from many miles of river and stream. Other departments mentioned that they were recommending only the largest bodies of water. These indicated that some of the finest panfishing might be found in much smaller lakes, streams or ponds.

Therefore, while it is practically impossible to include every small pond or stream in such a survey, I am nevertheless convinced that the following summary should serve as an extremely helpful guide to most readers.

ALABAMA

Bluegill   Guntersville Reservoir, Yates Reservoir, Thurlow Reservoir, Pickwick Reservoir, all state-owned fishing lakes.

Green Sunfish   Statewide distribution in streams, reservoirs, and ponds, no records of localized abundance.

Redear Sunfish   Guntersville Reservoir, Yates Reservoir, Thurlow Reservoir, Pickwick Reservoir, most state-owned fishing lakes.

Longear Sunfish   Found statewide, no records of abundance.

Yellowbreast or Redbreast Sunfish   Coosa, Tallapoosa, Apalachicola river systems. Recently introduced in Tenn. River. No records of abundance.

Spotted Sunfish   Found South of Tenn. River, no records of abundance.

Black Crappie   Weiss Reservoir, Guntersville Reservoir, Lake Eufaula, Millers Ferry Reservoir, Lake Jordan, Lay Lake, Pickwick Reservoir.

White Crappie   Same as black crappie.

Rock Bass   Found statewide in cool, clear streams, moderate gradients, gravel to rubble bottoms. No knowledge of abundance in various streams.

Warmouth Bass   Throughout the state, no records of abundance.

Yellow Perch   Guntersville Reservoir, Lake Harding, Lake Eufaula, Mobile Bay drainage.

White Bass   Lake Eufaula, Jordan Lake, Guntersville Reservoir, Pickwick Reservoir, Logan Martin Reservoir.

Yellow Bass   Inland Lake, Guntersville Reservoir, Mobile-Tensaw rivers.

Black Bullhead   Tenn. River system, Mobile Bay drainage system, no records of abundance.

Brown Bullhead   Statewide, no records of abundance.

Yellow Bullhead   Statewide, no records of abundance.

ALASKA

None of the species of panfish discussed in this book are found in the fresh waters of Alaska.

ARIZONA

Bluegill   Alamo Lake, Apache Lake, Arivaca Lake, Lake Havasu, Pena Blanca Lake.

Green Sunfish   Apache Lake, Canyon Lake, Lake Pleasant, Parker Canyon Lake, and Saguaro Lake.

Redear Sunfish   Arivaca Lake, Imperial Reservoir, Lower Colorado River, Parker Canyon Lake, and Patagonia Lake.

Black Crappie   Bartlett Lake, Lake Havasu, Lake Mead, San Carlos Lake, Roosevelt Lake.

White Crappie   Lake Pleasant.

Warmouth Bass   Apache Lake, Imperial Reservoir, Lower Colorado River.

Yellow Perch   Lyman Lake, McClelland Lake, Pecks Lake, Stoneman Lake.

White Bass   Lake Pleasant.

Yellow Bass   Canyon Lake, Apache Lake, Saguaro Lake.

Black Bullhead   Alamo Lake, Apache Lake, Canyon Lake, Roosevelt Lake, White Mountain Lake.

Yellow Bullhead   Mormon Lake, Lower Lake Mary, Upper Lake Mary.

ARKANSAS

Bluegill   Conway Lake, Harris Brake Lake, Lake Atkins, Lake Ashbaugh, Lake Overcup.

Green Sunfish   Statewide. Extremely common in ditches in East Arkansas.

Readear Sunfish   Conway Lake, Lake Atkins, Storm Creek Lake, Lake Atkins, Lake Erling.

Longear Sunfish   Most common sunfish in streams in Ozark and Ouachita streams. Statewide in smaller numbers. Same streams as rock bass.

Yellowbreast or Redbreast Sunfish   Not common, occasionally occurring in headwaters and streams of the White and Arkansas river systems.

Spotted Sunfish   Throughout Eastern and Southern Arkansas, in most delta streams and ditches.

Black Crappie   Lake Des Arc, Lake Erling, Lake Overcup, Lake Conway.

White Crappie   Millwood Lake, Blue Mountain Lake, Lake Conway, Overcup Lake.

Rock Bass   Buffalo River, Kings River, Strawberry River, Crooked Creek, Caddo River.

Warmouth Bass   Des Arc Lake, Millwood Lake, Gillham Reservoir, Arkansas River Oxbow lakes, White River Oxbow lakes.

White Bass   Beaver Lake, Bull Shoals Lake, Lake Hamilton, Greeson Lake, Arkansas River system.

Yellow Bass   Millwood Lake, Mississippi River Old River Lakes, Mallard Lake.

Black Bullhead   Statewide.

Brown Bullhead   Statewide, but not as common as other two bullheads. Most collected have been from headwaters of Gulf Coast plains streams in South Arkansas.

Yellow Bullhead   Same as for black bullhead.

CALIFORNIA

Bluegill   Clear Lake, San Antonio Reservoir.

Green Sunfish   No significant fishery.

Redear Sunfish   Nacimiento Lake, San Antonio Reservoir.

Pumpkinseed Sunfish   Big Bear Lake.

Sacramento Perch   Crowley Lake, Lake Almanor.

Black Crappie   Clear Lake, Lake Nacimiento, Lake Isabella.

White Crappie   Clear Lake, Lake Isabella.
Warmouth Bass   No significant fisheries.
Yellow Perch   Copco Lake, Iron Gate Reservoir.
White Bass   Lake Nacimiento, Lake Kaweah.
Black Bullhead   Folsom Lake.
Brown Bullhead   Clear Lake, Folsom Lake.
Yellow Bullhead   No significant fishery.

COLORADO

Bluegill   Pueblo Reservoir, found throughout state.
Green Sunfish   John Martin Reservoir, Pueblo Reservoir, Chatfield Reservoir.
Pumpkinseed Sunfish   Found throughout east slope of Colorado.
Sacramento Perch   Barr Lake.
Black Crappie   Bonny Reservoir, Sterling Reservoir, Pueblo Reservoir, Timber Reservoir, Chatfield Reservoir.
White Crappie   Navaho Reservoir.
Yellow Perch   Sanchez Reservoir, Narraquinup Reservoir, Chatfield Reservoir, Cheeseman Reservoir, Cherry Creek Reservoir.
White Bass   Bonny Reservoir, John Martin Reservoir, not widespread elsewhere.
Black Bullhead   Pueblo Reservoir, Engineers Reservoir, common throughout east slope of the state.

CONNECTICUT

Bluegill   Pachaug Pond, Candlewood Lake, Hopeville Pond, Pataganset Lake, Beachdale Pond.
Green Sunfish   None listed.
Pumpkinseed Sunfish   Most warmwater ponds.
Yellowbreast or Redbreast Sunfish   None listed.
Black Crappie   Bantam Lake, Mashapang Lake, Lake of Isles, Pataganset Lake, Lake Lillinonah.
White Crappie   Only a few around.
Rock Bass   East Twin Lake.
Yellow Perch   Candlewood Lake, Mooduc Reservoir, Quaddick Reservoir, Highland Lake, Rogers Lake.
White Perch   Bantam Lake, Lake Lillinonah, Lake Zoar, Squantz Pond.
Black Bullhead   None listed.
Brown Bullhead   Anderson Pond, Beachdale Pond, Black Pond, Bantam Lake, Powers Lake.

DELAWARE

Bluegill   Garrison Lake, Silver Lake (Dover), Records Pond, Beck Pond, Noxontown Lake.

Pumpkinseed Sunfish   Same as bluegill.
Black Crappie   Garrison Lake, Lake Como, Lums Pond, Red Mill Pond, Records Pond.
White Crappie   Lums Pond.
Rock Bass   Brandywine Creek.
Yellow Perch   Lums Pond, Moores Lake, Red Mill Pond, Records Pond, Trap Pond.
White Perch   Any tidal stream, Lake Como, Moores Lake, Noxontown Pond, Red Mill Pond.
Brown Bullhead   Andrews Lake, Garrison Lake, most tidal streams in fresh water, Red Mill Pond, Silver Lake (Dover).
Yellow Bullhead   Rare everywhere.

FLORIDA

The Game and Fish Commission sent information listing the prime fishing areas in each of five geographic regions in Florida. They are as follows:

NORTHWEST REGION

Apalachicola River   Bluegill, Redear Sunfish, Redbreast Sunfish, White Bass.
Lake Talquin   Bluegill, Redear Sunfish, Black Crappie.
Lake Jackson   Bluegill, Redear Sunfish, Black Crappie.
Hurricane Lake   Bullhead (Brown and Yellow).
Juniper Lake   Bluegill.

NORTHEAST REGION

Orange Lake   Bluegill, Redear Sunfish, Black Crappie, Warmouth Bass.
Lochloosa Lake   Bluegill, Redear Sunfish, Black Crappie.
Santa Fe River   Redbreast Sunfish.
Suwannee River   Redbreast Sunfish.
Newnans Lake   Bluegill, Redear Sunfish, Black Crappie.

CENTRAL REGION

W. Lake Tohopekaliga   Bluegill, Redear Sunfish, Black Crappie.
Lake Kissimmee   Bluegill, Redear Sunfish, Black Crappie.
Lake George   Bluegill, Redear Sunfish, Black Crappie.
Lake Panasoffkee   Bluegill, Redear Sunfish.
Oklawaha River   (Including Rodman Reservoir)—Bluegill, Redear Sunfish.

SOUTH REGION

Winter Haven Chain of Lakes   Bluegill, Crappie.
Lake Pierce   Bluegill, Black Crappie.

Lake Reedy
Lake Clinch
Lake Istokpoga   Bluegill, Black Crappie.
Lake Weohyakapka   Redear Sunfish, Black Crappie.

EVERGLADES REGION

Lake Okeechobee   Bluegill, Black Crappie, Bullheads.
Everglades Conservation Areas   Bluegill, Redear Sunfish, Warmouth Bass, Bullhead.
Lake Osborne   Bluegill, Black Crappie, Bullhead.
Blue Cypress Lake   Bluegill, Redear Sunfish, Spotted Sunfish, Black Crappie, Bullhead.
Lake Trafford   Redear Sunfish.

GEORGIA   (From a previous survey)

Bluegill   Lake Lanier, Lake Seminole, Lake Clark Hill, Lake Allatoona and Lake Burton.
Warmouth Bass   Okeefenokee Swamp, private ponds and all south Georgia rivers.
White and Black Crappie   Lake Allatoona, Lake Lanier, Lake Seminole, Lake Sinclair and Jackson Lake.
Longear Sunfish   Satilla River, Oconee River and Ochmulgee River.
Yellow Perch   Lake Burton, Lake Clark Hill, Lake Lanier, Lake Rabon and Lake Seed.
White Bass   Bartlett's Ferry, Goats Rock, Lake Allatoona, Lake Clark Hill and Lake Lanier.
Bullhead   Lake Nottley, Lake Sinclair and Bartlett's Ferry.

HAWAII

Bluegill   Wahiawa Reservoir, Oahu; Waita Reservoir, Kauai; Wailua Reservoir, Kauai; Tanaka Reservoir, Kauai; Puu Kaele Reservoir, Kauai.

IDAHO

Bluegill   No specific waters listed.
Green Sunfish   No specific waters listed.
Pumpkinseed Sunfish   No specific waters listed.
Black Crappie   No specific waters listed.
White Crappie   No specific waters listed.
Yellow Perch   No specific waters listed.
Black Bullhead   No specific waters listed.
Brown Bullhead   No specific waters listed.

ILLINOIS

Bluegill Carlyle Lake, Collins Lake, Crab Orchard Lake, Horseshoe Lake (Alexander Co.), Rend Lake.
Green Sunfish Carlyle Lake, Crab Orchard Lake, Lake Shelbyville, Lake Springfield, Rend Lake.
Redear Sunfish Dawson Lake, Horseshoe Lake, Mill Creek, Sam Parr Lake, Washington Co. Lake.
Pumpkinseed Sunfish Fox Lake, Fox Chain-O-Lakes Area, Grass Lake, Lake Marie, Nippersink Lake, Pistakee Lake.
Longear Sunfish Embarras River, Kaskaskia River, Little Wabash River, Vermilion River, Wabash River.
Spotted Sunfish Too sparse to include in a fishing publication.
Black Crappie Horseshoe Lake (Alexander Co.), Carlyle Lake, Mermet Lake, Fox Lake, Lake Shelbyville.
White Crappie Carlyle Lake, Clinton Lake, Collins Lake, Rend Lake, Lake Shelbyville.
Rock Bass Fox River, Iroquois River, Kankakee River, Rock River, Vermilion River.
Warmouth Bass Fox Lake, Mermet Lake, Kaskaskia River, Horseshoe Lake (Alexander Co.), Little Wabash River.
Yellow Perch Lake Michigan, Fox Lake, Fox River, Mississippi (Jo Daviess Co. and Carroll Co.).
White Bass Carlyle Lake, Crab Orchard Lake, Lake Shelbyville, Lake Springfield, Sangchris Lake.
Yellow Bass Horseshoe Lake (Alexander Co.), Fox Lake, Kaskaskia River, Illinois River, Sangamen River.
Black Bullhead Fox Lake, Collins Lake, Stump Lake (Jersey Co.), Illinois River, Kaskaskia River.
Brown Bullhead Fox Lake, Fox River, Anderson Lake, Horseshoe Lake (Alexander Co.), Illinois River.
Yellow Bullhead Fox Lake, Kaskaskia River, Illinois River, Horseshoe Lake (Alexander Co.), LaMoine River.

INDIANA

Bluegill Brush Creek, Knightstown, Manitou, Shock Lake, Springs Valley.
Green Sunfish No lake we want to talk about.
Redear Sunfish Bean Blossom Lake.
Pumpkinseed Sunfish No one lake.
Longear Sunfish Almost any river in the state.
Black Crappie Not available.
White Crappie Any of our reservoirs.
Rock Bass Tippecanoe River.
Warmouth Bass Not available.
Yellow Perch Lake Michigan, Loon, Yellow Creek, Prairie Creek.
White Bass Freeman, Harden Reservoir, Brookville.
Yellow Bass Monroe Reservoir.

Black Bullhead   There aren't any lakes that are outstanding. They are where you find them.

Brown Bullhead   There aren't any lakes that are outstanding. They are where you find them.

Yellow Bullhead   There aren't any lakes that are outstanding. They are where you find them.

IOWA

Bluegill   West Okoboji, Mississippi River, Red Haw Lake, Lake Icaria, Big Creek Lake.

Green Sunfish   Battle Creek Lake, Manteno.

Redear Sunfish   Lake Iowa, Lake Viking, Meadow Lake, Thayer Lake, Miami Lake.

Pumpkinseed Sunfish   Waters not listed.

Black Crappie   Clear Lake, Green Valley Lake, Lake Icaria, Big Creek Lake, Mississippi River.

White Crappie   Storm Lake, Rathbun Reservoir, Lake Odessa, Lake Miami, Mississippi River.

Rock Bass   Maquoketa River, Turkey River, Cedar River, Upper Iowa River, Mississippi River.

Warmouth Bass   Red Haw Lake, Nodawa Lake.

Yellow Perch   Spirit Lake, West Okoboji Lake, Clear Lake, Mississippi River, Lake Anita.

White Bass   Storm Lake, Red Rock Reservoir, Coralville Reservoir, Rathbun Reservoir, Mississippi River.

Yellow Bass   Clear Lake, Arrowhead Lake, Lake Manawa, Hartwick Lake, North Twin Lake.

Black Bullhead   Spirit Lake, Clear Lake, East Okoboji Lake, Blackhawk Lake, Hawthorne Lake.

KANSAS

Bluegill   Barber State Fishing Lake, Cowley State Lake, Pottawatomie State Lake No. 2, Mined Land Lakes (Strip Pits), Many community lakes.

Green Sunfish   Mined lakes and streams.

Redear Sunfish   Miami state fishing lake, Mined Land Lakes (Strip Pits).

Pumpkinseed Sunfish   Found in streams and lakes statewide. Not an appreciable sport fishery.

Longear Sunfish   Streams southeastern Kansas and eastern Flint Hills.

Black Crappie   Federal Reservoirs, most lakes—state and community.

Rock Bass   Spring River.

Warmouth Bass   Southeast Kansas, little significant fishery.

Black Bullhead   Statewide ponds, lakes, reservoirs, and streams.

Brown Bullhead   Not a significant fishery.

Yellow Bullhead   Not a significant fishery.

KENTUCKY

Bluegill   Strip pits in Western Ky. are best for big bluegill, otherwise found in all water of Ky.
Green Sunfish   Not a desirable panfish to most Ky. anglers, more of a nuisance.
Redear Sunfish   Beaver Lake, Ponds in Shelby County.
Pumpkinseed Sunfish   Most Lakes.
Longear Sunfish   Everywhere.
Yellowbreast or Redbreast Sunfish   Are few, but are in some eastern Ky. streams.
Black Crappie   Not given.
White Crappie   Berkley Lake, Kentucky Lake, Barren River Lake.
Rock Bass   Most nonpolluted creeks.
Warmouth Bass   All major reservoirs, and in most creeks.
Yellow Perch   Ohio River.
White Bass   Barren Lake, Kentucky River, Dix River.
Yellow Bass   Cumberland River in Western Ky., Tennessee River in western Ky.
Black Bullhead   In all farm ponds and lakes.
Brown Bullhead   Mill Creek Lake.
Yellow Bullhead   In all farm ponds and lakes.

LOUISIANA

Bluegill   Spring Bayou, Atchafalaya Basin, Toledo Bend, Old River, Lake Bistineau. Found statewide.
Green Sunfish   Statewide, but this species is not pursued by fishermen.
Redear Sunfish   Archafalaya Basin, Lake Bistineau, DeArbonne Lake, Toledo Bend, Spring Bayou. Found statewide.
Longear Sunfish   Dorcheat Bayou, Bodeau Bayou, Six Mile Creek, Black Lake Creek. Found statewide.
Yellowbreast or Redbreast Sunfish   Toledo Bend Only.
Spotted Sunfish, Spotted Bream   Statewide—all impoundments and backwater areas, but not sought after by sportsmen.
Black Crappie   Toledon Bend, Lake Bistineau, Lake Claiborne, Caddo Lake, Chicot Lake. Found statewide.
White Crappie   Spring Bayou, Larto—Saline, Sabine River, Cross Lake, Atchafalaya Basin. Found statewide.
Warmouth Bass   Atchafalaya Basin, Dorcheat Bayou, Lake Bistineau.
White Bass   Toledo Bend, Catahoula Lake, Caddo Lake, Old River, Black River.
Yellow Bass   Toledo Bend, Cross Lake, Lake Bistineau, Black Lake, Lake Bruin.
Black Bullhead   Statewide, all impoundments, but very little interest by anglers.
Brown Bullhead   Cypress, Lake Bistineau, Black Bayou, Dorcheat Bayou, Ivan Lake.

Yellow Bullhead   Statewide, all impoundments, very little fishing pressure.

MAINE

Pumpkinseed Sunfish   Found in over 694 lakes throughout the state and is abundant in waters in which it occurs. Of little interest.

Yellowbreast or Redbreast   Has a smaller distribution than the pumpkinseed, but still found in over 186 lakes, and is abundant in waters in which it occurs. Of little interest to fishermen.

Black Crappie   Found in only three drainages: the Sebago Lake drainage, the Sebasticook River drainage, and in the Little Ossipee River drainage. Abundant in all of the lakes and ponds they occupy. Found in 12 lakes.

Yellow Perch   Found in 772 surveyed lakes and ponds. Abundant in waters in which they occur. Of little interest to Me. fishermen.

White Perch   Found statewide, very popular panfish.

Brown Bullhead   Occurs in 750 surveyed lakes and ponds. Excellent eating but not popular with fishermen.

MARYLAND

Bluegill   St. Mary's Lake, Unicorn Lake, Wye Mills Lake, Smithville Lake, Urieville Lake.

Green Sunfish   Loch River Reservoir, Liberty Reservoir, Prettyboy Reservoir, Deep Creek Lake, Tridelphia Reservoir.

Redear Sunfish   Wheatley Lake.

Pumpkinseed Sunfish   Chester River, Unicorn Lake, Wye Mills Lake, Urieville Lake, Smithville Lake.

Yellowbreast or Redbreast Sunfish   Potomac River, Urieville Lake, Monocacy River, Patuxent River, Patapsco River.

Black Crappie   Loch Raven Reservoir, Liberty Reservoir, Prettyboy Reservoir, Conowingo Reservoir, Tridelphia Reservoir.

White Crappie   Loch Raven Reservoir, Liberty Reservoir, Prettyboy Reservoir, Tridelphia Reservoir, Conowingo Reservoir.

Rock Bass   Toms Creek, Potomac River, Middle Creek, Big Pipe, Monocacy River.

Warmouth Bass   Cedarville Pond, Loch Raven Reservoir. Scarce.

Yellow Perch   Deep Creek Lake, Loch Raven Reservoir, Severn River, Chester River, Wye River.

White Perch   Chesapeake Bay, Susquehanna River, Potomac River, Chester River, Choptank River.

Brown Bullhead   Deep Creek Lake, Loch Raven Reservoir.

Yellow Bullhead   Deep Creek Lake.

MASSACHUSETTS

Bluegill   Warners Pond, Lake Rohunta, Cheshire Lake, Bare Hill Pond, Long Pond.

Green Sunfish Very rare, not abundant anywhere.

Redear Sunfish Rare, not abundant.

Pumpkinseed Sunfish Warners Pond, Wequanquiet Pond, Wachusett Reservoir, Quabbin Reservoir, Pontoosuc Lake. Present almost everywhere.

Longear Sunfish Rare, not abundant.

Yellowbreast or Redbreast Sunfish Rare, not abundant.

Black Crappie Wildewood Lake, Little Chauncy Pond, East Brimfield Reservoir, Quabbin Reservoir, Connecticut River.

Rock Bass Quabbin Reservoir, Wachusett Reservoir, Onota Lake, Westfield River Drainage, Stockbridge Bowl.

Yellow Perch Quabbin Reservoir, Congamond Lakes, Onota Lake, Long Pond, Lake Cochituate. Extremely widespread.

White Perch Norton Reservoir, Quabbin Reservoir, Great Herring Pond, Billington Sea, Lake Cochituate. Widespread.

Brown Bullhead Warners Pond, Quabbin Reservoir, Otis Reservoir, Masapee-Wakeby Pond, Conn. River.

Yellow Bullhead Warners Pond, East Brimfield Reservoir, Charles River, Sudbury River, Westfield River.

MICHIGAN

Bluegill Found in most waters of the state.

Green Sunfish Found in many lakes of lower peninsula.

Redear Sunfish Private farm ponds.

Pumpkinseed Sunfish Found in many lakes of lower peninsula.

Longear Sunfish Records not kept on this small sunfish, so best lakes not known.

Black Crappie Found throughout the state.

White Crappie Found throughout the state.

Rock Bass Throughout the state in both inland and Great Lakes waters.

Warmouth Bass Located in some southern lakes.

Yellow Perch Southern Lake Michigan, Little Bay DeNoc, Les Cheneaux Island area, Saginaw Bay, Lake St. Clair.

White Bass Lake Erie, Detroit River, Lake St. Clair.

White Perch Sparse in Lake Erie only.

Black Bullhead Throughout state.

Brown Bullhead Throughout state.

Yellow Bullhead Throughout state.

MINNESOTA

Bluegill Pelican Lake, Osakis. Abundant distribution statewide.

Green Sunfish Abundant distribution statewide.

Pumpkinseed Sunfish Abundant distribution statewide.

Black Crappie Abundant distribution statewide.

White Crappie Abundant distribution statewide.

Rock Bass Abundant distribution statewide.

Warmouth Bass   Mississippi River in southeast, Minn.
Yellow Perch   Lake Winnibigoshish, Lake Mille Lacs, abundant distribution statewide.
White Bass   Waters not listed, but is a popular species.
Yellow Bass   Lower stretches of Mississippi River along the Minnesota, Wisconsin and Iowa border.
Black Bullhead   Abundant distribution statewide.
Brown Bullhead   Abundant distribution statewide.
Yellow Bullhead   Abundant distribution statewide.

MISSISSIPPI

Bluegill   Farm ponds in state.
Green Sunfish   Not considered a desirable fish in Miss.
Redear Sunfish   Farm ponds, Little Eagle Lake.
Longear Sunfish   Southern Miss. streams.
Spotted Sunfish   No significant populations.
Black Crappie   Sardis Reservoir, Enid Reservoir, Grenada Reservoir, Ross Barnett Reservoir, Eagle Lake, but not outstanding populations.
White Crappie   Found in same waters as those listed for black crappie above.
Rock Bass   No significant populations.
Warmouth Bass   Old Delta Oxbow Lakes.
White Bass   Enid Reservoir, Grenada Reservoir, Eagle Lake, Old Delta Oxbow Lakes.
Yellow Bass   Same as for white bass.
Black Bullhead   Considered trash fish in Miss.
Brown Bullhead   Considered trash fish in Miss.
Yellow Bullhead   Considered trash fish in Miss.

MISSOURI

Bluegill   Best waters not listed.
Green Sunfish   Best waters not listed.
Redear Sunfish   Best waters not listed.
Pumpkinseed Sunfish   Best waters not listed.
Longear Sunfish   Best waters not listed.
Spotted Sunfish   Limited distribution in sluggish streams in southeastern lowlands. Of little fishing importance.
Black Crappie   Widespread, sporadic distribution. Most prevalent in Ozark reservoirs and pools of the Miss. River.
White Crappie   Best waters not listed.
Rock Bass   Best waters not listed.
Warmouth Bass   Mainly found in southeastern lowlands. Most abundant in weedy ditches and swamps. Minor importance, but significant numbers are caught in Clearwater Lake and Lake Wappapello.
White Bass   Best waters not listed.
Yellow Bass   Found only in Miss. River, most common above the confluence with Mo. River (north of St. Louis).

Black Bullhead   Best waters not listed.
Brown Bullhead   Best waters not listed.
Yellow Bullhead   Seldom found in high numbers, but is widespread in the state.

MONTANA

Bluegill   Castle Rock Lake, Dengel Reservoir, Peterson Stock Dam.
Green Sunfish   Slow-moving streams and shallows of lakes, primarily in southern part of state.
Pumpkinseed Sunfish   Island Lake, Blanchard Lake, Peterson Reservoir, Kicking Horse Lake, Ninepipe Reservoir.
Black Crappie   Tongue River and Reservoir, Castle Rock Lake, Fort Peck Reservoir, Nelson Reservoir, Fresno Reservoir.
White Crappie   Tongue River Reservoir, Castle Rock Lake, Fort Peck Reservoir.
Rock Bass   Tongue River contains only population in state.
Yellow Perch   Baker Lake, Glasgow Air Base Reservoir, Box Elder Reservoir, Nelson Reservoir, Canyon Ferry Reservoir, Whitetail Reservoir.
Black Bullhead   Baker Lake, Tongue River Reservoir, South Sandstone Reservoir, Kawsnay Reservoir, Frazier Lake, Fatzinger Reservoir.
Yellow Bullhead   Tongue River Reservoir, South Sandstone Reservoir.

NEBRASKA

Bluegill   One of the most common sunfish in the state.
Green Sunfish   One of the most widely distributed fish in the state.
Redear Sunfish   Limited numbers in a few stocked ponds.
Sacramento Perch   Introduced in Ell, Hudson, and Smiths lakes in Cherry County. Limited.
Black Crappie   Entire state, but not as abundant as white crappie.
White Crappie   Entire state. An important sport fish.
Rock Bass   Only a few found in Enders and Kimball reservoirs, Cedar River, and some Sand Hills lakes.
Yellow Perch   Stocked throughout state, found in many Sand Hills lakes, reservoirs, river systems, and ponds.
White Bass   Has become quite common in the Platte and Republican reservoirs.
Black Bullhead   One of the most widely distributed fish in the state. Found in majority of lakes, ponds, streams.
Brown Bullhead   Found in a few private ponds in state's eastern section.
Yellow Bullhead   Not as widespread as black bullhead.

NEVADA

Bluegill   Lake Mead, Lake Mohave, Rye Patch Reservoir, Ft. Churchill Cooling Ponds.

Green Sunfish Rye Patch Reservoir, Lake Park Pond—Reno, Truckee River (lower section), Washoe Lake, Lahontan Reservoir.
Redear Sunfish Tule Pond.
Pumpkinseed Sunfish Dufferna Pond.
Sacramento Perch Pyramid Lake, Walker River, Washoe Lake.
Black Crappie Lake Mead, Lake Mohave.
White Crappie Lahontan Reservoir, Echo Canyon Reservoir, Rye Patch Reservoir.
Yellow Perch Harmon Reservoir, Indian Lakes, Lahontan Reservoir, Echo Canyon Reservoir.
White Bass Lahontan Reservoir, Rye Patch Reservoir, Indian Lakes, Sheckler Reservoir.
Black Bullhead Ft. Churchill Cooling Ponds, Still Water Marsh, Squaw Valley Reservoir, Humboldt River, Indian Lake.
Brown Bullhead Vegas Wash (Lake Mead), Nesbitt Lake, Weber Reservoir, Wall Canyon Reservoir.

NEW HAMPSHIRE

Bluegill Forest Lake, Lake Winnipesaukee, Spofford Lake, Deer Meadow Pond, Connecticut River.
Pumpkinseed Sunfish Statewide.
Yellowbreast or Redbreast Sunfish Uncommon and not fished for.
Black Crappie Balch Pond, Clement Pond. This is an uncommon species.
Rock Bass Connecticut River.
Yellow Perch Statewide.
White Perch Winnisquam Lake, Wentworth Lake, Winnipesaukee Lake.
Brown Bullhead Statewide.
Yellow Bullhead Statewide.

NEW JERSEY

Bluegill Spruce Run Reservoir, Lake Hopatcong, Farrington Lake, Assumpink Lake, Round Valley Reservoir.
Pumpkinseed Sunfish Union Lake, Swartswood Lake, Round Valley Reservoir, Assumpink Lake, Prospertown Lake.
Yellowbreast or Redbreast Sunfish Delaware River, Lake Hopatcong, Raritan River (South Branch), Swartswood Lake, Pompton River.
Black Crappie Delaware River, Farrington Lake, Greenwood Lake, Lake Musconetcong, Ramaps Lake.
White Crappie Delaware River.
Rock Bass Delaware River, Lake Hopatcong, Raritan River (South Branch), Pompton River, Greenwood Lake.
Yellow Perch Lake Hopatcong, Spruce Run Reservoir, Saxton Falls Lake, Metedeconk River, Tuckahoe Impoundment #3.
White Perch Lake Hopatcong, Round Valley Reservoir, Wanaque Reservoir, Tuckahoe Impoundment #3, Cranberry Lake.
Brown Bullhead Carnegie Lake, Round Valley Reservoir, Lake Hopatcong, Lake Musconetcong, Mirror Lake.

NEW MEXICO

Bluegill   Navajo Reservoir, Cochiti Reservoir, Conchas Reservoir, Ute Reservoir, Elephant Butte Reservoir.
Green Sunfish   Statewide, Elephant Butte Reservoir.
Redear Sunfish   Bear Canyon Reservoir only.
Longear Sunfish   Elephant Butte Reservoir, Lower Rio Grande, Lake Sumner.
Black Crappie   Elephant Butte Reservoir, Conchas Reservoir, Ute Reservoir.
White Crappie   Elephant Butte Reservoir, Navajo Reservoir, Conchas Reservoir, Ute Reservoir, Cochiti Reservoir.
Rock Bass   Lower Pecos River.
Warmouth Bass   Elephant Butte Reservoir, Navajo Reservoir, Caballo Reservoir, Rio Grande, drains near Las Cruces.
Yellow Perch   Charette Lake, Elephant Butte Reservoir, Stubblefield Reservoir.
White Bass   Elephant Butte Reservoir, Ute Reservoir, Caballo Reservoir, Lake Sumner, McMillian Reservoir.
Black Bullhead   Statewide.
Brown Bullhead   Lower Rio Grande drains.
Yellow Bullhead   Lower Pecos River.

NEW YORK

Bluegill   All watersheds except Adirondack, found in Saratoga Lake and Hudson River watershed. Many good lakes.
Green Sunfish   Rare in lower Hudson watershed.
Pumpkinseed Sunfish   Statewide.
Longear Sunfish   Western New York, Tonawanda Creek. Not an important sportfish.
Yellowbreast or Redbreast Sunfish   Hudson, Mohawk, and Delaware river drainage.
Black Crappie   Hudson and Susquahanna watersheds, St. Lawrence River and western New York, Saratoga Lake, Chautauqua Lake, Whitney Point Reservoir, Canandaigua Lake.
White Crappie   Hudson River, Mohawk River.
Rock Bass   All medium to large rivers.
Warmouth Bass   Small populations in Woodbury Creek and Sawkill Creek. Not worth a fishing trip.
Yellow Perch   Oneida Lake, Lake Erie, St. Lawrence River, Chautauqua Lake, and many others.
White Bass   Oneida Lake, Lake Erie.
White Perch   Hudson River, Mohawk River, Oneida Lake, eastern Lake Ontario, St. Lawrence River, Long Island estuaries.
Black Bullhead   Not a major species, some in western part of state and in Lake Ontario tributaries.
Brown Bullhead   Distributed statewide, especially good areas are

St. Lawrence River tributaries, Adirondack and Catskill Mountain ponds.

Yellow Bullhead   Southeastern counties, Cayuga Lake, and scattered in Susquahanna drainage.

NORTH CAROLINA

Bluegill   Farm ponds, reservoirs, city water supply lakes.
Green Sunfish   Never attains any size.
Redear Sunfish   Farm ponds, reservoirs, city water supply lakes.
Pumpkinseed Sunfish   Coastal streams.
Yellowbreast or Redbreast Sunfish   Coastal streams, southeastern North Carolina.
Black Crappie   Reservoirs, city water supply lakes.
White Crappie   Reservoirs, city water supply lakes.
Rock Bass   Foothill streams of northwestern North Carolina.
Warmouth Bass   Coastal streams.
Yellow Perch   Never attains any size.
White Bass   Piedmont reservoirs and tributary streams.
White Perch   Sounds, coastal streams in northern part of the state.
Black Bullhead   Reservoirs, not classed as gamefish.
Brown Bullhead   Piedmont and coast, not abundant, not classed as gamefish.
Yellow Bullhead   Piedmont reservoirs, coastal streams, not classed as gamefish.

NORTH DAKOTA

Bluegill   Jamestown Reservoir, Danzig Reservoir, Van Oosting Dam, Cedar Lake, and Dickinson Reservoir.
Rock Bass   Sheyenne River (only really good area) and Red River (only fair).
Crappie   Heart Butte Reservoir, Lake Ashtabula, Garrison Reservoir, Long Lake, and Danzig Reservoir.
Yellow Perch   Lake Darling (terrific), Lake Ashtabula (terrific), Jamestown Reservoir and Garrison Reservoir. Catches of 50-150/day are common in the best waters.
White Bass   Heart Butte Reservoir (only one that is good).
Black Bullhead   Lake Ashtabula, Jamestown Reservoir, and Rice Lake.

OHIO

Bluegill   Farm ponds, Portage Lakes, Ohio Power Recreation Area ponds, Alum Creek Lake, Lake LaSuAn.
Green Sunfish   St. Joseph River, Maumee River embayments, Scioto River embayments, farm ponds.
Redear Sunfish   Buckeye Lake, Pippin Lake, Paint Creek Lake.
Pumpkinseed Sunfish   Lake Erie, Maumee River, Buckeye Lake, Ross Lake, Indian Lake.

Longear Sunfish Hocking River, Paint Creek, Scioto River drainage, Mahoning River.

Black Crappie Lake Erie, Ohio River, Buckeye Lake, Sandusky River.

White Crappie Lake Erie, Pleasant Hill Reservoir, O'Shaunasee Reservoir, Indian Lake, Buckeye Lake.

Rock Bass Ohio River, Huron River, Maumee River, Scioto River, Great Miami River.

Yellow Perch Lake Erie, Findlay Reservoirs 1, 2.

White Bass Lake Erie, Bresler Reservoir, Sandusky River, Maumee River, Delaware Reservoir.

White Perch Lake Erie (only area).

Black Bullhead Lake Erie and tributaries, Scioto River, Maumee River, Ohio River.

Brown Bullhead Lake Erie and tributaries, Ohio River, Scioto River, Maumee River.

Yellow Bullhead Lake Erie and tributaries, Sunfish Creek, Grand Lake, St. Marys.

OKLAHOMA

Bluegill American Horse Lake, Watonga Lake, Altus Lugart Lake, Ft. Cobb Reservoir, Lake Humphreys.

Green Sunfish Mill Creek, Ft. Gibson Reservoir, Grand Reservoir, Hudson Reservoir, Robert S. Kerr Reservoir.

Redear Sunfish American Horse Lake, Lake Bluestem, Holdenville Lake, Hulah Reservoir, Okemah Lake.

Longear Sunfish Robert S. Kerr Reservoir, Clear Creek Reservoir, Oolowah Reservoir, Pine Creek Reservoir, Ft. Gibson Reservoir.

Yellowbreast or Redbreast Sunfish Found in only a few rivers in extreme southeastern Oklahoma.

Spotted Sunfish Little river drainage in southeastern Oklahoma.

Black Crappie Altus Lugert Lake, Lake Bluestem, Ft. Cobb Reservoir, Lake Humphreys, Robert S. Kerr Reservoir.

White Crappie Ponca City Lake, Clear Creek Reservoir, Grand Reservoir, Oologah Reservoir, Lawtonka Lake.

Rock and Warmouth Bass Illinois River.

Warmouth Bass Best waters not listed.

Yellow Perch Mountain Lake, Ardmore Lake, Lake Pawhauska, Lake Fairfax.

White Bass Texoma Reservoir, Murray Reservoir, Arbuckle Reservoir, Washita River, Eufaula Reservoir.

Yellow Bass Known in only a few lakes in Wagoner, Muskogee, and McCurtain counties.

Black Bullhead Altus Lugert Lake, Eufaula Reservoir, Lake Fuqua, Robert S. Kerr Reservoir, Webber Falls Reservoir.

Brown Bullhead Streams in McCurtain County in southeastern Oklahoma.

Yellow Bullhead Foss Reservoir, Lake Fuqua, Heyburn Lake, Robert S. Kerr Reservoir, Lake Konowa.

OREGON

Bluegill Tenmile Lakes, Siltcoos Lake, Tahkenitch Lake, many small lakes and ponds, Willamette River Oxbow Lakes.
Green Sunfish Only locally abundant, provides no fishing.
Redear Sunfish Experimentally stocked at St. Louis public fish ponds and Reynolds Pond.
Pumpkinseed Sunfish Widely distributed but abundant nowhere.
Sacramento Perch Locally common in Lost River.
Black Crappie Owyhee Reservoir, Brownlee Reservoir, Siltcoos Lake.
White Crappie Willamette River backwaters, Columbia River backwaters, Sauvie Island Lakes.
Warmouth Bass Widely distributed but not commonly caught due to low abundance.
Yellow Perch Siltcoos Lake, Tahkenitch Lake, Brownlee Reservoir, Columbia River.
Black Bullhead Uncommon.
Brown Bullhead Siltcoos Lake, Sauvie Island Lakes.
Yellow Bullhead Uncommon.

PENNSYLVANIA

Bluegill Widely introduced, forms the foundation of sunfish harvest, population quality fluctuates.
Green Sunfish Common but not abundant in lakes, streams, and rivers, desirable size rare, not considered an attractive fish for anglers.
Redear Sunfish Populations scarce, but individual fish are of nice size, not considered a target species.
Pumpkinseed Sunfish Native, occurring in all types of waters, individual quality somewhat less than bluegills, second in importance in sunfish harvest.
Longear Sunfish None or very rare.
Yellowbreast or Redbreast Sunfish Widely distributed in warmwater streams and lakes, quality of fishing varies with fishing pressure.
Black Crappie Widely introduced, stunting frequently a problem.
White Crappie Introduced less successfully than black crappie, more abundant in a few lakes.
Rock Bass Abundant and desirable populations in all rivers and larger warmwater streams. Lake populations are of poor quality.
Warmouth Bass None or extremely rare.
Yellow Perch Abundant in all lakes and ponds, stunting is always a problem.
White Bass Few populations confined to larger northwestern lakes.
White Perch Few populations confined to southeastern rivers, estuaries, and lakes.
Black Bullhead Limited, isolated populations in northwestern Pa. and Lake Erie, is not considered a target species.
Brown Bullhead An abundant and underutilized species in Pa., very good to excellent populations exist in most lakes.

Yellow Bullhead Not abundant or frequent. When they exist populations are attractive.

RHODE ISLAND

Bluegill Statewide.
Pumpkinseed Sunfish Statewide.
Yellowbreast or Redbreast Sunfish Alton Pond, Ashville Pond, Carbuncle Pond, Gorton Pond, Olney Pond.
Black Crappie Chapman Pond, Slatersville Reservoir, Flat River Reservoir, Waterman Reservoir, Olney Pond.
Rock Bass Not common.
Yellow Perch Statewide distribution.
White Perch Chapmen Pond, Worden Pond, Indian Lake, Stillwater Reservoir, Tucker Pond.
Brown Bullhead Statewide.
Yellow Bullhead Blackstone River.

SOUTH CAROLINA

Bluegill Santee Cooper, Lake Murray, Lake Wateree, Clark Hill Reservoir, Hartwell Reservoir.
Green Sunfish Same as bluegill. Not considered to make up a substantial percentage of catch.
Redear Sunfish Same areas as bluegill.
Pumpkinseed Sunfish Same areas as bluegill, not considered a gamefish by many people.
Yellowbreast or Redbreast Sunfish Edisto River, Black River, Pee Dee River, Combanee River, Waccamaw River.
Black Crappie Santee Cooper, Lake Wateree, Lake Murray, Clark Hill Reservoir, Hartwell Reservoir.
White Crappie Same areas as above.
Warmouth Bass Common in most waters throughout state.
Yellow Perch Lake Jocassee, Santee Cooper, Hartwell Reservoir, Toxaway Lake, Keowee Lake, Lake Murray.
White Perch Lake Murray, Salada River, Congaree River, Wateree River, Lake Wateree.
Black Bullhead Common in most low country rivers and lakes.
Brown Bullhead Same as above.
Yellow Bullhead Same as above.

SOUTH DAKOTA

Bluegill Big Stone Lake, Enemy Swim Lake, East Vermillion Lake, Lake Menno and Dante Lake.
Rock Bass Big Stone Lake.
White and Black Crappie Lake Traverse, Fort Randall Reservoir, Lewis and Clark Lake, Big Stone Lake, and Lake Poinsett.
Other Sunfish Little or no fishing for any of these. Both pumpkin-

seed and green sunfish are found in the state.

Yellow Perch   Roy Lake, Nine Mile Lake, Cottonwood Lake (Spink County), Lake Cochrane and Lake Traverse.

White Bass   Big Stone Lake and Shadehill Reservoir.

Black Bullhead   Lake Byron, Lake Badger, Spirit Lake, Oak Lake, Nine Mile Lake, and many others.

TENNESSEE

Bluegill   Cumberland Plateau Lakes, Watts Bar Reservoir, Lake Graham, Kentucky Reservoir, Norris Reservoir.

Green Sunfish   Private ponds, most rivers and reservoirs.

Redear Sunfish   Private ponds, Cumberland Plateau Lakes.

Pumpkinseed Sunfish   Private ponds, most rivers and reservoirs.

Longear Sunfish   Pigeon River.

Yellowbreast or Redbreast Sunfish   Holston River.

Spotted Sunfish, Spotted Bream   Rivers.

Black Crappie   Waters not listed.

White Crappie   Kentucky Lake, Reelfoot Lake, Douglas Reservoir, Watts Bar Reservoir, Chickamauga Reservoir.

Rock Bass   Stones River, Sequatchie River, Obed River, Daddy's Creek, Falling Water River.

Warmouth Bass   Private ponds and most reservoirs.

Yellow Perch   Nickajack Reservoir, Reelfoot Lake.

White Bass   Old Hickory Reservoir, Dale Hollow Reservoir, Kentucky Lake, Norris Reservoir.

Yellow Bass   Watts Bar Reservoir.

Black Bullhead   Private ponds.

Brown Bullhead   Chickamauga Reservoir.

Yellow Bullhead   Chickamauga Reservoir.

TEXAS

Bluegill   Toledo Bend, Quitman, Hawkins, Lake Fork, Town Lake.

Green Sunfish   No fishery, fish too small.

Redear Sunfish   Tyler East, Tyler West, Athens, Hawkins, Toledo Bend.

Longear Sunfish   Private ranches, West Texas.

Yellowbreast or Redbreast Sunfish   Town Lake, Lake Austin, Colorado River below city of Austin, Guadalupe River, private ranches in west Texas.

Spotted Sunfish, Spotted Bream   No fishery, fish too small.

Black Crappie   Palestine Lake, Lake Fork Lake, Murvaul Lake, Toledo Bend Lake, Texoma Lake.

White Crappie   Waco Lake, Sam Rayburn Lake, Whiteriver Lake, Upper Colorado River, O.C. Fisher Lake.

Rock Bass   Guadalupe River, Canyon Reservoir (an introduced species).

Warmouth Bass   Scattered and incidental.

Yellow Perch   Lake Meredith and Lake Greenbelt (these are experimental only).
White Bass   Livingston Lake, Trinity River, Whitney Lake, Upper Colorado River, Cedar Creek Lake.
Yellow Bass   Lake O' The Pines, Caddo Lake, Wright Patman Lake, Bob Sandlin Lake, Ellison Lake.
Black Bullhead   Lake Fork Reservoir, Bob Sandlin, Lake Steinhagen.
Yellow Bullhead   Lake Fork Reservoir, Bob Sandlin Reservoir, Lake Steinhagen.

UTAH

Bluegill   Pelican Lake, Pineview Reservoir, Gunnison Reservoir.
Green Sunfish   Steinaker Reservoir, Lake Powell.
Sacramento Perch   Garrison Reservoir (Pruess Lake).
Black Crappie   Lake Powell, Pineview Reservoir, Willard Bay Reservoir, Gunlock Reservoir, Cutler Reservoir.
Yellow Perch   Yuba Reservoir (Sevier Bridge), Deer Creek Reservoir, Gunnison Reservoir.
White Bass   Utah Lake.
Black Bullhead   Utah Lake, Pineview Reservoir.

VERMONT

Bluegill   Best waters not listed.
Pumpkinseed Sunfish   Best waters not listed.
Black Crappie   Best waters not listed.
Rock Bass   Best waters not listed.
Yellow Perch   Best waters not listed.
White Perch   Best waters not listed.
Brown Bullhead   Best waters not listed.

VIRGINIA

Bluegill   All impounded water.
Green Sunfish   Kerr Reservoir, Gaston Reservoir, Leesville Reservoir.
Redear Sunfish   Many farm ponds, Kerr Reservoir, Gaston Reservoir, Brunswick Reservoir, Conners Reservoir.
Pumpkinseed Sunfish   Most impounded waters.
Longear Sunfish   Streams in Tenn. River drainage.
Yellowbreast or Redbreast Sunfish   James River, Rappahanock River, Appomattox River.
Spotted Sunfish   Waters East of I-95.
Black Crappie   Kerr Reservoir, Gaston Reservoir, Anna Reservoir, Flannagan Reservoir, Claytor Reservoir.
White Crappie   Claytor Reservoir, Flannagan Reservoir, S. Holston Reservoir.
Rock Bass   New and James River drainages.
Warmouth Bass   All eastern drainages.

Yellow Perch   In most waters, is a nuisance species.
White Bass   Claytor Reservoir, S. Holston Reservoir, South Mountain Reservoir, Kerr Reservoir, Laswell's Reservoir.
White Perch   Anna Reservoir, Back Bay, Gaston Reservoir.
Black Bullhead   Small populations statewide.
Brown Bullhead   Carvin's Cover, eastern waters.

WASHINGTON

Bluegill   Moses Lake, Potholes Reservoir, Silver Lake, Hummel Lake, Fazon Lake.
Green Sunfish   Sacheen Lake, Diamond Lake, Loon Lake.
Redear Sunfish   None. We are thinking of importing.
Pumpkinseed Sunfish   Hicks Lake, Lake Cassidy, Eloika Lake, Alkali Lake, Napowsin Lake.
Black Crappie   Moses Lake, Potholes Reservoir, Kapowsin Lake, Silver Lake (Cowlitz Co.), Long Lake.
White Crappie   Silver Lake (Cowlitz Co.), Lake Washington, have been planted in Sprague Lake.
Rock Bass   Steilacoom Lake, Kapowsin Lake, Lake St. Clair.
Warmouth Bass   Silver Lake (Cowlitz Co.).
Yellow Perch   Lake Washington, Lake Sammamish, Silver Lake (Cowlitz Co.), Banks Lake, Campbell Lake.
Brown Bullhead   Lake Cassidy, Lake Terrell, Lake Stevens, Lake Washington, Lake Sawyer.
Yellow Bullhead   Lackamas, Lona Lake, Mound Lake, Yellepit Potholes Reservoir.

WEST VIRGINIA

Bluegill   Plum Orchard Lake, Bluestone Lake, Sleepy Creek Lake, Burnsville Lake, Sutton Lake.
Green Sunfish   Occur in virtually all impoundments throughout West Virginia.
Pumpkinseed Sunfish   Shenandoah River, Ohio River backwaters, Little Kanawha River, Hughes River, Middle Island Creek.
Longear Sunfish   Ohio River backwaters, Elk River, Guyandotte River, Tug Fork, Kanawha River.
Yellowbreast or Redbreast Sunfish   Shenandoah River, South Branch of Potomac River, Greenbrier River, New River, Cacapon River.
Black Crappie   Stonecoal Lake, Tygart Lake, Summersville Lake, East Lynn Lake, R. D. Bailey Lake.
White Crappie   Bluestone Lake, Sutton Lake, Burnsville Lake, R. D. Bailey Lake, Stonecoal Lake.
Rock Bass   New River, Greenbrier River, Cacapon River, South Branch of Potomac River, Gauley River.
Warmouth Bass   Ohio River backwaters.
Yellow Perch   Tygart Lake.

White Bass   Ohio River, Kanawha River, Bluestone Lake, New River, Hawks Nest Lake.

Black and Brown Bullheads   Black and brown bullheads have overlapping characteristics in the Ohio River drainage, therefore it is unclear whether black and/or brown bullheads occur. They are common in most small impoundments in West Virginia. Slow-flowing streams and backwaters of large streams generally contain these fish.

Yellow Bullhead   Distributed generally throughout the state in small impoundments and slow-flowing streams, and in backwaters of large streams.

WISCONSIN

Bluegill   Lake Poygan, Big Lake Butte des Morts, Lake Onalaska (Miss. River).

Green Sunfish   Not commonly sought for sport fishing in Wisconsin.

Pumpkinseed Sunfish   Common throughout southern Wisconsin, not actively sought, caught incidental to bluegill or crappie in smaller lakes.

Black Crappie   Lake Monona, Lake Winnebago, Lake Poygan, Lake Winneconne, Holcombe Flowage.

White Crappie   Lake Monona, Lake Koshkonong.

Rock Bass   Rock Lake (Lake Mills), Lake Geneva.

Warmouth Bass   Not commonly sought for sport fishing in Wisconsin. Some in Partridge Crop Lake.

Yellow Perch   Lake Mendota, Lake Winnebago, Lake Poygon, Lake Winneconne, Big Lake Butte des Morts.

White Bass   Lake Koshkonong, Lake Pepin.

Yellow Bass   Swan Lake.

Black Bullhead   Generally not sought for sport fishing due to small size.

Brown Bullhead   Lake Winneconne, Big Lake Butte des Morts, Lake Poygan, Cedar Lake (St. Croix Co.).

Yellow Bullhead   Cedar Lake.

WYOMING

Bluegill   Festo Lake, Ocean Lake.

Green Sunfish   Primarily farm ponds in northeast Wyoming.

Pumpkinseed Sunfish   Sloans Lake, private farm ponds.

Black Crappie   Boysen Reservoir, Ocean Lake, Bighorn Reservoir, Gray Rocks Reservoir, Country Club Lake.

Rock Bass   Lake DeSmet, Healy Reservoir.

Yellow Perch   Glenoo Reservoir, Boysen Reservoir, Lake DeSmet, Lake Hattie, Ocean Lake.

Black Bullhead   Joe Johnson Reservoir, farm ponds in northeastern Wyoming.

INDEX

Weight-forward tapered lines, 161,
162
Wet flies:
    for bass, rock and warmouth, 51
    for bass, white and yellow, 98
    for bluegills, 16, 17-18
    for crappie, 36, 38
    fly fishing for panfish, 182
    types of, 174
    for yellow perch, 79
White bass, 83-98
    distribution of, 85-86
    feeding habits, 90-91
    fishing for, 92-95
    growth rate, 87
    habits and habitat, 88-92
    lures/flies for, 90
    physical characteristics, 83
    spawning, 91-92
White crappie, *See* Crappie.
White perch, 99-112
    distribution of, 102-103
    fly fishing for, 107-109
    growth rate, 104
    habits, 105-107
    live-bait fishing, 111
    overpopulation of, 104-105
    physical characteristics, 101-102
    spawning and growth, 103-105
    spinning tackle for, 109-111

Wobbling and darting spoons, 34,
138
Wooly worm, for bass, rock and
    warmouth, 51

Yellow bass, 83-98
    distribution of, 86, 87
    feeding habits, 90-91
    fishing for, 92-95
    lures/flies for, 90
    physical characteristics, 83-85
    spawning, 91-92
Yellowbreast (redbreast) sunfish,
    62-64
    bait for, 63
    distribution of, 63
    habitat, 63
    physical characteristics, 62-63
    spawning, 63-64
Yellow perch, 70-82
    bait, live, 78-81
    distribution of, 71, 73
    as food, 81-82
    feeding habits, 74-76
    fishing for, 76-78
    flies/lures for, 79-81
    habitat and habits, 71-76
    ice fishing for, 230-231
    physical characteristics, 70-71, 72
    spawning, 73